ANNALS OF THE NEW YORK ACADEMY OF SCIENCES
Volume 932

THE CLINICAL SCIENCE OF SUICIDE PREVENTION

Edited by Herbert Hendin and J. John Mann

The New York Academy of Sciences
New York, New York
2001

Library of Congress Cataloging-in-Publication Data

The clinical science of suicide prevention / edited by Herbert Hendin and J. John Mann.
    p. : cm. — (Annals of the New York Academy of Sciences ; ISSN 0077-8923; v. 932)
    Includes bibliographical references and index.
    ISBN 1-57331-330-0 (cloth : alk. paper) — ISBN 1-57331-331-9 (paper : alk. paper)
    1. Suicide—Prevention—Congresses. 2. Suicidal behavior—Prevention—Congresses. I. Hendin, Herbert. II. Mann, J. John (Joseph John). III. Series.
    [DNLM: 1. Suicide—prevention & control—Congresses. 2. Crisis Intervention—Congresses. WM 401 C641 2001]
    RC569 .C55 2001
    500 s—dc21
    [616.85'844505]   2001030935

GYAT / BMP

Printed in the United States of America
ISBN 1-57331-330-0 (cloth)
ISBN 1-57331-331-9 (paper)
ISSN 0077-8923

ANNALS OF THE NEW YORK ACADEMY OF SCIENCES
Volume 932
April 2001

THE CLINICAL SCIENCE OF SUICIDE PREVENTION

Editors
HERBERT HENDIN AND J. JOHN MANN

This volume is the result of a conference entitled **Suicide Prevention 2000** held on May 7–8, 2000, in New York, New York.

CONTENTS

Part IV. Suicide Crisis

Part V. Psychosocial Influences

Financial assistance was received from:

- ABBOTT LABORATORIES
- BRISTOL-MYERS SQUIBB COMPANY
- FOREST LABORATORIES, INC.
- JANSSEN PHARMACEUTICA INC.
- ELI LILLY AND COMPANY
- MERCK & CO., INC.
- PFIZER INC.
- SMITHKLINE BEECHAM PHARMACEUTICALS
- SOLVAY PHARMACEUTICALS, INC.
- WYETH-AYERST LABORATORIES

Introduction

J. JOHN MANN AND HERBERT HENDIN

Department of Neuroscience, New York State Psychiatric Institute, New York, New York 10032, USA

American Foundation for Suicide Prevention, New York, New York 10005, USA and Department of Psychiatry, New York Medical College, Valhalla, New York 10595, USA

Despite great advances in the psychopharmacologic treatment and psychotherapy of major psychiatric disorders in the modern era of medicine, suicide and suicide attempts persist as major causes of mortality and morbidity. They occur most frequently in the context of a mood disorder and almost never in the absence of a diagnosable psychiatric illness. Therefore, given the rise in prescription of psychotropic medications as an index of more widespread effective treatment of major psychiatric disorders, the suicide rate should begin to fall in the United States. It is beginning to fall, but not very much. This enigma was addressed in *Suicide Prevention 2000,* the American Foundation for Suicide (AFSP) conference that led to this book.

This volume of the *Annals of the New York Academy of Sciences* brings together what we currently know about the assessment and treatment of the suicidal patient. A combination of treatment strategies involving pharmacotherapy and psychotherapy as well as psychosocial and public health approaches is recommended. The volume is organized along the lines of major psychiatric diagnoses associated with suicide and aspects of the life cycle. In addition, there is a specific discussion of the role of psychotherapy and some of the psychosocial factors that appear to have an effect on suicide.

Why does the suicide rate decline so slowly when effective treatment is possible? What can be done to bring about a greater reduction in the rate of suicide and attempted suicide? Perhaps treatment is not being delivered to enough patients or in adequate doses to have an impact. Another possibility is that the patients who are at greatest risk for suicide are the ones who are not availing themselves of treatment. A potential corrective lies in the tendency of most individuals who commit suicide to inform someone close to them or to consult with a medical professional in the month or so prior to suicide. With such forewarning at least some future suicides may be saved by timely treatment interventions.

Yet most individual who commit suicide in the context of a major depression were not receiving adequate antidepressant treatment at the time of their

death. Estimates suggest that 10–15% of such individuals are being adequately treated at the time of death, and they therefore are presumably treatment resistant. The vast majority (85–90%) are not being adequately treated or treated at all. This indicates an opportunity for improved intervention and, therefore, a reduction in suicide rates.

In *The Depressed Suicidal Patient: Assessment and Treatment,* Drs. Charles Nemeroff, Michael Compton, and Joseph Berger highlight how frequently depression or mood disorder is the psychiatric disorder that is complicated by suicide or suicide attempts. Given that frequency, an optimal evaluation and treatment of such patients is the cornerstone of reduction of suicide rates. The authors discuss the evaluation of depression and the evaluation of suicidality. A critical component of the latter is a history of previous suicidal behavior. A table is provided that summarizes the risk factors for suicide in major depression. Although it must be acknowledged that such laundry lists are of limited clinical usefulness, at the same time they do provide a measure of the degree of risk facing the patient. What is sometimes more difficult to convey is the relative importance of particular risk factors and the interpretation of differences in severity of individual risk factors between patients.

Nemeroff and his colleagues discuss the neurobiological abnormalities that are associated with suicide. Many of these abnormalities, particularly those involving the serotonergic system, are common to suicidal individuals independent of the primary psychiatric disorder and are not specific for major depression.

The authors address from several standpoints the choices involved in treatment. One critical decision is where to treat the patient. The decision to hospitalize is always a difficult, but essential, first step. Hospitalization is part of a process of separating the patient from the means for suicide. There are steps that can be taken that will achieve the same goal at home, but not to the same degree of completeness. They include removing guns, knives, and pills.

Another major concern is optimization of the treatment of depression in the choice of medication. A factor in choosing medication is safety in case of an overdose. Certain medications, such as lithium, may have specific antisuicidal effects. One would hypothesize the same property for SSRIs. ECT is a remarkably potent antidepressant with a potential capacity for reducing suicide risk, although there is disagreement in the literature on that point. Psychotherapies are effective for antidepressant treatment, particularly milder forms of depression, and may be used alone or in conjunction with medication. Most depressed patients do not receive adequate treatment in terms of both dose and duration. Some patients need long-term maintenance treatment to prevent recurrence of depression, when the episodes are frequent or have the potential to be particularly severe and perhaps associated with suicidal

acts. The authors close with some discussion of special populations, such as children, the elderly and the medically ill. Comorbidity, which carries a higher risk for suicidal behavior, is also a major problem in the successful treatment of mood disorders.

In *Treating the Suicidal Patient with Bipolar Disorder: Reducing Suicide Risk with Lithium,* Drs. Ross Baldessarini, Leonardo Tondo and John Hennen describe bipolar disorder as a special form of mood disorder associated with manic episodes; its treatment includes antimanic medications and mood stabilizers, such as lithium and anticonvulsants. While very little is known about the potential antisuicidal effect of anticonvulsants, a good deal of information has accumulated indicating that lithium may have striking antisuicidal properties over and above its mood-stabilizing properties. The chapter describes some of the work of the authors, which indicates that the risk of suicidal acts in bipolar patients is significantly reduced when they are on lithium and returns to prelithium levels if lithium is discontinued.

At least one randomized control study has shown that lithium has advantages over carbamazepine in reducing suicidal acts in bipolar and unipolar patients. This study needs replication, but it is consistent with a large body of data based on naturalistic observations. One aspect of lithium treatment that is important to appreciate is that the patient must attend a lithium clinic or equivalent regularly and have blood tests to monitor the adequacy of the lithium dosage. Thus, this is the only psychotropic agent where adequate treatment is assured in the context of routine management. It is not clear what role this combination of regular psychiatric supervision and insuring an adequate dose of the medication plays in the efficacy of lithium in preventing suicidal behavior.

In *Treatment of Suicidality in Schizophrenia,* Dr. Herbert Meltzer reviews our knowledge of suicide in this disorder as a prelude to discussing recent treatment advances in our ability to prevent it. The rate of suicide and suicide attempts in schizophrenia is significantly elevated above that of the general population. Estimates are that 4–13% of patients with schizophrenia commit suicide and 25–50% make a suicide attempt. After discussing the epidemiology of suicidal behavior in schizophrenia, Dr. Meltzer reviews the risk factors for suicidal behavior in schizophrenics. In particular, he discusses relationships of suicidal behavior in schizophrenia to depression and hopelessness as well as to cognition and insight. There appears to be a lower level of insight into their illness in individuals who report suicidal ideation or suicide attempts. The treatment of schizophrenic patients who are at risk for suicide requires considerable further research. Meltzer describes some very promising preliminary results, however, using the atypical antipsychotic, clozapine.

Clozapine appears to reduce rates of suicidal behavior that is manifested in terms of suicide attempts and possibly unintentional self-harm. Other investigators have confirmed these findings, analyzing different large databases, and the result has been the commencement of an international suicide prevention trial. This is a large-scale, prospective, randomized, open-label single-blind parallel group study comparing the efficacy of clozapine with olanzepine in reducing suicidality in schizophrenia. This study is being conducted at 68 sites in 11 countries. It should be noted that another characteristic of clozapine treatment is that patients have to come regularly for blood tests, and this insures a level of compliance that may explain part of the antisuicidal effect of clozapine. However, much of the data that have been analyzed comes from controlled clinical trials where the level of patient care and supervision was comparable to that for the typical *versus* the atypical antipsychotic and, therefore, this effect may be less striking than it is in the lithium literature. Nevertheless, the prospect of an antisuicidal effect from atypical antipsychotics offers hope for the treatment of suicidal behavior in schizophrenia.

In *Borderline Personality Disorder: Suicidality and Self-Mutilation*, Drs. John Gunderson and Maria Ridolfi discuss the challenging problem of suicidality and self-mutilation in borderline personality disorder. Both suicide attempts and self-mutilation are, unfortunately, quite common and somewhat resistant to treatment in borderline personality disorder. The lifetime incidence of suicide itself is quite high in borderline personality disorder and has been estimated to be approximately 9%. That rate is about 400 times the rate of suicide in the general population and more than 800 times the rate of suicide in young females, according to Gunderson and Ridolfi. They report that self-mutilation is exceedingly frequent, as are suicide attempts or gestures. There is some discussion of the neurobiological factors underlying these behaviors and the psychosocial triggering context. A serotonin deficiency may underlie impulsive self-destructive acts, but the biology of the compulsive quality of self-mutilation is less understood. In this population, interpersonal crises frequently trigger suicide attempts or, as impulsive mild injuries have sometimes been termed, suicide gestures. Management is a major challenge, and some guidelines are provided. Management is easier when it involves more than a single therapist. There are some psychotherapies, such as dialectical behavior therapy, that have been shown to be potentially effective for the suicidal behavior independent of mood.

In *Treating the Substance-Abusing Suicidal Patient,* Drs. Jack Cornelius, Ihsan Salloum, Kevin Lynch, Duncan Clark and John Mann discuss the frequency of suicidal behavior in association with substance abuse. It should be noted that substance abuse is frequently comorbid with other psychiatric conditions, including mood disorders, psychoses, anxiety disorders, and personality disorders. Its presence increases the risk of suicidal behavior in any of the other conditions. In addition, there is significant morbidity and mortality due to suicidal behavior in patients whose primary problem is substance abuse. After an initial discussion of the prevalence of suicidal behavior amongst substance-abusing patients, there is a description of the clinical presentation followed by suggestions regarding pharmacotherapy. The section on pharmacotherapy describes a series of studies, including a double-blind placebo-controlled study of fluoxetine in depressed alcoholics, that appear to have produced some very promising results. There is also a description of the literature, including the use of tricyclic antidepressants in nonsuicidal depressed alcoholics and antidepressant medication involving substance abusers other than alcoholics. The chapter ends with a review of the role of psychotherapy and psychosocial interventions and, in general, clinicians will probably find that they need to integrate several strategies, including pharmacotherapy, if they are to be successful in treating these patients.

In *Treating Impulsivity and Anxiety in the Suicidal Patient,* Dr. Jan Fawcett starts from the premise that anxiety and impulsivity traits are risk factors for suicidal behavior in a variety of psychiatric disorders. Therefore, where these features are prominent, regardless of the specific psychiatric disorder, they are potential treatment targets in their own right. Fawcett presents a review of a range of clinical symptoms, in addition to anxiety and impulsivity, that may be related in terms of their risk for suicidal behavior. These include global insomnia and a history of prior suicidal behavior. There is a careful description of the clinical evaluation of these features, including suicidal ideation, and their potential value in predicting suicidal behavior. Fawcett makes the point that very often the highest risk patients are also the most determined to commit suicide, and they conceal critical information from their physician. Thus, a statement that the patient has a specific suicidal plan may be a very important predictor of risk, but the denial of such a plan does not rule out the risk of suicide. Some extremely suicidal patients will specifically conceal such intentions from their physician. In those cases, there is not much the physician can do. Dr. Fawcett makes the case that the careful use of antianxiety treatments and perhaps medications that can reduce impulsivity, such as lithium, may therefore be helpful in reducing suicide risk.

The dramatic rise in youth suicide in much of the Western world in the last half of the last century has made the problem a national and international priority, engaging individuals and organizations ranging from the Surgeon General of the United States to the World Health Organization. The rise (threefold in the United States) has been attributed to a variety of psychosocial causes including a weakening of the family, changes in the roles of and expectations of young men and young women, and a widespread increase in substance abuse. Epidemiologists have correlated it with a rise in the incidence of depression in young people 15–24.

How are clinicians to respond to the increasing number of youngsters at risk for suicide? In *Assessment and Treatment of the Youthful Suicidal Patient,* Dr. David Brent addresses a number of the features of suicidal behavior that are specific to young people. In young adolescents an attempt of low lethality does not mean that suicidal intent is low, because cognitive immaturity may make it difficult for the youngster to formulate and execute a lethal plan. Precipitating events for young adolescents are likely to be interpersonal conflict or interpersonal loss usually involving a parent or a peer. Ongoing physical or sexual abuse is a particularly ominous precipitant. The highest suicide intent is seen among attempters whose motivation to die is to escape a psychologically painful situation such as abuse at home.

The most common psychopathological conditions in young suicide attempters are mood disorders, anxiety, disruptive behavior (conduct disorders), and substance abuse disorders. Impulsivity, impulsive aggression, poor affective regulation, and poor problem-solving skills are a common combination of psychological characteristics seen in young suicidal patients. The parents of suicide attempters and suicides have higher than expected rates of mood disorder, substance abuse, aggressive behavior, and suicidal behavior. The presence of a firearm in the home and the availability of lethal amounts of medication have been associated with increased suicide risk.

Brent reviews the successes and failures of cognitive behavioral therapy, dialectical behavior therapy, medication, family therapy, and supportive therapy in reducing suicide ideation and suicide attempts and in alleviating depression. He concludes by recommending a combined approach that involves treatment of the underlying psychopathology, amelioration of cognitive distortion and difficulties with social skills, problem-solving and affect regulation, and family psychoeducation and intervention.

Despite the rise in the rates of suicide among the young, it is older persons who remain most at risk And while the suicide rates of young people in the past decade have shown a slight decline, the rates for those 65 or older have risen. Demographic projections make it likely that both the rate and the number of suicides in this age group will continue to rise. In *Suicide in Elders,* Drs. Yeates Conwell and Paul Duberstein address the multiple dimensions of suicide among older people with a view to understanding what can be done to reduce suicide in this age group.

Factors that they discuss as contributing to suicide risk among older persons include living alone, recent bereavement, personality traits such as lack of openness to experience, psychiatric illness usually affective in nature, and physical illness particularly when accompanied by functional impairment.

Seventy percent of older persons who commit suicide have seen a primary care physician in the month prior to their death. This striking fact, Conwell and Duberstein point out, presents a unique opportunity for physicians to intervene if they can recognize the depressive illness that is likely to be present. Primary care physicians have been shown to have difficulty in recognizing depression. Brief screening instruments, however, have been shown to help them to do so. The authors discuss the educational intervention program on the Swedish island of Gotland in which primary care physicians were educated in the recognition and treatment of depression with a resulting significant reduction in the suicide rate. They point out the strengths and weaknesses of that intervention and the efforts being made to replicate and improve it.

They also discuss the community outreach programs for older persons that give us an opportunity to help those who may not visit a general practitioner. Most of these programs include regular telephone contact by trained staff with individuals referred by social service, crisis hotlines, family members, or gatekeepers. Their services can include referrals, crisis interventions, and home visits for medical, psychiatric, nutritional, and family assessments. Two of the programs they discuss give evidence of having been able to reduce suicide rates in their areas. Conwell and Duberstein provide convincing evidence that the combination of community outreach and the recognition and treatment of depressive illness in primary care settings offers realistic hope of reducing suicide in older people.

Since the 1980s, when Dr. Aaron Beck demonstrated that hopelessness was the dimension of depression most correlated with risk of suicide, there has been increasing interest in the affective and behavioral factors that increase suicide risk. In *Recognizing and Responding to a Suicide Crisis,* Drs. Herbert Hendin, John Maltsberger, Alan Lipschitz, Professor Ann P. Haas, and Jennifer Kyle distinguish a suicide crisis defined as a time-limited occurrence signaling immediate danger of suicide and suicide risk, a broader term that includes such factors as age and sex, psychiatric diagnosis, and past suicide attempts and such traits and behaviors as impulsivity and substance abuse.

The authors draw on cases in which the patients were in treatment when they committed suicide to identify signs that warned of a suicide crisis. Three factors were identified as markers of the suicide crisis: a precipitating event; one or more intense affective states other than depression; and at least one of three behavioral patterns: speech or actions suggesting suicide, deterioration in social or occupational functioning, and increased substance abuse.

Consistently linked to the suicide crises were acute, intense affective states that appeared to have compounded patients' depression—feelings of desperation, an acute sense of abandonment, anxiety, rage, guilt, or humiliation. The acute affective state most associated with a suicide crisis was desperation. Defined as a state of anguish accompanied by an urgent need for relief, desperation was present in 85% of the patients.

In more than half the cases, the therapists did not recognize that their patients were in a suicide crisis. In most of these cases greater awareness of the crisis signs would likely have alerted the therapist to the patient's risk. Among the other patients in whom the suicide crisis was not recognized, problems in communication between patient and therapist often originating in therapeutic anxiety over the patient's possible suicide contributed to the lack of recognition. Case illustrations are presented in the chapter to indicate how this occurs. In many instances, therapists recognized that their patients were in a suicide crisis, but they experienced a variety of problems in responding that are also discussed with case illustrations.

In *When to Hospitalize Patients at Risk for Suicide*, Dr. Robert Hirschfeld addresses the critical decision of determining whether patients who are being evaluated for suicide risk present an imminent danger (within 48 hours) for suicide—a danger usually requiring their immediate hospitalization. As a necessary background for such a determination, he deals first with the general types of risk factors for suicide: Older, white males living alone are most at risk. Past suicide attempts, substance abuse, and a family history of suicide increase the risk. Patients with depression especially psychotic depression with auditory hallucinations commanding the patient to kill him- or herself and patients in mixed manic states are more likely to be at imminent risk. The impulsivity and aggression associated with borderline personality disorders or antisocial personality disorders also place patients at high imminent risk.

A variety of medical conditions such as cancer, epilepsy, multiple sclerosis, head injury, cardiovascular disease, dementia, and AIDS increase the risk for suicide. The risk is also heightened by intoxication, inability to resist impulses, hopeless cognitions, and severe depression, especially with comorbid anxiety symptoms.

In deciding whether a patient is at imminent risk, Hirschfeld points out that the most obvious thing to do is to ask the patient. Unlike patients in ongoing outpatient treatment who often conceal suicidal intentions out of fear of hospitalization, distressed patients presenting initially for help are more likely to respond frankly to such questioning.

Hirschfeld warns that a patient who needs to be hospitalized because of imminent suicide risk should not be left alone. There are many tragic instances of patients committing suicide while waiting for transfer to a hospital. He cautions that it is better to have an ambulance service or the police take the patient to the hospital rather than a family member who may be manipulated by the patient out of doing so.

The revolution in our biological knowledge of depression and our ability to treat even severe cases successfully with psychotropic medication has posed a challenge to both the theory and the practice of psychodynamically trained psychotherapists. Most have begun to meet the challenge and have recognized that medication makes many patients accessible to psychotherapy who otherwise would not be. Drs. Steven Roose and John T. Maltsberger are psychoanalysts who are helping to integrate the knowledge that advances in both neurobiology and psychodynamics are bringing to the treatment of suicidal patients.

In *What is in the Clinician's Mind,* Roose addresses some of the difficulties that a psychodynamically trained physician may encounter when evaluating a seriously depressed patient. If the physician is adverse to a medical model of illness in which diagnosis often dictates treatment and is only comfortable with an approach based on interpretation, then he or she will have difficulty in intervening—insisting on hospitalization, for example—in situations where it is required. The psychodynamic model leads some to regard depression not as an illness but simply as the affective consequence of a conflict that is subject to interpretation. Roose points that such a view may be motivated by a desire to avoid a level of activity or an assumption of power that is inherent in a medical model of illness. Such a theoretical orientation interferes with the ability to diagnose and treat suicidally depressed patients. To prevent this from occurring, "the dynamically-oriented physician must use the dynamic model of the mind when appropriate and recognize that in certain situations it is not germane."

A somewhat different problem can emerge when suicidal ideation or behavior takes place in an ongoing psychotherapy. Clinicians tend to believe that if you do the right thing in treating a suicidal patient, the patient will stay alive. Suicide is experienced as a failure and a source of shame. In accepting such responsibility the psychodynamic therapist is to a degree accepting the medical model of illness, but may not embrace an important component—the realization that not all severely ill patients can be saved. Lacking such a perspective, many psychotherapists avoid treating suicidal patients.

Roose believes that what may help the psychodynamic therapist overcome these problems is the psychodynamic treatment tht they have had as part of their training. They are trained to be aware of their feeling states in response to patients. This awareness can help them recognize whether countertransference in the form of taking refuge in theory, intellectualization, avoidance, or anxiety is influencing their behavior. If they can also include nondynamic models of illness in their thinking, they may be uniquely able to develop a treatment plan for the suicidal patient.

In *Treating the Suicidal Patient: Basic Principles*, Maltsberger describes some of the ways in which psychodynamic psychotherapy must adapt to deal with the psychopathology of suicidal patients, because a high percentage of those who are suicidal and seek psychotherapy suffer from "narcissistic character disorders of a borderline nature." They usually have problems in reality testing that contraindicate classical psychoanalysis with its emphasis on understanding the transference. The inability of these patients to contain affects without acting on them and their lack of a stable sense of self are further reasons to avoid treating them with a classic psychoanalytic approach.

The therapist must become an auxiliary ego to these patients, offering them narcissistic assistance and strengthening their ego through their identification with the therapist. This requires the therapist to care deeply for the patient and not to conceal this fact. In this context, the therapist must become aware of, but not act on, his or her countertransference reactions to the patient, being particularly cognizant of the anxiety and anger that suicidal patients can generate in their therapists. At the same time, the therapist must be able to help the patient contain anxiety, rage, and self-hatred without going into destructive action. This involves both calming patients and teaching them that there are better ways of obtaining help from others than by suicidal threats or self-injury. Reality testing that corrects perceptive distortions often about the therapist and setting limits on patient behavior, including hospitalization wshen necessary, must be part of the therapeutic approach. Time-limited treatments are not likely to lead to long term success.

In the United States, firearms, long the method chosen by most men who commit suicide, have in recent years become the method of choice of most women as well. Understandably, there has been interest in determining whether restriction of gun availability and accessibility holds significant promise for suicide prevention. In *Firearms and Suicide,* Dr. David Brent, who has been a major contributor to this research, provides an overview of our current knowledge and the evidence for it.

The suicide rate has been found to be higher in those parts of the country where more people own guns. States with more restrictive gun control laws have lower rates of firearm suicides, and although they have higher rates by other means, their suicide rate is lower overall. Studies of the effect of instituting state firearms control legislation, whether by requiring a waiting period, licensing requirements, and restricting availability based on psychiatric criminal records, have all been shown to have an effect in reducing a state's suicide rate primarily among youthful suicides.

Brent points out that the dramatic increase in youth suicide in the last half of the last century cannot be attributed simply to firearms. The increase in youth suicide has occurred in parts of the world where firearm ownership and firearms suicides are relatively rare. There has been a more widespread increase in drug and alcohol abuse, which has been shown to be strongly correlated with an increase in suicide. Brent's own work indicates a strong and deadly relationship between the use of firearms to commit suicide and substance abuse. The proportion of youthful suicide victims who were drinking at the time of their suicide has been increasing; those youth who were drinking at the time of their suicide were much more likely to use a gun than were those who were not.

The most convincing evidence that firearm availability increases the risk for suicide comes not from studies of the effects of legislation restricting firearms, but from studies of the effects of the presence of a gun in the home on suicide. Although three-quarters of gun owners keep a gun at least partly for self-protection, a study by Arthur Kellerman and his coworkers of 398 consecutive gun deaths occurring in homes where firearms were kept found that only two (.5%) of those killed were intruders; 12 (3%) were accidental gunshot deaths; 50 (12.6%) were homicides, primarily adults in the home who killed each other during a quarrel; and in 333 cases (83.2%) the guns were used by an adolescent or an adult to kill him- or herself.

Brent's work has established that the presence of a gun in the home is one of the strongest predictors of youth suicide independent of the presence in the youngster of a psychiatric disorder. Study of those who survive suicide attempts with guns indicates that for a high percentage of such patients the attempt was impulsive. Impulsive suicide attempts are common among the young and the presence of a gun makes it more likely that the attempt will be fatal. This seems to be one of the strongest reasons to restrict and license gun access.

For two decades an increasing body of research, first in the United States and then abroad, demonstrated that prominent, frequent, and sensational media coverage of suicide increases suicidal behavior, particularly among young people. The size of the increase is related to the celebrity of the suicide victim and the amount of publicity given to the story.

In *Suicide and the Media*, Professor Madelyn Gould, who has been an important contributor to research in this area, reviews the features in media coverage of suicide that have been shown to encourage imitative (copycat) suicides: detailed descriptions of methods employed, emphasis on the victim's engaging qualities, and emphasizing the "rewards" of the attempt such as getting even or gaining attention.

In summarizing the research findings of the past 20 years, Gould discusses ways in which the research was done and some of the methodologic problems involved in doing it. Most studies have relied on the effect on suicide rates of the publication of differing ways of treating stories of individual suicides. Determining whether those involved in suicidal behavior have actually been exposed to the media stories has begun to engage investigators. Some studies have measured the effect of newspaper strikes ("blackouts") on reducing suicide rates. The adoption by the media in Austria of guidelines written by mental health professionals for the coverage of stories on suicide has been shown to have had a significant impact in reducing suicide in the country.

In the 1980s, the Center for Disease Control (CDC) organized and utilized a national workshop on media coverage of suicide to develop and publish a set of guidelines on the reporting of suicide. In 2000 the American Foundation for Suicide Prevention (AFSP) enlisted Dr. Gould, who had participated in the original CDC workshop, to lead an effort to update those guidelines. Updated guidelines, discussed in her chapter, formed the starting point for a conference of concerned organizations sponsored by AFSP and the Annenberg School of Communications designed to develop a consensus on such guidelines. The conference, which included the CDC, the National Institute of Mental Health, the Office of the Surgeon General, the Substance and Mental Health Services Administration, the World Health Organization, and the American Association of Suicidology, has developed a preliminary draft to be found on the AFSP website (www.afsp.org) which also includes examples of appropriate and inappropriate coverage.

Stories about suicide can be helpful in efforts to prevent suicide by informing the public about the likely causes and warning signs of suicide, its relation to depression and other mental illnesses, and advances in treatment. Since this information can highlight opportunities to prevent suicide, the media guidelines not only are cautionary but also contain positive suggestions for coverage

The Clinical Science of Suicide Prevention rests on the knowledge that in the past decade specific treatments have been shown to reduce suicide and/or suicidal behavior in a variety of psychiatric conditions: bipolar disorder, schizophrenia, and borderline personality disorder. In the next decade we should be able to learn how effective our treatments of depression are in preventing suicide and in what way they need to be supplemented by treatments aimed at regulating associated affects and other psychopathologies that complicate depressive disorders.We must determine whether medication combined with psychotherapy improves compliance and enhances efficacy in treating depression and preventing suicide than either treatment alone.

The past decade has also seen a burgeoning interest in genetic research into suicide that may guide future treatments by identifying high risk patients and aiding the choice of medication. In addition, the study of the influence of psychosocial factors on suicide, whether in the form of firearm availability or the contagious influence of certain types of media coverage of suicide, has increasingly moved from the anecdotal to the scientific.

The comprehensive Suicide Prevention 2000 conference that led to this book was sponsored by the American Foundation for Suicide Prevention. AFSP has contributed to the remarkable advances in our knowledge over the past 10 years and looks forward to stimulating research and educational efforts to prevent suicide in the years to come.

The Depressed Suicidal Patient

Assessment and Treatment

CHARLES B. NEMEROFF, MICHAEL T. COMPTON, AND JOSEPH BERGER

Department of Psychiatry and Behavioral Sciences, Emory University School of Medicine, Atlanta, Georgia 30322, USA

ABSTRACT: Depressive disorders are associated with significant psychosocial impairment and disability. Depression should be thoroughly evaluated, as should current and past suicidality and potential risk factors for suicide. Mortality by suicide characterizes the course of major affective disorders in approximately 15% of those suffering from these illnesses. Several neurobiological correlates of suicidality have been discovered. Treatment of depression with suicidality may involve hospitalization, pharmacotherapy, electroconvulsive therapy, and psychotherapy. Special populations include children and adolescents, the elderly, medically ill patients, patients with comorbid personality disorders, and patients with comorbid substance abuse disorders. Clinicians encountering patients with depressive disorders should be proficient in the assessment and treatment of depression with suicidality.

KEYWORDS: Depression; Suicide

INTRODUCTION

A thorough understanding of the treatment of the depressed suicidal patient is imperative for psychiatrists, other physicians, and mental health professionals encountering these severely affectively ill patients. According to the National Comorbidity Survey, the lifetime prevalence of major depression in the general U.S. population is 17.1% for men and 21.3% for women.[1] Due to the high prevalence and significant morbidity and psychosocial impairment associated with this disorder, primary care and specialized physicians as well as psychiatrists should be proficient in the evaluation of depression. Suicidal thoughts and/or behaviors should be assessed in each patient with a depressive syndrome.

Address for correspondence: Dr. Charles B. Nemeroff, Emory University School of Medicine, Department of Psychiatry and Behavioral Sciences, 1639 Pierce Drive, Suite 4000, Atlanta, GA 30322. Voice: 404/727-8382; fax: 404/727-3233.
cnemero@emory.edu

EVALUATION OF DEPRESSION

The clinician's first task is a thorough assessment of the patient's depressive condition. A complete history should include current symptoms, psychiatric history (including a history of hypomanic or manic symptoms and the response to current or previous treatments), and medical, social, family, and substance use histories.[2] Review of systems, mental status examination, physical examination, and diagnostic tests as indicated should be obtained. Collateral history is often useful. Screening for depression is a vital function of primary care physicians[3] as well as mental health professionals.

Differential Diagnosis

As defined by the fourth edition of the *Diagnostic and Statistical Manual of Mental Disorders* (DSM-IV),[4] a major depressive episode is a period of at least 2 weeks' duration in which there is either depressed mood or anhedonia. The individual must also experience at least four additional depressive symptoms that represent a change from previous functioning. The symptoms cause clinically significant distress or impairment in social, occupational, or other important areas of functioning.

A major depressive episode can occur in the context of major depressive disorder or during the course of bipolar I disorder, bipolar II disorder, or schizoaffective disorder. Rates of suicidality may be different in these various diagnostic categories. In a review of six studies in which unipolar, bipolar I, and bipolar II patients were analyzed separately, the rate of suicidal behavior among bipolar patients (19%) was significantly higher than that among unipolar patients (12%).[5] The lifetime history of suicide attempts is significantly higher in bipolar II than bipolar I patients (24% vs. 17%). These and other studies suggest that bipolar II disorder imparts a particularly high risk for attempted or completed suicide.[5] Some of the excess risk may be due to comorbid substance use disorders, personality disorders, or anxiety disorders.

Aside from a major depressive episode, one must consider other conditions that cause a similar presentation of depressive symptoms. Such a depressive profile can be identified as a direct physiological effect of a substance ("with depressive features") or general medical condition ("with major depressive-like episode") or as related to other disorders such as dysthymic disorder or an adjustment disorder. The lifetime prevalence of suicide attempts in three depressive illnesses was studied in 176 young male patients.[6] Major depressive disorder was associated with a 27% lifetime prevalence of suicide attempts, but there was also a 17% prevalence in dysthymic disorder and 4% in adjustment disorder with depressed mood.

EVALUATION OF SUICIDALITY

A suicide attempt is an act of self-inflicted harm accompanied by explicit or implicit intent to cause death. Although the rate of suicide attempts is much higher, the incidence of completed suicide in primary affective disorders is estimated to be 15%.[7] Completed suicide is more frequent in men, likely because of the more violent means used, although attempts are more common in women. Of those who die annually by suicide, 72% are white males, 19% are white females, 7% are nonwhite males, and 2% are nonwhite females.[8]

Assessment of Current and Past Suicidality

Of primary importance in the clinical assessment of the depressed patient is a thorough evaluation of suicidal thoughts, plans, intent, and attempts. Practical interviewing strategies have been developed for efficiently eliciting suicidal ideation, such as the Chronological Assessment of Suicide Events (CASE) approach.[9] Evaluation of current suicidality should include extent and details of planning, lethality of such plans, intent to act on them, availability of means, and preparatory plans such as drafting a will, purchasing life insurance, or securing means.[10]

Because an important predictor of suicide attempt is a past personal history of suicide attempt (and past history of taking precautions against being discovered after an attempt[11]), the clinician should thoroughly evaluate details of any past suicidality. The treatment plan should weigh the presence or absence of a history of suicidal behavior as an important regulator of acute intervention and follow-up.[12] Suicidal ideation or acts are the variables with perhaps the strongest association with completed suicide, with a possible "dose-response" relationship between the extent to which the patient has acted on suicidal ideation and the risk of completed suicide.[13] Gathering collateral history from family and friends is an important aspect of a thorough assessment of suicidality.

Assessment of Risk Factors

A risk factor is a characteristic, variable, or hazard that increases the likelihood of development of an adverse outcome, that is measurable, and that precedes the outcome.[14] Aside from the evaluation of current and past suicidality, the clinician should consider whether or not the patient has certain other risk factors for suicide.

Most studies have assessed long-term risk factors, but clinicians frequently must assess acute or short-term risk.[10] It is not possible to predict accurately whether or when a particular individual with depression will attempt suicide.[4] Furthermore, interactions among risk factors may be complex, and such interactions are as yet poorly understood.[15] Thus, prediction is imprecise, and assessment of risk factors is a less informative tool than actual thorough clinical evaluation of suicidal thoughts and behaviors. Nonetheless, the identification of high-risk patients, an important aspect of the primary prevention of suicide, can be informed by thorough assessment of risk factors.

Potential Risk Factors for Suicide

Putative risk factors tend to have low specificity and predictive power, which may result in overdiagnosis of high suicide risk due to the relative rarity of suicide. Many studies have proposed multiple risk factors for suicide (TABLE 1), and various classifications for such risk factors have been put forth. For example, Blumenthal and Kupfer[16] proposed an overlapping model for considering major risk factors for suicide, which includes five factors with varying individual weights: (1) psychiatric diagnosis, (2) personality style, (3) psychosocial risk factors such as social supports, life events, and chronic medical illness, (4) genetic and family factors, and (5) neurochemical factors. Risk factors can also be divided into predisposing factors and potentiating factors.[3] Similarly, risk factors for suicide in major depression can be organized according to whether they affect the threshold for suicidal acts or they serve as triggers of suicidal acts.[10]

Some factors that may influence the threshold for suicidal behavior during an episode of major depression include: personal past history of suicide attempt, family history of suicide, early onset of depression, comorbid substance use disorders, comorbid cluster B personality disorders, chronic physical illness, marital isolation, parental loss through death before the age of 11, childhood history of physical or sexual abuse, corporal punishment in adolescence, presence of hopelessness, and low self-esteem.[10] Risk factors that may serve as triggers for suicidal behavior in major depression include: bipolar disorder, presence of psychosis, acute substance intoxication, social, financial, or family crisis or loss, and contagion or recent exposure to suicide.[10] Clinical variables that may be protective against suicidality include religious or moral constraints, concern about social disapproval, better coping skills, feelings of responsibility towards family, and living with children under the age of 18.[10]

There is a strong relationship between treatment history (specialty mental health care vs. primary care, inpatient vs. outpatient care) and suicide mortality, which almost certainly reflects the association between level of treatment and severity of illness.[17] The first 3 months after the onset of a major depressive episode and the first 5 years after the lifetime onset of major depressive

TABLE 1. Potential risk factors for suicide in major depression

Demographic factors

- Male gender
- White race
- Ages 24–35 or over 50

Factors associated with the depressive episode

- Suicidal thoughts or acts
- Lack of treatment or inadequate treatment of depressive episode
- Presence of hopelessness
- Low self-esteem, feelings of failure
- More severe depressive symptoms (diminished concentration, insomnia, anhedonia, but not diminished energy level)
- Recent bereavement
- Presence of psychosis
- Concomitant anxiety or panic attacks
- Being in the first 3 months after the onset of the depressive episode

Factors related to personality characteristics

- Personality variables including aggression, hostility, or impulsivity

Comorbidity

- Comorbid substance use disorders
- Comorbid borderline personality traits or disorder
- Comorbid conduct disorder or antisocial personality traits or disorder
- Comorbid general medical conditions
- Bipolar disorder or mood cycling
- Acute substance intoxication

Factors revealed by history

- Past personal history of suicide attempt
- Past history of taking precautions against being discovered after an attempt
- Presence of a family history of suicide
- Early onset of depression, being younger at first hospitalization, more previous hospitalizations
- Parental loss through death before the age of 11
- Childhood history of physical or sexual abuse
- Corporal punishment in adolescence

Psychosocial factors

- Being recently widowed/separated/divorced
- Chronic physical illness
- Social, financial, or family crisis or loss (negative live events)
- Unemployment or financial problems
- Lack of religious or moral constraints against suicide
- Not living with a child younger than 18
- Social isolation

Miscellaneous

- Access to means with greater lethality
- Contagion or recent exposure to suicide

disorder may represent the highest risk period for attempted suicide, independent of severity of depression.[18] Another important risk factor for suicide is lack of treatment or inadequate treatment of the depressive episode.[19] In an assessment of risk, one must consider the patient's degree of social isolation and access to means of suicide with greater potential lethality. Higher lethality may correlate with higher scores on the Hamilton Rating Scale for Depression (HAM-D) at the time of hospitalization,[18] and more severe depressive symptoms (diminished concentration, insomnia, loss of interest or pleasure,[20] but not diminished energy level[21]). Other potential risk factors include trait and state anxiety, impulsivity,[22] panic attacks, and mood cycling.[23] Hopelessness has been found to mediate the relationship between depression and suicide for attempters of all age groups. Demographic variables that have been associated with increased risk include white race, male gender, ages 24–35 or over 50, being recently widowed, separated, or divorced, and unemployment or financial problems.[16,21,24]

The preceding listed risk factors for suicide are not divided into long-term versus short-term risk factors here, although some studies have attempted to do so. Risk assessments are probabilistic determinations that can be rated as low (few risk factors present), moderate (several risk factors present), or high (many risk factors present).[25] If the suicide risk is ongoing and chronic, then improvement in modifiable risk factors should be a goal of treatment.[24] Documenting a competent suicide risk assessment that directs clinical interventions is important from professional and medicolegal perspectives.[25]

NEUROBIOLOGY OF SUICIDALITY

A lowered threshold for suicidal behavior may originate from familial/genetic vulnerability via specific neurobiological endophenotypes. Although the neurobiological substrates of suicidality continue to be the subject of intense research, a brief review of this topic is of interest for clinicians encountering suicidally depressed patients. The findings presented here comprise the current general consensus in the research literature (TABLE 2), though some findings have been disputed and others need replication. Very preliminary findings are omitted.

Dysfunction in central serotonin (5-hydroxytryptamine, 5-HT) systems may be a biochemical trait that is associated with lowered threshold for self- and externally directed aggressive behavior, and thus suicidality. Patients with major depression who have made suicide attempts have lower levels of 5-hydroxyindoleacetic acid (5-HIAA) in the brain stem[26] and in cerebrospinal fluid (CSF) compared to patients who have not.[27] This reduction in CSF 5-HIAA appears to correlate with lethality, more planning, and medical dam-

TABLE 2. Proposed neurobiological correlates of suicidality

Serotonergic dysfunction

- Decreased 5-HIAA concentrations in the brainstem
- Decreased 5-HIAA concentrations in cerebrospinal fluid
- Decreased binding of presynaptic serotonin transporter sites ([^{3}H]-imipramine binding)
- Increased binding of postsynaptic 5-HT$_2$ receptors in prefrontal cortex
- Increased 5-HT$_{1A}$ binding in the midbrain dorsal raphe and prefrontal cortex
- Blunted prolactin levels in response to fenfluramine challenge
- Increased density of serotonin neurons in the dorsal raphe nuclei
- Polymorphism in the gene for tryptophan hydroxylase

Noradrenergic dysfunction

- Increased β-adrenoreceptor binding in prefrontal cortex
- Fewer noradrenergic locus ceruleus neurons
- Increased tyrosine hydroxylase activity
- Decreased α$_1$-adrenergic binding in specific frontal and temporal gyri
- Increased α$_1$-adrenergic binding in specific layers of the prefrontal cortex
- Increased α$_2$-adrenergic binding in locus ceruleus

Dopaminergic dysfunction

- Reduced dopamine turnover in the basal ganglia (reduced DOPAC levels)
- Decreased HVA concentrations in cerebrospinal fluid
- Decreased urinary outputs of HVA, DOPAC, and sum dopamine

Hypothalamic-pituitary-adrenal axis hyperactivity

- Persistent dexamethasone suppression test nonsuppression
- Elevated CRF in CSF
- Reduced CRF binding sites in the frontal cortex

age of the attempt.[28,29] This finding has not been replicated when bipolar patients have been studied.[30]

Decreased CSF 5-HIAA may be a marker of the impulsive, aggressive, and violent nature of suicide. Measurements of CSF 5-HIAA in a group of 64 patients with various DSM-III-R diagnoses but no past suicidal behavior revealed that the aggressive group ($n = 35$) had significantly lower CSF 5-HIAA concentrations than the nonaggressive group.[31] Thus, there may be an association between disinhibited aggressive, impulsive, violent behavior and serotonergic dysfunction independent of suicidal behavior (a dimensional rather than a categorical model of psychopathology[32]).

Other measures indicate that central nervous system (CNS) serotonergic dysfunction is associated with suicidality. Such findings include: (1) decreased binding to serotonin transporter sites on presynaptic terminals (as measured by tritiated imipramine binding), (2) increased binding to postsynaptic 5-HT$_2$ receptors in the prefrontal cortex (possibly due to upregulation),

(3) increased binding to 5-HT$_{1A}$ receptors in the midbrain dorsal raphe and prefrontal cortex, (4) blunted prolactin response to fenfluramine challenge (a measure of overall serotonergic response—fenfluramine is a serotonin-releasing and uptake-inhibiting agent), (5) increased density of serotonin neurons in the dorsal raphe nucleus, and (6) a possible polymorphism in the gene for tryptophan hydroxylase.[32–36] Some of these findings, such as the upregulation of postsynaptic receptors, have been debated due to mixed findings across studies and methodologic limitations.[37,38]

Findings involving the adrenergic system in association with suicidality appear to be less well replicated, but include: (1) increased binding to β-adrenoreceptors in prefrontal cortex, (2) fewer noradrenergic locus ceruleus neurons, (3) increased tyrosine hydroxylase activity, (4) decreased α$_1$-adrenergic binding in specific frontal and temporal gyri, (5) increased α$_1$-adrenergic binding in specific layers of the prefrontal cortex, and (6) increased α$_2$-adrenergic binding in the locus ceruleus.[33,35,39] Increases in receptor binding may represent compensatory upregulation of postsynaptic elements in response to deficiencies in the presynaptic neurons innervating cortical targets.[33]

Although other neurotransmitter systems have not yet received as much attention in the research literature as serotonin and norepinephrine, some preliminary work has been conducted. In a postmortem study of 49 depressed subjects who committed suicide, concentrations of the dopamine metabolite dihydroxyphenylacetic acid (DOPAC) were significantly lower in the caudate, putamen, and nucleus accumbens of antidepressant-free suicides compared to controls and in the caudate in antidepressant-treated suicides.[40] Lower concentrations were largely restricted to those suicides who died by nonviolent methods. Other studies have shown lower CSF levels of homovanillic acid (HVA) in depressed patients attempting suicide[27] (which has also been associated with greater medical damage[28]), and lower urinary outputs of HVA, DOPAC, and total body output of dopamine in patients with depression who had attempted suicide compared to depressed patients who had not.[41]

Other findings point to an association between hypothalamic-pituitary-adrenal (HPA) axis hyperactivity and suicide. Such studies report elevated corticotropin-releasing factor (CRF) concentrations in CSF and reduced CRF binding sites in the frontal cortex of suicide victims.[42] Nemeroff et al.[43] studied the number and affinity of CRF binding sites in the frontal cortex of 26 suicide victims and 29 controls. There was a 23% reduction in the number of CRF binding sites in the frontal cortex of suicide victims compared with controls, consistent with the hypothesis that CRF is hypersecreted in depression, resulting in downregulation in the number of high-affinity CRF binding sites. We recently replicated this finding in a second study (Owens and Nemeroff, unpublished data). Predisposing suicide risk factors such as early parental loss may be mediated by prolonged hyperactivity of the HPA axis and extra-hypothalamic CRF circuits associated with the stress of separation on the developing brain.

TREATMENT OF DEPRESSION WITH SUICIDALITY

Although the treatment of depression has received much attention, the treatment of depression with associated suicidality has been relatively neglected in the research literature. Few studies have focused on the effects of pharmacotherapy on suicidal behavior, in part due to practical and ethical difficulties with such investigations.[44] In treatment studies of various psychiatric disorders, subjects considered to be at risk for suicide are usually excluded, leading to a lack of information on the treatment of individuals at risk for suicide.[45] Thus, there are few data on standards of care for preventing suicide or reducing the frequency or severity of parasuicidal acts (manipulative self-harming gestures where the individual reports not wanting to die).

The clinician should plan treatment around the acute phase, the continuation phase (once remission is achieved, to prevent relapse), and the maintenance phase (to prevent subsequent recurrences).[2] The therapeutic patient-caregiver relationship is a critical life-saving treatment component.[3] As the psychiatrist treats the depressive episode, the specific symptom of suicidality must be frequently reassessed and specifically targeted. The following review of the treatment of the suicidally depressed patient provides an outline for the management of this severely ill patient population.

Hospitalization

The most important initial step in the management of the depressed suicidal patient is to determine the level and intensity of care indicated according to the risk assessment. Hospitalization is an important treatment modality for the depressed suicidal patient, serving to allow initiation of aggressive treatment and to protect the patient from potential harm to self. If the patient is at significant risk for suicide but refuses hospitalization, involuntary hospitalization should be considered if the condition meets criteria of the local jurisdiction.[2] If hospitalization is not indicated, family members should be involved in treatment planning and to provide increased vigilance.[24]

Simply admitting a patient to the hospital should not be considered a guarantee of safety. The clinician must assess and initiate the appropriate degree of observation and precautions. Even patients who appear to be improving may attempt suicide in the hospital setting, and an apparent improvement in the patient's condition may reflect a resolution of conflict by the decision to die.[46] Thus, apparent improvement should not necessarily mean immediate decreased vigilance.

Another phase of increased risk arises when the hospitalized depressed patient is discharged from the hospital.[8,47] Close monitoring is required during the transition back to the outpatient setting. Discharge summaries should communicate past and recent suicidality and risk assessments to the outpatient clinician as accurately as possible to facilitate effective patient care.[12] The patient's record should provide a comprehensive assessment of long- and short-term indicators of suicide risk.

Reducing Availability of Methods

Some studies suggest that the availability of specific lethal means is a determinant of suicide rates[48] and that differences in availability may account for differences in overall suicide rates between communities.[49] After thoroughly evaluating suicidality, the clinician should take steps to reduce the access to means of suicide, such as having family members remove guns or caches of medication from the home.[10] Firearms are the most common methods used by both men and women to commit suicide in the United States, accounting for nearly 60% of all suicide deaths.[14] Although removing available methods may be an adjunct to treatment of the suicidal patient, it should not be considered definitive treatment, and targeted treatment must still be initiated, possibly including hospitalization.

Pharmacotherapy

Antidepressants

Three aspects of the pharmacological treatment of depression with suicidality are of special importance: (1) the effectiveness of some antidepressants over others in alleviating suicidal ideation, (2) the possibility that some antidepressants may actually provoke suicide, and (3) the lethality of various antidepressants when taken in overdose.

Although comparative trials are currently lacking, agents considered to be efficacious in the treatment of depression are likely efficacious in the alleviation of suicidality. Most controlled trials of antidepressants specifically have excluded suicidal patients.[47] Oquendo et al.[10] reviewed several studies suggesting that the serotonergic capacity of drugs is important to achieve an antidepressant effect in the presence of suicidal behavior; serotonergic medications such as selective serotonin reuptake inhibitors (SSRIs) may afford superior improvement in suicidal behaviors compared to other antidepressants. There is some suggestion from several studies that serotonergic agents may produce more rapid improvement in suicidal ideation.[47] These medications also offer the added benefit of a greater margin of safety in overdose (vide infra). Although the biological processes involved are obviously very complex, such findings from clinical studies of antidepressants, suggesting efficacy of serotonin-specific agents in depression and suicidality, support the aforementioned association of CNS serotonergic dysfunction with suicidality.

Although tricyclic antidepressants (TCAs) have greater inherent toxicity, it remains to be determined whether the elevated rates of death from overdoses are simply related to toxicity or whether there is some element of suicide provocation with these drugs.[50] There have been some reports in the literature suggesting that some antidepressants may provoke suicidal behavior, including benzodiazepines (although a meta-analysis of pooled data from 22 placebo- and/or active comparator- controlled studies of depression found no association with emergence or worsening of suicidal ideation[51]), maprotiline,[52] amitriptyline,[50] and fluoxetine. Various mechanisms have been proposed, including the one side effect, akathisia, and improvement in energy level during treatment.[47] However, reports have been confounded by the natural fluctuation of suicidal thoughts during the course of depression,[53] and no evidence for such an association was found in the randomized controlled trial literature. Indeed, results from controlled retrospective studies involving large numbers of patients do not support a differential negative effect of certain antidepressants on suicidal behavior.[54] The risk of suicide attempt does not appear to differ among antidepressants.

Overdose accounts for a significant percentage of suicide and suicide attempts, and antidepressant medications are the most common agents involved. It is well known that newer antidepressants including SSRIs are safe in overdose compared with older agents such as TCAs and monoamine oxidase inhibitors (MAOIs). TCAs are associated with a higher rate of death in the event of an overdose than the newer nontricyclic antidepressants.[55] Indeed, with the exception of illicit drugs, TCAs represent the leading cause of overdose death in the United States. It is generally accepted that 15–20 mg/kg of one of the older TCAs will be fatal.[56] The life-threatening effects of TCA poisoning are related mainly to cardiotoxicity (due to quinidine-like activity) and CNS toxicity.[54] The chance of death after an overdose appears to be greater for desipramine and dothiepin (not available in the United States) than for other TCAs.[55] Lethality of MAOIs is likely related to their ability to cause a serotonin syndrome.[56] When ranking antidepressant classes according to deaths from overdose per million prescriptions, TCAs are found to be the most toxic, with 34.14 deaths.[57] MAOIs were associated with 13.48 deaths per million prescriptions, 6.19 for second-generation antidepressants, and 2.02 for SSRIs. The SSRI data are confounded by overdose with multiple other medications.

The therapeutic index, that is, the degree of toxicity, of an agent is an important factor in the choice of an antidepressant for treatment of individuals at risk for suicide.[54] Newer antidepressants appear to be devoid of direct cardiotoxicity and are significantly less anticholinergic than TCAs. SSRIs taken alone rarely, if ever, cause death when taken in overdose. The low toxicity of newer antidepressants renders them first choice in treating depressed suicidal patients. Clinical management of the suicidal depressed patient requires choosing a clinically effective antidepressant that minimizes the possibility of both an overdose and a fatal outcome in the event of an overdose.[55]

Once pharmacotherapy with an antidepressant is initiated, the patient is faced with a period of no improvement (due to the time lag before improvement in depressive symptoms after starting an antidepressant) and the additional burden of side effects.[47] During this period, the patient may actually be at greater risk, and the patient must be monitored closely, possibly in an inpatient setting. The antidepressant regimen should be maximized with a goal of complete remission of suicidal ideation and depressive symptoms. Several studies have documented unacceptably high rates of inadequately treated depression in patients who have committed suicide.[47]

Lithium

Some studies indicate an effect of lithium on the suicidal component of depressive illnesses. Comparing 64 former psychiatric inpatients who had committed suicide within 1 year after their discharge with a group of carefully matched patients who had not, Modestin and Schwarzenbach[58] found that a significantly higher proportion of the patients who did not commit suicide had been receiving pharmacotherapy, and a significantly higher proportion of them were on lithium (11% of controls vs. 0% of suicides).

Suicidal behavior was analyzed in 378 randomized subjects in a prospective trial of 2.5 years' duration, focusing on the differential episode-preventing effects of lithium, carbamazepine, or amitriptyline in affective disorders.[44] Of the nine suicides and five attempted suicides in this study, none took place during lithium treatment. Several other studies support the possibility that long-term lithium treatment reduces mortality and suicidal behavior.

Tondo, Jamison, and Baldessarini[59] reviewed 28 relevant reports from the period 1974–1996, most of which suggest that prophylactic treatment with lithium may provide some protection against suicidal behavior. In these studies, risk of suicide and attempts averaged 3.2 per 100 patient-years without lithium versus 0.37 per 100 patient-years with lithium (an 8.6-fold difference). Despite many methodological limitations of such reports, lithium seems to confer a clear antisuicidal effect. It is unclear whether such benefit merely reflects the mood-stabilizing effects of lithium or represents a distinct action on suicidal behaviors through direct effects on aggression and impulsivity, perhaps mediated by enhancement of central serotonergic functioning.[59] Protection against suicide with lithium is incomplete, but rates of suicides plus suicide attempts during lithium treatment may approach general population base rates.[60]

Other Pharmacological Agents

The use of other pharmacological agents may be necessary for the treatment of persistent specific symptoms (e.g., insomnia, anxiety, psychotic symptoms), comorbid conditions (e.g., panic disorder, alcohol dependence or withdrawal), or worrisome side effects (e.g., akathisia). Patients with bipolar depression should be treated with a mood stabilizer or a combination of mood stabilizers, and antidepressants, although the use of antidepressants, particularly TCAs, in bipolar depression carries a risk of inducing hypomania/mania or cycle acceleration.[61] If the depression is accompanied by psychotic features, antipsychotic medication should be prescribed. Psychotically depressed patients may be more likely to attempt suicide using violent methods.[62]

Electroconvulsive Therapy

Electroconvulsive therapy (ECT) is likely an underutilized treatment in the current armamentarium for suicidal depression. Due to the severity of the condition and the need for rapid improvement, clinicians treating the suicidally depressed patient should always consider ECT as an option. In several patient populations, ECT may represent the treatment of choice, such as for severe or psychotic depression, during pregnancy, during concomitant medical illness when antidepressant medications are contraindicated, or in a patient with a preference for or excellent previous response to ECT.

Psychotherapy

The roles for various forms of psychotherapy in the management of depressed patients with suicidality have not yet been adequately studied. Psychotherapeutic interventions that improve compliance, provide psychoeducation, decrease hopelessness,[63] diminish cognitive distortions, enhance self-esteem, strengthen social supports, and promote interpersonal relationships should theoretically decrease the risk of suicide.[16] However, it has been suggested that psychotherapy and the reexamination of painful problems in vulnerable individuals may actually provoke suicidal behavior.[50]

Some studies have suggested the efficacy of psychotherapy on the suicidality associated with depression. One trial randomized 20 patients at high risk of repeated suicide attempts to either a cognitive-behavioral problem-solving treatment consisting of five sessions or to a treatment-as-usual control condition.[64] The group practicing the problem-solving technique improved significantly more than the control group on ratings of depression, hopelessness, suicidal ideation, and target problems.

Linehan[65] developed dialectical behavior therapy, a novel manualized psychotherapy combining treatment strategies from cognitive, behavioral, and supportive psychotherapies, that targets suicidal and parasuicidal behavior in borderline personality disorder patients. Dialectical behavior therapy, which includes both individual and group therapy, has been shown to reduce incidences of parasuicide and medically severe parasuicides, to decrease attrition from individual therapy, and to decrease inpatient psychiatric days as compared to treatment-as-usual in the community in a group of chronically parasuicidal women.[65]

Outpatient Aftercare

Clinical vigilance after the onset of a depressive episode is of utmost importance, because this phase of the illness may carry an increased risk of suicide.[18] Several studies document a very high rate of suicide during the first several months after beginning treatment for an index episode of depression. Resources should be used to develop more intensive follow-up and support systems for patients showing features of high risk over the first year after hospital discharge.[23] Once the depressed suicidal patient is stabilized, aftercare follow-up in the outpatient setting should be arranged. Crisis intervention through problem-oriented sessions, perhaps including relevant significant others, may reduce immediate psychosocial stressors. Improvement in depressive symptoms is not uncommonly uneven.[3] Patients should be warned that suicidal ideation may occasionally recur during the course of treatment and that in such an event they should immediately contact their doctor or another mental health professional.[33,53]

Aftercare is often complicated by poor compliance, and methods to improve compliance should be employed. Poor compliance with antidepressants would be expected to prolong the episode of depression, leaving the individual at a persistently higher risk of suicide.[56] Compliance may be improved by fixed aftercare appointments and continuity of care from the inpatient to the outpatient settings.[66]

SUICIDAL DEPRESSION IN SPECIAL POPULATIONS

Several groups of patients may require special attention in the case of suicidal depression. These are reviewed briefly below.

Children and Adolescents

The diagnosis of a major depressive episode in children and adolescents requires attention to several differences in symptoms distinct from those of adults. For example, the mood may be irritable rather than sad, rather than weight loss the child may fail to make expected weight gains, and drop in grades may reflect poor concentration.[4] Children and adolescents are more likely to present with behavioral problems, poor school performance, somatic complaints, irritability, rebelliousness, apathy, self-esteem problems, and social withdrawal.[2] Major depressive episodes can occur in conjunction with attention-deficit and other disruptive behavior disorders, separation anxiety disorder, and other childhood psychiatric disorders. When working with children and adolescents, collateral history from family and other sources is obviously extremely important, and the family unit itself may need specific intervention to help reduce the risk of further suicidal behavior.[67]

Risk factors related to completed suicide in adolescence include having a psychiatric disorder, tendency towards impulsive aggression, family history of suicidal behavior, comorbid substance use, and central serotonergic abnormalities.[67] Stressful events such as disciplinary crisis, disappointment or rejection, and high levels of anxiety, anger, hopelessness, or depression may also precipitate suicide attempts. Comorbid conduct disorder (and later antisocial personality traits) may also increase risk for suicidality.[16] Children coming from a nonintact family of origin and children with poor connection to school may also be at increased risk for attempting suicide.[67]

Elderly Patients

Geriatric depression frequently presents with clinical features distinct from those of the general adult population and with particular problems in assessment. For example, memory difficulties may be mistaken for early signs of dementia ("pseudodementia").[4] A thorough history should include a review of medications and medical conditions that could cause or contribute to a depressive syndrome.

The rates of completed suicide are higher in late life than at any other point in the life course; suicidal behavior is more lethal in the elderly.[68] Older depressed patients tend to be frailer, to be suffering from more physical illness and other losses, to be more socially isolated, to give fewer warnings of their suicidal plans, and to use more potentially deadly methods. Chronic physical disability, dependence on caregivers, loss of dignity, chronic pain, and the fear of being institutionalized are frequently cited factors contributing to demoralization, depression, and suicide.[69]

Because of the potentially higher lethality of suicide attempts in the elderly, patients who voice suicidality should be evaluated with hospitalization as a serious option. A complete work-up rules out common organic causes, and the depressive episode is then treated aggressively. Psychosocial interventions are also invaluable to assist in improving overall quality of life and to decrease social isolation. Interpersonal factors including strains in patient-relative relationships and difficulties related to the care of the depressed older patient may be risk factors for suicide attempts in older depressed patients.[70] Survivors of suicidal behavior in old age remain a high-risk group and require close monitoring.[69]

Medically Ill Patients

A major depressive episode can be especially difficult to evaluate when it occurs in an individual who has other medical disorders. Many signs and symptoms of a diverse number of diseases may be identical to those of major depressive disorder. Some investigators recommend that symptoms should count towards a major depressive episode except when they are clearly and fully accounted for by the medical condition.[4]

In a study of 196 patients with advanced terminal cancer, hopelessness (defined broadly to encompass the inability to find purpose in living) was correlated more highly with suicidal ideation than was the level of depression.[71] Many medical disorders have been reported to increase the risk of suicide, including: HIV/AIDS, Huntington's disease, malignant neoplasms, multiple sclerosis, peptic ulcer disease, renal disease requiring dialysis, spinal cord injury, and systemic lupus erythematosus.[72] Many such conditions have high comorbid prevalence rates of psychosis or substance use disorders, which are a link between the general medical condition and suicide. Physicians treating such patients should assess the patient for depression and associated suicidality, so that proper treatment can be initiated.[73]

Patients with Comorbid Personality Disorders

The prevalence of personality disorders is high among patients with depressive disorders, including major depressive disorder, adjustment disorder with depressed mood, and especially dysthymic disorder.[6]

Borderline personality traits are associated with recurrent suicide attempts and chronic suicidal behavior. Corbitt et al.[74] evaluated the relationship between personality disorders and suicidal behavior in 102 psychiatric inpatients with major depressive disorder, using standardized structured interviews. No differences were found between attempters and nonattempters in numbers of cluster A or cluster C criteria met. The presence and severity of borderline or cluster B personality psychopathology were positively related to indicators of suicidality. Also, greater borderline personality traits were associated with higher rates and earlier manifestations of suicidal behavior.

A recent study compared characteristics of 81 inpatients with borderline personality disorder, 49 patients with borderline personality disorder and a comorbid major depressive episode, and 77 inpatients with a major depressive episode alone.[75] No significant differences were found in the characteristics of suicide attempts between patients with borderline personality disorder and those with major depression. Patients with both disorders had the greatest number of suicide attempts and the highest level of objective planning. Impulsivity and hopelessness predicted lethal intent in all three groups, and hopelessness predicted objective planning in the group with both disorders. Although parasuicidal behaviors are common in borderline personality disorder, suicidal behaviors accompanied by intent to die should not be considered less serious than those of patients with major depression only.

Patients with Comorbid Substance Use Disorders

Patients with comorbid alcohol or drug abuse/dependence and depression are at particularly high risk for suicide.[76] One study found that the risk of alcoholics eventually committing suicide was over five times greater than that of nonalcoholics.[11] A series of 107 consecutive patients diagnosed as meeting criteria for both major depressive disorder and alcohol dependence who presented to an evaluation clinic were compared to two comparison groups of 5,625 consecutive nonalcoholic patients with major depression and 497 consecutive nondepressed alcoholics.[77] The depressive symptom that most strongly distinguished the two groups was suicidality, which was 59% more severe in depressed alcoholics than in nonalcoholic depressed patients. Regarding other depressive symptoms, the magnitude of the difference was smaller (low self-esteem was 22% more common in depressed alcoholics) or not significantly different. The depressed alcoholic patients were also significantly distinguished from nonalcoholic depressed patients in the degree of impulsivity and functional impairment. Substance abuse may also limit or counteract expected decreases in suicidal rates with treatment.[76]

Hospitalization is often necessary for such patients, but depressive symptoms often decrease substantially within a few weeks or once the withdrawal syndrome is over. The abuse of alcohol, tobacco, cocaine, and heroin has been shown to be associated with increased rates of suicidal behavior.[76] Substance abuse is also more common in patients with bipolar disorder or borderline personality disorder, two disorders that also confer increased risk of suicide.

Other Special Populations

Special consideration must also be given to depression and suicidality when they occur in the context of grieving/bereavement, during an adjustment disorder with depressed mood, during pregnancy and the postpartum period, when associated with the premenstrual syndrome (premenstrual dysphoric disorder), with concomitant anxiety or panic attacks, and in the context of bipolar disorder.

In a study of 296 women of reproductive age from different strata of society in India, suicidal ideas and/or death wish during the premenstrual period were reported by 30 (10%) subjects.[78] Premenstrual symptoms such as depression, irritability, mood swings, sense of losing control, and water retention were significantly more often reported by women who had suicidal ideas as compared with women without suicidal ideas. Other studies have also found increased rates of suicidality in females during the luteal and menstrual phases of their cycles. Although pregnancy and the puerperium may be associated with a decreased risk of suicide,[72] women are at risk for depression and psychosis around the time of delivery, and specialized treatment may be necessary.

In a study of 100 consecutive patients with panic disorder referred to an anxiety clinic, Lepine *et al.*[79] found that 42% had attempted suicide at some time during their lives, 14.3% of whom required hospitalization in an intensive care unit. The patients were referred to a clinic specializing in anxiety; 52% of the patients with panic disorder had experienced at least one episode of major depression at some time during the course of their illness (71.4% of suicide attempters), and 31% of patients with panic disorder had a lifetime diagnosis of alcohol and/or other substance abuse (45.2% of suicide attempters). Consistent with other literature, more female than male patients, and more single, divorced, or widowed than married patients attempted suicide.

Bipolar depressed patients tend to have a higher incidence of suicidality, especially patients with bipolar II disorder[21] (vide supra). Given the evidence that lithium treatment is associated with remarkably reduced rates of life-threatening or fatal suicidal acts in patients with severe recurrent mood disorders,[59] clinicians should consider lithium as the first-line agent in bipolar depression.[61]

CONCLUSIONS

A thorough understanding of the treatment of the depressed suicidal patient is an important skill for clinical psychiatrists. The depressive episode should be completely evaluated, and differential diagnoses should be considered. The degree of suicidality must be thoroughly assessed, and potential risk factors should be reviewed. Experimental evidence suggests that suicidality may be neurobiologically mediated, and central serotonergic dysfunction may be especially relevant. Further research into these neurobiological correlates of suicidality may advance the development of appropriate suicide-specific interventions.

The patient with suicidal depression should be considered for stabilization in the hospital setting. Aggressive treatment should be initiated with pharmacologic, psychotherapeutic, and psychosocial treatment modalities. Lithium, ECT, or specific psychotherapy strategies may provide benefit in certain patients. Special populations, including the young and the elderly, and patients with comorbid medical illness, substance use disorders, or personality disorders require special attention. The treatment of suicidal behavior during depression has not yet been adequately evaluated in the research literature, and research into this important area should be supported.

REFERENCES

1. KESSLER, R.C., K.A. MCGONAGLE, S. ZHAO, *et al.* 1994. Lifetime and 12-month prevalence of DSM-III-R psychiatric disorders in the United States: results from the National Comorbidity Survey. Arch. Gen. Psychiatry **51:** 8–19.
2. AMERICAN PSYCHIATRIC ASSOCIATION. 2000. Practice guideline for the treatment of patients with major depressive disorder (revision). Am. J. Psychiatry **157:** 1–45.
3. JACOBS, D.G. 2000. A 52-year-old suicidal man. JAMA **283:** 2693–2699.
4. AMERICAN PSYCHIATRIC ASSOCIATION. 1994. Diagnostic and Statistical Manual of Mental Disorders, 4th Ed. American Psychiatric Association. Washington, DC.
5. RIHMER, Z. & P. PESTALITY. 1999. Bipolar II disorder and suicidal behavior. Psychiatr. Clin. North Am. **22:** 667–673.
6. SPALLETTA, G., A. TROISI, M. SARACCO, *et al.* 1996. Symptom profile, axis II comorbidity and suicidal behavior in young males with DSM-III-R depressive illnesses. J. Affect. Disorders **39:** 141–148.
7. GUZE, S.B. & E. ROBINS. 1970. Suicide in primary affective disorders. Br. J. Psychiatry **117:** 437–438.
8. FAWCETT, J., D.C. CLARK & K.A. BUSCH. 1993. Assessing and treating the patient at risk for suicide. Psychiatr. Ann. **23:** 244–254.
9. SHEA, S.C. 1998. The chronological assessment of suicide events: a practical interviewing strategy for the elicitation of suicidal ideation. J. Clin. Psychiatry **59** (Suppl. 20): 58–72.
10. OQUENDO, M.A., K.M. MALONE & J.J. MANN. 1997. Suicide: risk factors and prevention in refractory major depression. Depression Anxiety **5:** 202–211.

11. BECK, A.T. & R.A. STEER. 1989. Clinical predictors of eventual suicide: a 5- to 10-year prospective study of suicide attempters. J. Affect. Disorders **17:** 203–209.
12. MALONE, K.M., K. SZANTO & E.M. CORBITT. 1995. Clinical assessment versus research methods in the assessment of suicidal behavior. Am. J. Psychiatry **152:** 1601–1607.
13. POWELL, J., J. GEDDES, J. DEEKS, *et al.* 2000. Suicide in psychiatric hospital inpatients: risk factors and their predictive power. Br. J. Psychiatry **176:** 266–272.
14. MOSCICKI, E.K. 1997. Identification of suicide risk factors using epidemiologic studies. Psychiatr. Clin. North Am. **20:** 499–517.
15. YOUNG, M.A., L.F. FOGG, W.A. SCHEFTNER, *et al.* 1994. Interactions of risk factors in predicting suicide. Am. J. Psychiatry **151:** 434–435.
16. BLUMENTHAL, S.J. & D.J. KUPFER. 1986. Generalizable treatment strategies for suicidal behavior. Ann. N.Y. Acad. Sci. **487:** 327–340.
17. SIMON, G.E. & M. VONKORFF. 1998. Suicide mortality among patients treated for depression in an insured population. Am. J. Epidemiol. **147:** 155–160.
18. MALONE, K.M., G.L. HAAS, J.A. SWEENEY, *et al.* 1995. Major depression and the risk of attempted suicide. J. Affect. Disorders **34:** 173–185.
19. ISOMETSÄ, E.T., M.M. HENRIKSSON, H.M. ARO, *et al.* 1994. Suicide in major depression. Am. J. Psychiatry **151:** 530–536.
20. FAWCETT, J., W.A. SCHEFTNER, L. FOGG, *et al.* 1990. Time-related predictors of suicide in major affective disorder. Am. J. Psychiatry **147:** 1189–1194.
21. BULIK, C.M., L.L. CARPENTER, D.J. KUPFER, *et al.* 1990. Features associated with suicide attempts in recurrent major depression. J. Affect. Disorders **18:** 29–37.
22. APTER, A., R. PLUTCHIK & H.M. VAN PRAAG. 1993. Anxiety, impulsivity, and depressed mood in relation to suicidal and violent behavior. Acta Psychiatr. Scand. **87:** 1–5.
23. FAWCETT, J., W. SCHEFTNER & D. CLARK. 1987. Clinical predictors of suicide in patients with major affective disorders: a controlled prospective study. Am. J. Psychiatry **144:** 35–40.
24. HIRSCHFELD, R.M.A. & J.M. RUSSELL. 1997. Assessment and treatment of suicidal patients. N. Engl. J. Med. **337:** 910–915.
25. SIMON, R.I. 1998. Psychiatrists awake! Suicide risk assessments are all about a good night's sleep. Psychiatric Ann. **28:** 479–485.
26. NORDSTRÖM, P. & M. ÅSBERG. 1992. Suicide risk and serotonin. Int. Clin. Psychopharmacol. **6 :** 12–21.
27. ROY, A., J. DEJONG & M. LINNOILA. 1989. Cerebrospinal fluid monoamine metabolites and suicidal behavior in depressed patients: a 5-year follow-up study. Arch. Gen. Psychiatry **46:** 609–612.
28. MANN, J.J., K.M. MALONE, J.A. SWEENEY, *et al.* 1996. Attempted suicide characteristics and cerebrospinal fluid amine metabolites in depressed inpatients. Neuropsychopharmacology **15:** 576–586.
29. MANN, J.J. & K.M. MALONE. 1997. Cerebrospinal fluid amines and higher-lethality suicide attempts in depressed inpatients. Biol. Psychiatry **41:** 162–171.
30. MANN, J.J. & V. ARANGO. 1992. Integration of neurobiology and psychopathology in a unified model of suicidal behavior. J. Clin. Psychopharmacol. **12:** 2S–7S.

31. STANLEY, B., A. MOLCHO, M. STANLEY, *et al.* 2000. Association of aggressive behavior with altered serotonergic function in patients who are not suicidal. Am. J. Psychiatry **157:** 609–614.
32. COCCARO, E.F., L.J. SIEVER, H.M. KLAR, *et al.* 1989. Serotonergic studies in patients with affective and personality disorders: correlates with suicidal and impulsive aggressive behavior. Arch. Gen. Psychiatry **46:** 587–599.
33. ARANGO, V., M.D. UNDERWOOD & J.J. MANN. 1992. Alterations in monoamine receptors in the brain of suicide victims. J. Clin. Psychopharmacol. **12:** 8S–12S.
34. MANN, J.J. & S. KAPUR. 1991. The emergence of suicidal ideation and behavior during antidepressant pharmacotherapy. Arch. Gen. Psychiatry **48:** 1027–1033.
35. MANN, J.J. & D.M. STOFF. 1997. A synthesis of current findings regarding neurobiological correlates and treatment of suicidal behavior. Ann. N.Y. Acad. Sci. **836:** 352–363.
36. STOCKMEIER, C.A., L.A. SHAPIRO, G.E. DILLEY, *et al.* 1998. Increase in serotonin-1A autoreceptors in the midbrain of suicide victims with major depression—postmortem evidence for decreased serotonin activity. J. Neurosci. **18:** 7394–7401.
37. CHEETHAM, S.C., M.R. CROMPTON, C.L.E. KATONA, *et al.* 1988. Brain 5-HT$_2$ receptor binding sites in depressed suicide victims. Brain Res. **443:** 272–280.
38. STOCKMEIER, C.A., G.E. DILLEY, L.A. SHAPIRO, *et al.* 1997. Serotonin receptors in suicide victims with major depression. Neuropsychopharmacology **16:** 162–173.
39. ARANGO, V., M.D. UNDERWOOD & J.J. MANN. 1997. Biologic alterations in the brainstem of suicides. Psychiatr. Clin. North Am. **20:** 581–593.
40. BOWDEN, C., S.C. CHEETHAM, S. LOWTHER, *et al.* 1997. Reduced dopamine turnover in the basal ganglia of depressed suicides. Brain Res. **769:** 135–140.
41. ROY, A., F. KAROUM & S. POLLACK. 1992. Marked reduction in indexes of dopamine metabolism among patients with depression who attempt suicide. Arch. Gen. Psychiatry **49:** 447–450.
42. FAWCETT, J., K.A. BUSCH, D. JACOBS, *et al.* 1997. Suicide: a four-pathway clinical-biochemical model. Ann. N.Y. Acad. Sci. **836:** 288–301.
43. NEMEROFF, C.B., M. J. OWENS, G. BISSETTE, *et al.* 1988. Reduced corticotropin releasing factor binding sites in the frontal cortex of suicide victims. Arch. Gen. Psychiatry **45:** 577–579.
44. THIES-FLECHTNER, K., B. MÜLLER-OERLINGHAUSEN, W. SEIBERT, *et al.* 1996. Effect of prophylactic treatment on suicide risk in patients with major affective disorders: data from a randomized prospective trial. Pharmacopsychiatry **29:** 103–107.
45. LINEHAN, M.M. 1997. Behavioral treatments of suicidal behaviors: definitional obfuscation and treatment outcomes. Ann. N.Y. Acad. Sci. **836:** 302–328.
46. GOH, S.E., P.H. SALMONS & R. M. WHITTINGTON. 1989. Hospital suicides: are there preventable factors? Profile of the psychiatric hospital suicide. Br. J. Psychiatry **154:** 247–249.
47. MALONE, K.M. 1997. Pharmacotherapy of affectively ill suicidal patients. Psychiatr. Clin. North Am. **20:** 613–624.
48. BRENT, D.A., J.A. PERPER, C.J. ALLMAN, *et al.* 1991. The presence and accessibility of firearms in the homes of adolescent suicides: a case-control study. JAMA **266:** 2989–2995.

49. MARZUK, P.M., A.C. LEON, K. TARDIFF, *et al.* 1992. The effect of access to lethal methods of injury on suicide rates. Arch. Gen. Psychiatry **49:** 451–458.

50. MONTGOMERY, S.A. 1997. Suicide and antidepressants. Ann. N.Y. Acad. Sci. **836:** 329–338.

51. JONAS, J.M. & A.E. HEARRON. 1996. Alprazolam and suicidal ideation: a meta-analysis of controlled trials in the treatment of depression. J. Clin. Psychopharmacol. **16:** 208–211.

52. MONTGOMERY, S.A., D.B. MONTGOMERY, M. GREEN, *et al.* 1992. Pharmacotherapy in the prevention of suicidal behavior. J. Clin. Psychopharmacol. **12 :** 27S–31S.

53. MANN, J.J., F.K. GOODWIN, C.P. O'BRIEN, *et al.* 1993. Suicidal behavior and psychotropic medication: accepted as a consensus statement by the ACNP council, March 2, 1992. Neuropsychopharmacology **1:** 177–183.

54. MOLCHO, A. & M. STANLEY. 1992. Antidepressants and suicide risk: issues of chemical and behavioral toxicity. J. Clin. Psychopharmacol. **12 :** 13S–18S.

55. KAPUR, S., T. MIECZKOWSKI & J.J. MANN. 1992. Antidepressant medications and the relative risk of suicide attempt and suicide. JAMA **268:** 3441–3445.

56. HENRY, J.A. 1997. Epidemiology and relative toxicity of antidepressant drugs in overdose. Drug Safety **16:** 374–390.

57. HENRY, J.A., C.A. ALEXANDER & E.K. SENER. 1995. Relative mortality from overdose of antidepressants. Br. Med. J. **310:** 221–224.

58. MODESTIN, J. & F. SCHWARZENBACH. 1992. Effect of psychopharmacotherapy on suicide risk in discharged psychiatric inpatients. Acta Psychiatr. Scand. **85:** 173–175.

59. TONDO, L., K.R. JAMISON & R.J. BALDESSARINI. 1997. Effect of lithium maintenance on suicidal behavior in major mood disorders. Ann. N.Y. Acad. Sci. **836:** 339–351.

60. TONDO, L. & R.J. BALDESSARINI. 2000. Reduced suicide risk during lithium maintenance treatment. J. Clin. Psychiatry **61 :** 97–104.

61. COMPTON, M.T. & C.B. NEMEROFF. 2000. The treatment of bipolar depression. J. Clin. Psychiatry **61** (Suppl. 9): 57–67.

62. ISOMETSÄ, E., M. HENRIKSSON, H. ARO, *et al.* 1994. Suicide in psychotic major depression. J. Affect. Disorders **31:** 187–191.

63. BECK, A.T., G. BROWN & R.J. BERCHICK. 1990. Relationship between hopelessness and ultimate suicide: a replication with psychiatric outpatients. Am. J. Psychiatry **147:** 190–195.

64. SALKOVSKIS, P.M., C. ATHA & D. STORER. 1990. Cognitive-behavioural problem solving in the treatment of patients who repeatedly attempt suicide: a controlled trial. Br. J. Psychiatry **157:** 871–876.

65. LINEHAN, M.M., H.E. ARMSTRONG, A. SUAREZ, *et al.* 1991. Cognitive-behavioral treatment of chronically parasuicidal borderline patients. Arch. Gen. Psychiatry **48:** 1060–1064.

66. MÖLLER, H.J. 1992. Attempted suicide: efficacy of different aftercare strategies. Int. Clin. Psychopharmacol. **6 :** 58–69.

67. GREENHILL, L.L. & B. WASLICK. 1997. Management of suicidal behavior in children and adolescents. Psychiatr. Clin. North Am. **20:** 641–666.

68. CONWELL, Y. 1997. Management of suicidal behavior in the elderly. Psychiatr. Clin. North Am. **20:** 667–683.

69. DRAPER, B.M. 1995. Prevention of suicide in old age. Med. J. Aust. **162:** 533–534.

70. ZWEIG, R.A. & G.A. HINRICHSEN. 1993. Factors associated with suicide attempts by depressed older adults: a prospective study. Am. J. Psychiatry **150:** 1687–1692.
71. CHOCHINOV, H.M., K.G. WILSON, M. ENNS, *et al.* 1998. Depression, hopelessness, and suicidal ideation in the terminally ill. Psychosomatics **39:** 366–370.
72. HARRIS, E.C. & B.M. BARRACLOUGH. 1994. Suicide as an outcome for medical disorders. Medicine **73:** 281–296.
73. MCHUGH, P.R. 1994. Commentary: suicide and medical afflictions. Medicine **73:** 297–298.
74. CORBITT, E.M., K.M. MALONE, G.L. HAAS, *et al.* 1996. Suicidal behavior in patients with major depression and comorbid personality disorders. J. Affect. Disorders **39:** 61–72.
75. SOLOFF, P.H., K.G. LYNCH, T.M. KELLY, *et al.* 2000. Characteristics of suicide attempts of patients with major depressive episode and borderline personality disorder: a comparative study. Am. J. Psychiatry **157:** 601–608.
76. TONDO, L., R.J. BALDESSARINI, J. HENNEN, *et al.* 1999. Suicide attempts in major affective disorder patients with comorbid substance use disorders. J. Clin. Psychiatry **60:** 63–69.
77. CORNELIUS, J.R., I.M. SALLOUM, J. MEZZICH, *et al.* 1995. Disproportionate suicidality in patients with comorbid major depression and alcoholism. Am. J. Psychiatry **152:** 358–364.
78. CHATURVEDI, S.K., P.S. CHANDRA, G. GURURAJ, *et al.* 1995. Suicidal ideas during the premenstrual phase. J. Affect. Disorders **34:** 193–199.
79. LEPINE, J.P., J.M. CHIGNON & M. TEHERANI. 1993. Suicide attempts in patients with panic disorder. Arch. Gen. Psychiatry **50:** 144–149.

Treating the Suicidal Patient with Bipolar Disorder

Reducing Suicide Risk with Lithium

ROSS J. BALDESSARINI,[a] LEONARDO TONDO,[a,b] AND JOHN HENNEN[a]

[a]*International Consortium for Research on Bipolar Disorders; Department of Psychiatry & Neuroscience Program, Harvard Medical School, and the Bipolar & Psychotic Disorders Program, Mailman Research Center, McLean Division of Massachusetts General Hospital, Belmont, Massachusetts 02478, USA*

[b]*Department of Psychology, University of Cagliari and Lucio Bini Stanley Foundation International Research Center, Cagliari, Sardinia*

ABSTRACT: Bipolar disorder is associated with increased mortality because of complications of commonly comorbid substance use and stress-sensitive medical disorders as well as accidents and very high rates of suicide. Long-term lithium treatment may be associated with reduced suicidal risk. We review and summarize findings that help to quantify relationships between the presence versus the absence of lithium maintenance and suicides or attempts in patients with bipolar or other major affective disorders. Results from 33 studies (1970–2000) yielded 13-fold lower rates of suicide and reported attempts during long-term lithium treatment than without it or after it was discontinued. Although greatly reduced, these rates remain above those estimated for the general population. Evidence for substantial, if incomplete, protection against suicide with lithium is supported by more compelling evidence than that for any other treatment provided for patients with mood disorders. Studies of commonly used, but incompletely evaluated, alternative treatments are required, and further protection against premature mortality can be anticipated with better protection against bipolar depression.

KEYWORDS: Bipolar disorder; Depression; Lithium; Maintenance treatment; Manic-depressive disorders; Mortality rates; Suicide

INTRODUCTION AND BACKGROUND

Major affective disorders are potentially lethal diseases owing to several causes. These include accidents, violence, and medical complications of very

Address for correspondence: Dr. R.J. Baldessarini, Mailman Research Center, McLean Hospital, 115 Mill Street, Belmont, MA 02478. Voice: 617-855-3203; fax: 617-855-3479.
rjb@mclean.org)

common comorbid substance abuse, as well as premature mortality associated with cardiopulmonary and other presumably stress-sensitive medical diseases.[1–6] A particularly significant, and potentially preventable, cause of death is suicide, currently a leading cause of death among young adults and adolescents.[5,6] International annual suicide rates among 24 developed nations were recently reported to average (± SD) 16.6 ± 7.5 per 100,000 population, or 0.0166 ± 0.0075% per year, with substantial variation between countries, regions, ethnic groups, ages, and the sexes.[6,7] The suicide rate in the United States is approximately 0.0112% per year, with Native American and elderly white men at highest risk.[5] Potentially lethal suicide *attempts* are much more prevalent and occur in perhaps 10–15% of those who eventually die of suicide.[8] The population lifetime prevalence of suicide attempts has ranged from 2–15% and varies with the level of lethality and the apparent seriousness of intent as well as with probably high rates of underreporting.[2,6] The reported ratio of attempts to completed suicides averages 18:1 in the general population, but only about 3:1 among persons with mood disorders.[5] Given these considerations, we estimated the overall annual international rate of suicide plus nontrivial suicide attempts to be 0.315% per year (0.0166 + [18 × 0.0166]).

Psychiatric illnesses, particularly mood disorders, with or without comorbid substance abuse, are strongly associated with suicide.[1–3,8–12] In both major depression and bipolar disorder, suicide may account for approximately 1 in 4 or 5 deaths in severely depressed or ever-hospitalized patients; suicide is less frequent with less severe illness, and about twice more likely in men than in women.[5,6,11,12] With lifetime prevalence in the general population at 8% for major depression and at least 2% for bipolar disorders (types I and II),[13–15] major affective disorders account for a high proportion of all suicides and, in turn, present high mortality risks in persons with such disorders, as well as representing an extraordinary cost burden to society in direct medical costs and indirect costs representing disability and premature death.[9,16–18] Remarkably, only a minority of persons with major mood disorders that are both common and potentially lethal, but eminently treatable, are diagnosed, often after years of delay, and only a minority of those diagnosed are adequately treated.[10,19–21] A further irony is that despite the enormity of the public health problem represented by suicide, studies of the effects of psychiatric interventions on fatality rates in major affective illness remain uncommon and limited, and they remain inadequate to guide specific clinical recommendations or effective preventive policies.[6,10,22]

Reasons for limited research into the effectiveness of interventions into suicide have been reviewed previously.[6,10] In addition to the infrequency of suicidal acts in feasibly accessible clinical samples, there is the ethical impossibility of controlled prospective studies when fatality is a potential outcome, particularly after rapid discontinuation of ongoing treatments.[23–25] To manage such challenges, most studies of treatment effects on suicide have been naturalistic or have considered the suicidal act as an unintended outcome in controlled trials of therapeutic options that were similarly plausible at the time of the study.[10,26–28]

Despite broad application of treatments with demonstrated effectiveness in clinical depression, including antidepressant drugs, electroconvulsive treatment (ECT), and cognitive-behavioral or interpersonal psychotherapy, and even though it seems probable clinically that modern mood-altering treatments can be life-saving in the short-term, evidence that such treatments alter long-term mortality rates in major depression or bipolar disorder is remarkably limited. The last half-century of broad clinical use of antidepressant and antimanic treatments has yielded little evidence of reductions of long-term rates of suicide or other causes of premature mortality associated with the major affective illnesses just considered.[1,4,6,10,22,26–33] A particularly striking paradox is that the introduction of safer modern antidepressants with low lethality on acute overdose since the 1980s was not followed by measurable reduction of suicide rates, since there are many other lethal means of committing suicide.[34,35]

A final paradox is that even though suicidal behavior is strongly associated with depressive-dysphoric states in bipolar as well as major depressive disorders, treatment of bipolar depression, in particular, remains remarkably poorly studied.[36] Indeed, bipolarity, and even suicidality itself, are routine exclusion criteria in trials of new treatments for depression. Moreover, studies of proposed mood-stabilizing agents have tended to focus on acute mania and recurrences of mania rather than on the more lethal condition of bipolar depression. Even lithium continues not to carry an FDA-sanctioned indication for depression, despite abundant evidence of its effectiveness in both phases and subtypes of bipolar illness.[37–40]

META-ANALYSIS OF REPORTED EFFECTS OF LITHIUM TREATMENT ON SUICIDAL BEHAVIOR

Although information indicating reductions in long-term risks of suicides and attempts for most interventions is very limited and largely inconclusive, there is substantial evidence that maintenance treatment with lithium salts is associated with marked reductions of risk, particularly in bipolar manic-depressive illness.[6,10,29,41–44] We now present an updated meta-analysis of the available literature pertaining to suicides and attempts in patients with major affective disorders under comparable conditions with or without long-term treatment with lithium. It is similar in approach to a preliminary summary that we reported earlier in the *Annals*,[29] but it greatly expands the information considered and includes previously unreported findings from our own case series. We specifically consider rates of suicides and attempts with and without lithium treatment and compare these risks to those reported for the general population as an indication of the degree of success in preventing suicidal behavior during lithium treatment.

In computerized literature searches and references cited in identified reports, we found 33 studies reported over the last three decades (1970–2000), including 55 treatment arms (plus 3 studies with suicides and attempts scored separately) with data permitting estimation of annual rates of suicide attempts or fatalities in persons with bipolar or other recurrent major mood disorders with or without treatment with lithium (TABLE 1).[45–77] Direct comparisons were provided for risks with and without lithium maintenance treatment under matching conditions of diagnosis, follow-up, and assessment in 19 reports.[45,46,48,51–53,55,58,65–68,70,72–77]

Before summarizing the findings from this collection of studies, several characteristics and potential limitations of the data should be noted. These include highly variable sample size, inconsistent reporting on risks with and without lithium, and the general lack of study designs aimed specifically at assessing suicidal risk. Nearly all of the studies (29 of 33) involve patient-subjects with conditions that included affective disorders other than bipolar disorder of type I or II, especially major depressive and schizoaffective disorders, without defining diagnosis-specific effects of lithium treatment on suicidal risk. Pooling of rates of suicides and attempts varying in seriousness of means and lethality of intent can potentially be misleading, particularly without stratification by known or suspected risk factors, such as prior attempts and substance use comorbidity. Most studies provided imprecise information concerning times at risk, requiring estimated averages. Adherence to recommended treatment was not necessarily consistently assured by assays of serum lithium concentrations, and exposure to other simultaneous or intermittent treatments was not controlled or even necessarily reported. It may also be particularly important that 8 of the 19 comparison studies reported on suicidal risks during versus after discontinuing lithium maintenance.[65,67,68,72,75–77] Such comparisons may involve increased morbid and suicidal risks in the without-lithium condition, because of the reported effects of treatment discontinuation.[23–25,42] Despite these shortcomings, several interesting and generally consistent findings arise from these data.

Overall, the 33 studies with data concerning suicidal acts with or without lithium maintenance treatment yielded substantially lower annual rates of suicidal behavior during maintenance treatment with lithium (TABLE 1). It is striking that all but 1 of the 19 reports with observations with and without lithium treatment found greater rates of suicidal acts without treatment; the sole exception found no suicides or attempts at all among relatively small numbers of subjects.[45] The estimated rate of suicides with versus without lithium treatment differed nearly fivefold (0.793 vs. 0.167 fatalities per 100 patient-years, or % per year). Also, based on studies that reported on suicides and attempts separately, the rate of suicide attempts was nearly 10-fold lower during lithium maintenance treatment (4.021 vs. 0.407 % per year). Based on all reported data, an overall estimate of all suicidal acts (attempts plus deaths), the difference with and without treatment was more than 13-fold (2.57 vs. 0.197% per year). The overall rates for all suicidal acts are not simple sums of the separate rates for suicides and attempts, because not all studies provided data for all three outcomes. These several rates, their 95% confidence intervals (CI) based on random-effects modeling in response to the high variance in outcomes across studies,[78] the number of studies providing data, and the average numbers of subjects and average estimated exposure times are summarized in TABLE 2.

COMPARISON OF SUICIDE RATES WITH THOSE IN THE GENERAL POPULATION

The comparisons summarized in TABLES 1 and 2 indicate large reductions in risk of both suicides and attempts with versus without lithium treatment. These results were compared with reported average suicide rates for the general population just reported and those derived from recent reports from 24 developed nations that yielded a mean international rate of 0.0166% per year (95% CI = 0.0136–0.0196% per year).[6,7] Inasmuch as the reported ratio of suicide attempts to fatalities in the general population averages 18-fold,[6] an estimated population rate for suicide attempts is 0.289% per year (95% CI = 0.245–0.353% per year). Not only was the rate of suicide attempts during long-term lithium treatment relatively low (0.407% per year; 95% CI = 0.154–0.660% per year) compared to the rate in untreated patients, but also it was less than twice the estimated population base rate (0.289% per year; 95% CI = 0.245–0.353% per year, with overlapping confidence intervals; FIG. 1). However, the average rate of suicides during lithium treatment, although nearly five times lower than that without such treatment or after discontinuing it, remained 10 times above the international base rate (0.167; 95% CI = 0.109–0.224 % per year vs. 0.017% per year; 95% CI = 0.014–0.011% per year; FIG. 1).

This last finding, if the estimates are valid, indicates that despite major sparing of mortality during long-term lithium treatment, the risk of suicide during treatment is nevertheless substantially above the base rate in the general population. An estimate of suicidal risk among persons with major affective disorders is 0.523% per year (95% CI = 0.435–0.627% per year) based on their approximate average standard mortality ratio of 32.0 times above the general population rate of 0.0166% per year.[6,8] This estimate of 0.523% per year accords well with the estimated suicide rate without lithium, and the confidence intervals of the two estimates overlap (0.793% per year; 95% CI = 0.592–0.995% per year; TABLE 2).

The moderately (52%) higher estimated suicide rate in the data reported here without lithium treatment (TABLES 1 and 2) compared to estimates derived from other studies of major affective disorders calls for comment. This difference may reflect case selection factors that might increase suicide risk. These may include patients evaluated at specialized referral and research centers and considered sufficiently ill to require long-term maintenance treatment and follow-up. Also, at least three of the studies involved selection of patients with previous suicide attempts who are presumably at high risk for future suicidal acts.[65,67,75] Finally, nine of the studies involving lithium discontinuation may also contribute to unusually high suicide rates in the absence of lithium (TABLE 1).[65,67,68,70,72,73,75–77] However, the effect of lithium discontinuation may be limited overall, because the average rate of all suicidal acts in the nine studies that involved lithium discontinuation in the no-lithium treatment condition was not significantly greater than that in the 24 other studies that apparently did not involve lithium discontinuation (0.510 ± 0.460 vs. 0.338 ± 0.668% per year, respectively; F[1; 31 df] = 0.50, NS).

An additional finding in the present analysis is a confirmation of the previously reported observation that the ratio of suicide attempts to suicides is evidently much greater in the general population than among persons with major affective disorders. In contrast to the 18:1 ratio found in the general population, even with probable underreporting of suicide attempts, the ratio in the present data was only 2.44:1 (TABLE 2). This low ratio may imply that suicidal behavior in patients with major affective disorder is more lethal than in the general population, even though many suicides in the general population probably represent undiagnosed depression or bipolar illness and their various associated and potentially contributing comorbidities.

Attainment of population base rates or, ideally, reaching zero risk of suicidal acts during long-term treatment is obviously far from having been accomplished. It may not even be a realistic goal, even if treatment efficacy itself were not imperfect. Practical limitations include highly inefficient case finding, frequent denial of illness and need for treatment, and the improbability of sustaining indefinitely prolonged and uninterrupted maintenance treatment even in persons who are willing to accept long-term treatment and medical supervision. We recently reported that failure rates involving at least one recurrence of mania or bipolar depression during closely supervised lithium maintenance treatment in our research center averaged 38% within 1 year and 54% by 2 years.[40]

TABLE 1. Summary of reports on lithium and suicidal behavior

Study	Diagnosis	Quality	Total n	Act Type	With lithium Acts/N/y	%/y	Without lithium Acts/N/y	%/y
Baastrup, 1970[a,45]	MAD	37.5	123	S+A	0/84/0.42	**0.000**	0/39/0.41	**0.000**
Prien et al., 1974[b,46]	MAD	100	289	S	0/146/2.00	**0.000**	2/143/2.00	**0.699**
Bech et al., 1976[47]	MAD	25.0	40	S	1/40/7.00	**0.357**	...	
Kay & Petterson, 1977[48]	MAD	25.0	192	S	0/123/2.33	**0.000**	3/69/11.4	**0.381**
Poole et al., 1978[49]	MAD	25.0	99	A	0/99/5.00	**0.000**	...	
Glen et al., 1979[50]	MAD	37.5	784	S	8/784/4.83	**0.211**	...	
Ahlfors et al., 1981[51]	MAD	62.5	126	S	0/14/1.33	**0.000**	3/112/1.25	**2.143**
Venkoba-Rao et al., 1982[a,52]	MAD	50.0	47	A	0/47/8.50	**0.000**	2/47/8.50	**0.501**
Hanus & Zaplatálek, 1984[a,53]	MAD	50.0	95	A	4/95/5.10	**0.826**	25/95/5.10	**5.160**
Norton & Whalley, 1984[a,54]	MAD	37.5	791	S	8/791/2.17	**0.466**	...	
Lepifker et al., 1985[a,55]	UP	50.0	35	A	0/33/8.30	**0.000**	7/33/8.30	**2.556**
Jamison, 1986[56]	MAD	37.5	9000	S	4/9000/1.00	**0.044**	...	
Page et al., 1987[57]	BPD	25.0	79	S	6/79/12.1	**0.628**		
Schou & Weeke, 1988[a,58]	MAD	50.0	57	A	0/9/1.00	**0.000**	10/48/8.58	**2.428**
Wehr et al., 1988[59]	BPD	250	70	S	2/70/7.55	**0.378**	...	
Coppen et al., 1991[60]	MAD	37.5	103	S+A	0/103/11.0	**0.000**	...	
Nilsson & Axelsson, 1991[61]	MAD	25.0	37	A	0/37/7.00	**0.000**	...	
O'Connell et al., 1991[62]	BPD	37.5	248	S	4/248/8.00	**0.202**	...	
Vestergaard & Aagard, 1991[63]	MAD	25.0	50	S	5/50/5.00	**2.000**	...	
Modestin & Schwartzen-bach, 1992[64]	MAD	25.0	64	S+A	0/64/12.1	**0.000**	...	
Müller-Oerlinghausen et al., 1992[a,c,d,65]	MAD	50.0	68	A	4/68/8.00	**0.735**	7/68/8.00	**1.287**
	MAD	50.0	...	S	2/68/8.00	**0.368**	4/68/8.00	**0.735**
Rihmer et al., 1993[a,66]	BPD	50.0	36	A	6/36/7.20	**2.315**	61/36/7.20	**23.53**
	BPD	50.0	...	S	1/36/7.20	**0.386**	3/36/7.20	**1.157**
Felber & Kyber, 1994[a,c,67]	BPD	50.0	71	S+A	7/71/6.98	**1.412**	64/71/7.19	**12.54**
Lenz et al., 1994[a,c,68]	MAD	75.0	695	S	9/695/6.66	**0.194**	23/430/6.25	**0.856**
Müller-Oerlinghausen, 1994[69]	MAD	37.5	394	S	7/394/14.2	**0.125**	...	
Sharma & Markar, 1994[c,70]	BPD	50.0	114	S	2/57/8.50	**0.413**	6/57/9.00	**1.170**
Ahrens et al., 1995[71]	BPD+SA	37.5	611	S	7/611/6.60	**0.174**	...	
Koukopoulos et al., 1995[a,c,72]	BPD	62.5	432	S	3/343/12.2	**0.072**	5/89/2.75	**2.043**
Nilsson, 1995[a,c,73]	MAD	75.0	362	S	6/230/14.2	**0.184**	9/132/8.40	**0.812**
Thies-Flechtner et al., 1996[b,74]	BPD+SA	100.0	285	S+A	0/139/2.50	**0.000**	8/146/2.50	**2.192**
Bocchetta et al., 1998[a,c,d,75]	BPD+SA	50.0	115	S+A	2/68/6.92	**0.425**	5/47/5.60	**1.900**
Coppen & Farmer, 1998[a,c,76]	MAD	62.5	115	S	1/103/5.25	**0.185**	1/12/9.00	**0.926**
Tondo et al., 2000[a,c,77]	MAD	75.0	426	A	7/426/4.27	**0.385**	87/324/6.65	**4.038**
	MAD	75.0	...	S	4/426/4.27	**0.220**	9/222/3.85	**1.053**

NOTE: Data derived from 33 studies with 55 treatment arms (33 with and 22 without lithium), involving a total of 13,725 subjects corrected for studies reporting suicides (S) and attempts (A) separately in the same persons and for subjects observed both on and off lithium in some studies[a] with a bipolar (BPD), major affective (MAD), or schizoaffective (SA) disorders.
[b]Random-assignment, double-blind trial design. Data indicate suicidal acts/number of subjects at risk/average years of exposure, with resulting rates (acts/100 patient-years, or %/year). Quality assessment scoring (% of maximum score) is defined in text.
[c]Studies involving lithium discontinuation (n = 9).
[d]High-risk studies with patients selected for previous suicide attempts (n = 3).

TABLE 2. Estimated rates of suicidal acts with and without lithium maintenance treatment[a]

Outcome	With lithium	Without lithium
Suicides		
Rate	**0.167**	**0.793**
(95% CI)	(0.109–0.224)	(0.592–0.995)
Studies	21	11
Subjects	14,308	1,370
Exposure (years)	3.11	5.93
Attempts		
Rate	**0.407**	**4.021**
(95% CI)	(0.154–0.660)	(2.040–6.003)
Studies	898	651
Exposure (years)	5.06	6.96
All acts		
Rate	**0.197**	**2.570**
(95% CI)	(0.128–0.266)	(1.751–3.389)
Studies	33	19
Subjects	15,157	1,998
Exposure (years)	3.27	5.60

[a]Pooled estimates of rates are derived from a random-effects model using data summarized in TABLE 1, with weighted estimates based on the inverse of study-specific variance and adjustment for between-studies variance, because between-study variance was significant for most of the conditions listed (average Q = 72.1 [mean df = 16 df], $p < 0.001$).[78] Average exposure times are weighted by the number of subjects in each study. Confidence intervals (CI) are not strictly directly comparable, because some studies involved patients under both conditions of treatment, and some patients may have made >1 attempt in some studies. Rates for without versus with lithium treatment differed by 4.75-fold for suicides, 9.88-fold for attempts, and 13.05-fold overall, and the untreated ratio of rates for attempts per suicide was 2.44.

BASIS OF PROTECTION AGAINST SUICIDE BY LITHIUM TREATMENT

Interpretation remains open for the very substantial apparent protection against suicide attempts and suicides with long-term lithium treatment in patients with a variety of severe recurrent mood disorders reported here. An "antisuicidal" effect of lithium may merely be incidental to the overall clinical benefits of long-term mood stabilization with lithium. This view is supported by strong associations between suicidal behavior and recurrences of depressive or mixed-dysphoric mood states in patients with bipolar disorder[42–44] and evidence that lithium is effective in preventing both depressive and manic phases of the disorder.[36–40]

Lithium may have specific neuropharmacological properties not necessarily found with alternative proposed mood-stabilizing treatment. One such possibility is the potentiation of cerebral serotonergic function in limbic fore-

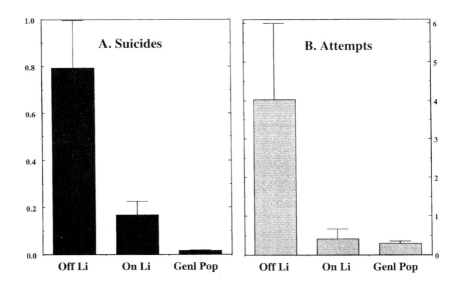

FIGURE 1. Rates of **(A)** suicide and **(B)** suicide attempts among major affective disorder patient-subjects without versus with long-term lithium maintenance treatment compared to reported estimates of rates in the general population. Rates are in suicidal acts per 100 patient-years (% per year) with their 95% confidence intervals (CI). Note that the suicide attempt rates on lithium versus population base rates do not differ significantly, but that treated rates for suicide are 10 times above the international suicide rate in the general population.

brain.[36] This effect may tend to offset the proposed deficiencies in cerebral serotonergic functioning associated with suicidal and other violent behavior.[79] Such serotonin-mediated effects are unknown with anticonvulsants, and it may be relevant that carbamazepine, the only mood-stabilizing agent other than lithium that has been evaluated for antisuicidal effects to date, was found to be much less effective than lithium in a large, randomized trial involving mainly patients with bipolar disorder.[27,74]

In addition to the specific neuropsychopharmacological benefits of the long-term mood-stabilizing effects of lithium treatment, interpersonal and psychosocial factors may also contribute to an antisuicide effect. Psychosocial treatments have been much less well investigated in bipolar disorder than in major depression and other common psychiatric disorders, but emerging research data support their utility when combined with clinically effective pharmacological treatments.[80] The clinical management of long-term lithium maintenance treatment over time typically involves close monitoring of patients receiving the treatment and a degree of collaboration that may be greater than that with other less potentially risky treatments. The personal interactions involved may themselves support improvements in emotional stability, interpersonal relationships, vocational functioning, self-esteem, and perhaps reduced comorbid substance abuse, thus contributing to a suicide-sparing effect of treatment.

It also follows that the incomplete protection from suicidal behavior found during lithium treatment (FIG. 1) may reflect both imperfect compliance and incomplete protection against recurrences of affective illness by all currently available methods of treatment of bipolar disorder.[36,40] Incomplete protection against bipolar depression and mixed dysphoric-agitated states is particularly important, because suicidal behavior in patients with bipolar disorder is much more strongly associated with depressive and dysphoric states than with pure mania or hypomania.[42–44]

CONCLUSIONS

The data just reviewed provide strong and highly consistent support for a major reduction in risk of suicide and attempts during long-term lithium maintenance treatment, not only in patients with bipolar disorder, but also in those with other current major affective disorders as well. This conclusion arises from more than 30 studies over as many years, involving a total of nearly 14,000 mood-disordered patients. Although virtually none of the studies analyzed was designed specifically to test for treatment effects on suicidal risk, the consistency and magnitude of the results obtained are highly compelling. Moreover, despite the possibility that the contrast between with- versus without-lithium conditions was biased by the reported impact of rapidly discontinued lithium, such an effect of discontinuation was not supported by direct comparison of studies in which this possibility was more or less likely.

It is very important to emphasize that this effect of lithium may not generalize to other mood-stabilizing or antidepressant treatments. Differences between specific treatments may arise from pharmacodynamic and efficacy differences between treatments, particularly against bipolar depression. In addition, differences in the manner in which different treatments are administered and monitored may contribute to differences in the treatment-specific outcomes. In turn, this consideration calls for further studies of the effects of psychosocial and other nonpharmacological aspects of comprehensive care required by patients with major affective disorders as a means of further limiting long-term suicide risk.

It is also important to emphasize that the reduction of suicidal risk, particularly of completed suicides, during long-term lithium treatment was incomplete and that the average suicide rate during lithium maintenance treatment remained substantially above the base rate in the general population. This limitation further emphasizes the need for even better treatments as well as better and earlier case finding and support of long-term adherence to available treatments. Because suicidal risk is associated mainly with depressive or mixed bipolar episodes, it follows that better protection against bipolar depression is a key to limiting suicidal behavior in bipolar disorders.

Ethical considerations severely constrain the design and conduct of prospective, randomized, controlled studies when death is an anticipated outcome. Nevertheless, the present findings indicate that naturalistic studies of the therapeutics of suicide are feasible, and even controlled comparisons are possible when equally clinically plausible alternative treatments are offered.

ACKNOWLEDGMENTS

This work was supported by National Institutes of Health Grant MH-47370, a grant from the Bruce J. Anderson Foundation, and by the McLean Hospital Private Donors Neuropharmacology Research Fund (to RJB); and by grants from the Theodore & Vada Stanley Foundation and a NARSAD Investigator Award (to LT). Based on a presentation at a national symposium, Suicide Prevention 2000, in New York, NY, May, 2000, organized by the American Foundation for Suicide Prevention (AFSP). Some material reviewed is derived from previous reports, as specified in the text.

REFERENCES

1. COPPEN, A. 1994. Depression as a lethal disease: prevention strategies. J. Clin. Psychiatry **55:** 37–45.
2. DIECKSTRA, R.F. 1993. The epidemiology of suicide and parasuicide. Acta Psychiatr. Scand. Suppl. **371:** 9–20.
3. DIECKSTRA, R.F. & W. GULBINAT. 1993. The epidemiology of suicidal behavior: a review of three continents. World Health Stat. Quart. **46:** 52–68.
4. ANGST, J., R. SELLARO & F. ANGST. 1998. Long-term outcome and mortality of treated vs. untreated bipolar and depressed patients: a preliminary report. Int. J. Psychiatr. Clin. Pract. **2:** 115–119.
5. JAMISON, K.R. 1999. Night Falls Fast. Alfred A. Knopf. New York.
6. TONDO, L. & R.J. BALDESSARINI. 2000. Reduced suicide risk during lithium maintenance treatment. J. Clin. Psychiatry **61:** 97–104.
7. MAKINEN, I.H. & D. WASSERMAN. 1997. Suicide prevention and cultural resistance: stability in European countries' suicide ranking, 1970–1988. Ital. J. Suicidol. **7:** 73–85.
8. CONWELL, Y. & R.E. HENDERSON. 1996. Neuropsychiatry of suicide. *In* Neuropsychiatry. B.S. Fogel, R.B. Schiffer & S.M. Rao, eds. :485–521. Williams & Wilkins. Baltimore.

9. HARRIS, E.C. & N. BARRACLOUGH. 1997. Suicide as an outcome for mental disorders: a meta-analysis. Br. J. Psychiatry **170**: 205–228.
10. BALDESSARINI, R.J. & K.R. JAMISON. 1999. Effects of medical interventions on suicidal behavior: summary and conclusions. J. Clin. Psychiatry **60**: 117–122.
11. CLARK, D.C. & A.E. GOEBEL-FABBRI. 1998. Lifetime risk of suicide in major affective disorders. *In* Harvard Medical School Guide to Assessment and Intervention in Suicide. D.G. Jacobs, ed. :270–286. Jossey-Bass. San Francisco.
12. MOSCIKI, E.K. 1998. Epidemiology of suicide. *In* Harvard Medical School Guide to Assessment and Intervention in Suicide. D.G. Jacobs, ed. :40–51. Jossey-Bass. San Francisco.
13. KESSLER, R.C., K.A. MCGONIGLE, S. ZHAO *et al.* 1994. Lifetime and 12-month prevalence of DSM-III-R psychiatric disorders in the US: results from the national comorbidity study. Arch. Gen. Psychiatry **51**: 8–19.
14. BEBBINGTON, P. & R. RAMANA. 1995. The epidemiology of bipolar disorder. Soc. Psychiatry Psychiatr. Epidemiol. **30**: 279–292.
15. BALDESSARINI, R.J. 2000. A plea for integrity of the bipolar disorder concept. Bipolar Disorders **2**: 3–7.
16. WYATT, R.J. & I. HENTER. 1995. An economic evaluation of manic-depressive illness. Soc. Psychiatry Psychiatr. Epidemiol. **30**: 213–219.
17. GREENBERG, P.E., L.E. STIGLIN, S.N. FINKELSTEIN & E.R. BERNDT. 1993. The economic burden of depression in 1990. J. Clin. Psychiatry **54**: 405–418.
18. KIND, P. & J. SORENSEN. 1993. The costs of depression. Int. Clin. Psychopharmacol. **7**: 191–195.
19. MCCOMBS, J.S., M.B. NICHOL, G.L. STIMMEL, *et al.* 1990. Cost of antidepressant drug therapy failure: a study of antidepressant use patterns in a Medicaid population. J. Clin. Psychiatry **51**: 60–69.
20. ISACSSON, G., G. BOËTHIUS & U. BERGMAN. 1992. Low level of antidepressant prescription for people who later commit suicide: 15 years of experience from a population-based drug database in Sweden. Acta Psychiatr. Scand. **85**: 444–448.
21. SUOMINEN, K.H., E. ISOMETSÄ, M.M. HENDRIKSSON, *et al.* 1998. Inadequate treatment for major depression both before and after attempted suicide. Am. J. Psychiatry **155**: 1778–1780.
22. GUNNELL, D. & S. FRANKEL. 1994. Prevention of suicide: aspirations and evidence. Br. Med. J. **308**: 1227–1233.
23. VIGUERA, A.C., R.J. BALDESSARINI & J. FRIEDBERG. 1998. Risks of interrupting continuation or maintenance treatment with antidepressants in major depressive disorders. Harvard Rev. Psychiatry **5**: 293–306.
24. BALDESSARINI, R.J. & L. TONDO. 1998. Effects of lithium treatment in bipolar disorders and post-treatment-discontinuation recurrence risk. Clin. Drug Invest. **15**: 337–351.
25. BALDESSARINI, R.J., L. TONDO & A.C. VIGUERA. 1999. Effects of discontinuing lithium maintenance treatment. Bipolar Disorders **1**: 17–24.
26. TEICHER, M.H., C.A. GLOD & J.O. COLE. 1993. Antidepressant drugs and the emergence of suicidal tendencies. Drug Safety **3**: 186–212.
27. GREIL, W., W. LUDWIG-MAYERHOFER, N. ERAZO *et al.* 1997. Lithium vs. carbamazepine in the maintenance treatment of bipolar disorders—a randomized study. J. Affect. Disorders **43**: 151–161.

28. MALONE, K.M. 1997. Pharmacotherapy of affectively ill suicidal patients. Psychiatr. Clin. North Am. **20:** 613–625.
29. TONDO, L., K.R. JAMISON & R.J. BALDESSARINI. 1997. Antisuicide effects of lithium. Ann. N.Y. Acad. Sci. **836:** 339–351.
30. MÜLLER-OERLINGHAUSEN, B. & A. BERGHÖFER. 1999. Antidepressants and suicidal risk. J. Clin. Psychiatry **60:** 94–99.
31. PRUDIC, J. & H.A. SACKEIM. 1999. Electroconvulsive therapy and suicide risk. J. Clin. Psychiatry **60:** 104–110.
32. KAHN, A., H.A. WARNER & W.A. BROWN. 2000. Symptom reduction and suicide risk in patients treated with placebo in antidepressant clinical trials. Arch. Gen. Psychiatry **57:** 311–317.
33. BALDESSARINI, R.J., D. IOANITESCU, J. RAGADE, et al. 2001. Suicidal risk and antidepressant treatment: a meta-analysis. Submitted for publication.
34. FREEMANTLE, N., A. HOUSE, F. SONG, et al. 1994. Prescribing selective serotonin reuptake inhibitors as strategy for prevention of suicide. Br. Med. J. **309:** 249–253.
35. OHBERG, A., J. LONQVIST, S. SARNA et al. 1995. Trends and availability of suicide methods in Finland: proposals for restrictive measures. Br. J. Psychiatry **166:** 35–43.
36. BALDESSARINI, R.J. & F.I. TARAZI. 2001. Drugs for the treatment of psychiatric disorders. In Goodman and Gilman's The Pharmacological Basis of Therapeutics, 10th Ed. Chapts. 19 & 20. J.G. Hardman, L.E. Limbird, P.B. Molinoff, R.W. Ruddon & A.G. Gilman, eds. McGraw-Hill Press. New York. In press.
37. BALDESSARINI, R.J., L. TONDO, T. SUPPES et al. 1996. Pharmacological treatment of bipolar disorder throughout the life-cycle. In Bipolar Disorder through the Life-Cycle. K.I. Shulman, M. Tohen & S. Kutcher, eds. :299–338. Wiley & Sons. New York.
38. TONDO, L., R.J. BALDESSARINI, J. HENNEN & G. FLORIS. 1998. Lithium maintenance treatment: depression and mania in bipolar I and II disorders. Am. J. Psychiatry **155:** 638–645.
39. TONDO, L, R.J. BALDESSARINI & G. FLORIS. 2001. Long-term clinical effectiveness of lithium maintenance treatment in types I and II bipolar manic-depressive disorders. Br. J. Psychiatry. In press.
40. BALDESSARINI, R.J., M. TOHEN & L. TONDO. 2000. Maintenance treatment in bipolar disorder. Arch. Gen. Psychiatry **57:** 490–492.
41. CRUNDWELL, J.K. 1994. Lithium and its potential benefit in reducing increased mortality rates due to suicide. Lithium **5:** 193–204.
42. TONDO, L., R.J. BALDESSARINI, G. FLORIS, et al. 1998. Lithium treatment and risk of suicidal behavior in bipolar disorder patients. J. Clin. Psychiatry **59:** 405–414.
43. BALDESSARINI, R.J. & L. TONDO. 1998. Antisuicidal effect of lithium treatment in major mood disorders. In Harvard Medical School Guide to Assessment and Intervention in Suicide. D.G. Jacobs, ed.: 355–371. Jossey-Bass. San Francisco.
44. BALDESSARINI, R.J., L. TONDO & J. HENNEN. 1999. Effects of lithium treatment and its discontinuation on suicidal behavior in bipolar manic-depressive disorders. J. Clin. Psychiatry **60:** 77–84.
45. BAASTRUP, P.C., J.C. POULSEN, M. SCHOU, et al. 1970. Prophylactic lithium: double-blind discontinuation in manic-depressive and recurrent-depressive disorders. Lancet **1:** 326–330.

46. PRIEN, R.F., C.J. KLETT & C.M. CAFFEY. 1974. Lithium prophylaxis in recurrent affective illness. Am. J. Psychiatry **131**: 198–203.
47. BECH, P., P.B. VENDSBORG & O. RAFAELSEN. 1976. Lithium maintenance treatment of manic-melancholic patients: its role in the daily routine. Acta Psychiatr. Scand. **53**: 70–81.
48. KAY D.W.K. & U. PETTERSON. 1977. Manic-depressive illness. Acta Psychiatr. Scand. **269**: 55–60.
49. POOLE, A.J., H.D. JAMES & W.C. HUGHES. 1978. Treatment experiences in the lithium clinic at St. Thomas' Hospital. J. Roy. Soc. Med. **71**: 890–894.
50. GLEN, A.I.M., M. DODD, E.B. HULME & N. KREITMAN. 1979. Mortality on lithium. Neuropsychobiology **5**: 167–173.
51. AHLFORS, U.G., P.C. BAASTRUP, S.J. DENCKER, *et al.* 1981. Flupentixol decanoate in recurrent manic-depressive illness: a comparison with lithium. Acta Psychiatr. Scand. **64**: 226–237.
52. VENKOBA-RAO, A., N. HARIHARASUBRAMANIAN, S. PARVATHI-DEVI, *et al.* 1982. Lithium prophylaxis in affective disorder. Indian J. Psychiatry **23**: 22–30.
53. HANUS, K. & M. ZALPETÁLEK. 1984. Suicidal activity of patients with affective disorders in the course of lithium prophylaxis. Cesk. Psychiatrie **80**: 97–100.
54. NORTON, B. & L.H. WHALLEY. 1984. Mortality of a lithium treatment population. Br. J. Psychiatry **145**: 277–282.
55. LEPKIFKER, E., N. HORESH & S. FLORU. 1985. Long-term lithium prophylaxis in recurrent unipolar depression: a controversial indication. Acta Psychiatr. Belg. **85**: 434–443.
56. JAMISON, K.R. 1986. Suicide and bipolar disorders. Ann. N.Y. Acad. Sci. **487**: 301–315.
57. PAGE, C., S. BENAIM & F. LAPPIN. 1987. A long-term retrospective follow-up study of patients treated with prophylactic lithium carbonate. Br. J. Psychiatry **150**: 175–179.
58. SCHOU, M. & A. WEEKE. 1988. Did manic-depressive patients who committed suicide receive prophylactic or continuation treatment at the time? Br. J. Psychiatry **153**: 324–327.
59. WEHR, T.S., D.A. SACK, N.E. ROSENTHAL & R.W. COWDRY. 1988. Rapid cycling affective disorder: contributing factors and treatment responses in 51 patients. Am. J. Psychiatry **145**: 179–184.
60. COPPEN, A., H. STANDISH-BARRY, J. BAILEY, *et al.* 1991. Does lithium reduce mortality of recurrent mood disorders? J. Affect. Disorders **23**: 1–7.
61. NILSSON, A. & R. AXELSSON. 1990. Lithium discontinuers: clinical characteristics and outcome. Acta Psychiatr. Scand. **82**: 433–438.
62. O'CONNELL, R.A., J.A. MAYO, L. FLATOW, *et al.* 1991. Outcome of bipolar disorder on long-term treatment with lithium. Br. J. Psychiatry **159**: 123–129.
63. VESTERGAARD, P. & J. AAGAARD. 1991. Five-year mortality in lithium-treated manic-depressive patients. J. Affect. Disorders **21**: 33–38.
64. MODESTIN, J. & F. SCHWARTZENBACH. 1992. Effect of psychopharmacotherapy on suicide risk in discharged psychiatric inpatients. Acta Psychiatr. Scand. **85**: 173–175.
65. MÜLLER-OERLINGHAUSEN, B., B. MÜSER-CAUSEMANN & J. VOLK. 1992. Suicides and parasuicides in a high-risk patient group on and off lithium long-term medication. J. Affect. Disorders **25**: 261–270.

66. RIHMER, Z., W. RUTZ & J. BARSI. 1993. Suicide rate, prevalence of diagnosed depression and prevalence of working physicians in Hungary. Acta Psychiatr. Scand. **88:** 391–394.

67. FELBER, W. & A. KYBER. 1994. Suizide und Parasuizide während und ausserhalb einer Lithium prophylaxe. *In* Ziele und Ergebnisse der medikamentosen Prophylaxe affektiver Psychosen. B. Müller-Oerlinghausen & A. Berghöfer, eds. :53–59. G. Thieme Verlag. Stuttgart.

68. LENZ, G., B. AHRENS, E. DENK, *et al.* 1994. Mortalität nach Ausschneiden aus der Lithiumambulanz (Increased mortality after drop-out from lithium clinic). *In* Ziele und Ergebnisse der medicamentösen Prophylaxe affecktiver Psychosen. B. Müller-Oerlinghausen & A. Berghöfer, eds. :49–52. G. Thieme Verlag. Stuttgart.

69. MÜLLER-OERLINGHAUSEN, B. 1994. Die "IGSLI" Studie zur Mortalität lithium behandelter Patienten mit affektiven Psychosen. *In* Ziele und Ergebnisse der medikamentosen Prophylaxe affektiver Psychosen. B. Müller-Oerlinghausen & A. Berghöfer, eds. :35–39. G. Thieme Verlag. Stuttgart.

70. SHARMA, R. & H.R. MARKAR. 1994. Mortality in affective disorder. J. Affect. Disorders **31:** 91–96.

71. AHRENS, B., B. MÜLLER-OERLINGHAUSEN, M. SCHOU, *et al.* 1995. Excess cardiovascular and suicide mortality of affective disorders may be reduced by lithium prophylaxis. J. Affect. Disorders **33:** 67–75.

72. KOUKOPOULOS, A., D. REGINALDI, G. MINNAI, *et al.* 1995. The long-term prophylaxis of affective disorders. *In* Depression and Mania: From Neurobiology to Treatment. G. Gessa, W. Fratta, L. Pani, & G. Serra, eds. :127–147. Raven Press. New York.

73. NILSSON, A. 1995. Mortality in recurrent mood disorders during periods on and off lithium: a complete population study in 362 patients. Pharmacopsychiatry **28:** 8–13.

74. THIES-FLECHTNER, K., B. MÜLLER-OERLINGHAUSEN, W. SEIBERT, *et al.* 1996. Effect of prophylactic treatment on suicide risk in patients with major affective disorders. Pharmacopsychiatry **29:** 103–107.

75. BOCCHETTA, A., R. ARDAU, C. BURRAI, *et al.* 1998. Suicidal behavior on and off lithium prophylaxis in a group of patients with prior suicide attempts. J. Clin. Psychopharmacol. **18:** 384–389.

76. COPPEN, A. & R. FARMER. 1998. Suicide mortality in patients on lithium maintenance therapy. J. Affect. Disorders **50:** 261–267.

77. TONDO, L. & R.J. BALDESSARINI. 2000. Rates of suicidal behavior in patients with major affective disorders with and without long-term treatment with lithium. Unpublished observations.

78. DER SIMONIAN, R. & N.M. LAIRD. 1986. Meta-analysis in clinical trials. Controlled Clin. Trials **7:** 177–188.

79. MANN, J.J., M. OQUENDO, M.D. UNDERWOOD & V. ARANGO. 1999. The neurobiology of suicide risk. J. Clin. Psychiatry **60:** 7–11.

80. HUXLEY, N., S.V. PARIKH & R.J. BALDESSARINI. 2000. Effectiveness of psychosocial treatments in bipolar disorder: state of the evidence. Harvard Rev. Psychiatry **8:** 126–140.

DISCUSSION OF PAPERS BY DR. NEMEROFF *et al.* AND DR. BALDESSARINI *et al.*

J. JOHN MANN (*Chairman*): Dr. Nemeroff, ECT is supposedly the most effective antidepressant. Can you say a word about that?

CHARLES B. NEMEROFF (*Emory University, Atlanta, GA*): There's no question that ECT, compared with other treatments, is the most effective in terms of complete remission. It has been perfected over time or improved upon, so that many of the side effects associated with the older methods of administering ECT using electrodes, bilaterally in the old days, more unilaterally today, have been dealt with; memory loss has been cut down, and much more refined methods in terms of seizure induction, using muscle-paralyzing agents, are used, so that there is no overt seizure. All of that has led to patient compliance with treatments. At our site, as an example, we administered 4,000 ECT treatments last year, two of three on an outpatient basis. Many of our patients who have failed on medications now receive inpatient treatment with ECT and a tapering dose of ECT to end up with first a once-a-week treatment and then once every 2 weeks. Bill MacDonald in our group is currently looking at combination antidepressant treatment ECT to try to spread out the treatments. Our biggest problem is with patients in rural areas who travel great distances to get their treatment and then are unable to drive home for a few hours after treatment; those treatments will be scrutinized closely. There's no question that ECT, and now some of its related somatic new treatment paradigms such as rapid transcranial magnetic stimulation, another method to activate neurons in the brain, which Dr. Mann has pioneered, is an extraordinarily effective treatment of depression. Ross would like to add a comment.

ROSS J. BALDESSARINI: I agree with everything Charlie has said. ECT continues to be a very important treatment for acutely suicidal patients, but there are no data to indicate that ECT reduces long-term suicide rates.

MANN: Charlie, could you comment on the role of antipsychotic medications in the treatment of suicidally depressed patients and the question of typical versus atypical?

NEMEROFF: In the delusionally depressed patient, the 20% of patients who actually have a psychotic ideation, antipsychotic treatment is absolutely essential in combination with antidepressant treatment. The question is whether there is a role for atypical antipsychotics in nondelusional suicidal depressed patients. Perhaps Dr. Gunderson will discuss the use of low doses of atypical antipsychotics of an atypical type. This was termed years ago by more dynamic psychiatrists as "ego glue." Many persons with depressive symptoms or even syndromes and comorbid personality disorders do extremely well with very low doses of olanzapine 5 mg, risperidone 0.5 mg, or clothiapine 25 or 50 mg. These drugs tend to reduce mood lability and impulsivity, which

I find to be extremely helpful. However, as Dr. Baldessarini would be quick to point out, there are little in the way of controlled data in this regard. In one open study with risperidone, eight patients who were refractory depressives had risperidone added to their treatment, and it seemed to have an ameliorative effect. There is an olanzapine study showing more rapid onset of action in combination with fluoxetine. We do need controlled studies. I think there is a role clinically.

BALDESSARINI: There is a dimension of suicidality at a clinical level where antipsychotic drugs may have special benefits. Nihilistic delusional thinking is one, and there is also a kind of anguish and turmoil—not quite anxiety and not quite psychosis—that can be highly lethal. Antipsychotic drugs and anxiolytics might have beneficial effects in such conditions. There is also a growing body of observations suggesting that the atypical antipsychotics may have interesting effects on mood per se, either an uplift or a normalization, something a little different from what we are used to with standard neuroleptics.

NEMEROFF: Though the data are scant.

BALDESSARINI: Surely!

MANN: This question really is addressed to both speakers. On the one hand, we heard that there's not much difference between the antidepressants; on the other hand, there was a hint that not all antidepressants may be equally efficacious in terms of lowering suicide rates. I know the data are pretty sparse, but to leave the audience with some sense of where to go with these two pieces of information, perhaps you could expand on that area?

NEMEROFF: There has never been a study powered statistically to ask the question does one antidepressant have more of an antisuicide effect than another and is one antidepressant actually more effective than another. All the comparator trials have recently been small numbers that have looked at side effects. My own belief, and this is not science but belief, is that the reduction in suicide is strictly related to efficacy, and I do believe that drugs that act as dual reuptake inhibitors of norepinephrine and serotonin are more effective in refractory and severe depression than those that act on a single site. There is some evidence based on the DUAG studies in Denmark to support that. However, I just completed a large study of venlafaxine, a dual uptake inhibitor, versus fluoxetine, in 300 patients. My colleague, Allen Schatzberg, did a 300-patient study in geriatric depression, and we found no evidence of any difference in efficacy in this 600-patient study; some differences in side effects, but none in efficacy. So at the current time I don't think we could say that one antidepressant is more effective than another. In a subset of a particular severely depressed population, that might be the case.

BALDESSARINI: There are a number of technical considerations that greatly complicate evaluations of treatment effects on suicidal risk. First, there is a wide gulf between thinking about suicide and carrying out suicidal acts. While suicidal ideation is very important to consider clinically, it is not necessarily closely related to suicidal acts. Studies aimed at detecting treatment effects on suicidal ideation may be relatively feasible in that such thoughts are common during acute depressive episodes, though the reliability of their assessment is often uncertain. Designing individual studies to detect treatment effects on suicidal acts would be a highly daunting task, both ethically and practically, and would require very large numbers and prolonged observation times. Our meta-analyses pertaining to lithium and suicide have considered only life-threatening suicidal acts and suicides and were able to detect treatment effects because pooling yielded large aggregate patient-time exposures. Another limitation to detecting treatment effects on suicidality in antidepressant trials is the ubiquitous exclusion of patient-subjects known to be currently suicidal. Other risk factors for suicide, including bipolarity, psychosis, and substance-use comorbidity, also are often bases for exclusion. Accordingly, suicidal behavior is rarely encountered in short-term efficacy trials of treatments for mood disorders.

From a clinical perspective, the close association of depression and suicide leads one to treat patients as if improving and stabilizing mood will diminish suicidal risk, even without research evidence that this is an effective strategy, at least with respect to most antidepressant treatments. Another factor that may contribute to reducing suicidal risk in clinical practice is the manner in which mood disorder patients tend to be treated. Bipolar disorder patients, especially if maintained on lithium, tend to be followed relatively closely medically, with regular follow-up visits, encouragement to continue treatment, monitoring for adverse effects, and blood testing—typically, over many years. In contrast, depression is commonly treated in a more intermittent manner and often with less consistent and close monitoring and regular long-term follow-up. These stylistic factors may contribute to the apparent differences in suicidal risk between affectively ill patients maintained on lithium and those treated with antidepressants.

MANN: If I might just ask a question that I think summarizes some of the questions here: in comparing these different antidepressants and lithium, how much account is taken into analyses of the relative efficacy of, say, SSRIs compared to tricyclics? In other words, do you have any data to indicate that if I have a depressed patient who is responding extremely well to an SSRI, does it mean that the SSRI is any less beneficial than a good response to a tricyclic or an MAO inhibitor?

NEMEROFF: I think Ross and I would agree that the sine qua non here is efficacy. If you have had remission with an SSRI, you are just as protected from suicidality as you are with remission from an MAO or a tricyclic. The question is, do you have remission or not? There I see too many patients who are on a low dose of an antidepressant or two antidepressants and simply do not have remission, and because psychiatrists and nonphysician mental health practitioners do not routinely measure disease severity as we do, they don't know on a given visit whether a patient is in remission or not. It's the biggest problem we have in the field. If I were going to leave you with one take-home message, it's this: you wouldn't go to an internist who looked at your face to see how ruddy it was to determine your blood pressure or who decided to taste your urine to see if you were in a diabetic crisis. You want somebody who is measuring your disease severity. It takes 1 minute of a self-rating scale to measure someone's depression, yet 90+% of practitioners do not give their patients a rating scale for depression, so they simply don't know whether patients are in remission or not. It's unfathomable to me why this is the norm in our practice in the community standard, because it's far below what I would consider competence. So, if a patient's in remission, they should be just fine.

BALDESSARINI: I have nothing to disagree with about that. My emphasis might be a bit different in that spending quality time with patients and knowing them well matters a lot and may be more powerful in limiting suicidal risk than formal rating scales. Although rating scales are essential, for research can add documentaton to monitor clinical progress and can serve as a reminder to consider ongoing risk factors, in my opinion they are best considered as adjunctive to the primary clinical relationship, particularly in efforts to prevent suicide.

MANN: I want to endorse this idea of doing a brief assessment of the patient's view of the severity of the illness with a self-rating scale, because in our studies the patient's report as to how depressed, hopeless, or suicidal they are feeling is a much better guide as to the risk of suicidal behavior than the clinician's objective assessment using classical scales such as the Hamilton depression scale. In other words, the patients themselves have a better fix on how badly they are feeling in terms of the risk of suicidal behavior than just making a global assessment of the objective severity of depression. If you have a patient who presents to you for the first time, and the easier case obviously is the bipolar patient who is depressed, and is seeking maintenance treatment because of a history of say 6 or 7 years of mood fluctuations, either highs or lows, or a unipolar patient, where does lithium fit into your thinking in terms of a recommendation to a clinician for the maintenance treatment to put the patient on?

BALDESSARINI: This is a difficult question to deal with. My presentation emphasized what the available research evidence indicates, namely, that long-term treatment of manic-depressive (including bipolar and some nonbipolar) patients has been consistently associated with a much lower risk of suicide and suicide attempts. However, in the real world of clinical practice at the present time, at least in this country, lithium is often not a readily accepted treatment option for many patients and clinicians. In addition to the known risks of adverse effects of lithium and the need for regular monitoring of blood lithium levels and other medical variables, there appears to be something of a social stigma surrounding its use in the United States. Moreover, lithium has always been a classic "orphan drug," with limited industrial backing for research and promotion of its use. The clinical situation now is also similar for older antidepressants, including the tricyclics and particularly the MAO inhibitors—agents that tend to be avoided or deferred when simpler choices are available. Moreover, to some extent, contemporary medical economics and an associated tendency towards briefer and less frequent contacts with a prescribing psychiatrist, also favor the use of the simplest and least time-requiring available treatments. Nevertheless, despite these issues, lithium and older antidepressants continue to be very useful treatments that should not be abandoned or neglected.

MANN: Somebody has asked an interesting question. When you are treating patients with lithium, you have to see them often and ask a lot of questions, because it's a little trickier to manage than some of the other medications and the psychotherapeutic implications of all that extra interest may be contributing to its antisuicidal effect.

BALDESSARINI: Again, the interpersonal and clinical aspects of the care of manic-depressive patients may well be part of the benefit of lithium maintenance treatment, including its association with reduced risk of suicide. It seems unwise to think of lithium as a specific biological "magic bullet" for suicide. Comprehensive and sustained care, and prevention or timely treatment of recurring depressive or mixed dysphoric-agitated episodes are surely critically important mediators in any beneficial effects of lithium or other treatments on suicide risk.

Treatment of Suicidality in Schizophrenia

HERBERT Y. MELTZER

*Division of Psychopharmacology, Vanderbilt University School of Medicine,
Psychiatric Hospital at Vanderbilt, Nashville, Tennessee 37212, USA*

ABSTRACT: Between 4 and 13% of people with schizophrenia commit suicide and between 25 and 50% make a suicide attempt, a reflection of the devastating toll this syndrome takes on the quality of life, that is, the subjective and objective sense of well-being. Many risk factors for suicide in schizophrenia have been identified, the most important of which are previous suicide attempts, depression, hopelessness, substance abuse, and male gender. Insight into having a serious mental illness and less severe cognitive impairment are also associated with increased risk for suicide in schizophrenia, most likely when accompanied by feelings of hopelessness. Typical neuroleptic drugs have not been shown to reduce the risk of suicide. However, several types of evidence suggest that clozapine, an atypical antipsychotic drug, appreciably reduces the suicide attempt and completion rates in schizophrenia and schizoaffective disorder, perhaps by as much as 75–85%. Other atypical antipsychotic drugs may have a similar effect, but direct evidence is lacking. Improvement in positive and negative symptoms, reduced extrapyramidal side effects (EPS), a direct antidepressant action, improved cognitive function, and improved compliance may contribute to reduced suicidality. The International Suicide Prevention Trial (InterSePT) is a large prospective, randomized study intended to compare the effectiveness of clozapine with that of olanzapine in reducing suicide and suicide-related events in schizophrenic and schizoaffective patients. Some information about suicidality in the patient sample is reported here.

KEYWORDS: Antipsychotic; Clozapine; Depression; Drug therapy; Insight; Risperidine; Schizophrenia; Suicide

INTRODUCTION

Suicide is the leading cause of premature death in schizophrenic patients.[1–3] Bleuler[4] stated his view that the suicidal drive is the most serious of all schizophrenic symptoms at a time (1911) when, because of the unavail-

Address for correspondence: Dr. Herbert Y. Meltzer, Director, Division of Psychopharmacology, Vanderbilt University School of Medicine, Psychiatric Hospital at Vanderbilt, 1601 23rd Ave. South, Suite 306, Nashville, TN 37212. Voice: 615-327-7049.
herbert.meltzer@mcmail.vanderbilt.edu

ability of antipsychotic drugs, positive symptoms must have been extremely prominent relative to other aspects of the schizophrenic syndrome. Thus, suicide represents a substantial risk to patients and their families and a great challenge for clinicians. In addition, suicide and suicide attempts represent a significant economic burden, because of the costs of autopsies, funerals, lost income of the victims and their families, and treatment costs for the survivors and possibly family members. The cost associated with lost productivity from individuals who commited suicide in the United States was estimated at $7 billion per year in 1991, whereas treatment of suicide attempts and investigation of completed suicides have been estimated to cost $190 million per year.[5]

Reduction in the suicide rate in this group of patients remains an important aim, and understanding the factors that predispose schizophrenic patients to suicidal behavior may lead to improvements in their management and rehabilitation. This review of suicide in schizophrenia discusses epidemiology, risk factors, and the effect of antipsychotic drug treatment, particularly clozapine, which has been shown to reduce the suicide rate in many studies.

EPIDEMIOLOGY OF SUICIDE IN SCHIZOPHRENIA

The suicide attempt rate in schizophrenia was estimated at 25–50% lifetime.[1–3] The completed suicide rate in the US general population is estimated at 11.4 per 100,000.[6] The rate of completed suicide among patients with schizophrenia is usually reported to be between 9 and 13%, 25 times greater than that in the general population, based on data from cohort studies for various periods between 1921 and 1975.[7] The methodology used to determine this rate was challenged by Inskip et al.,[8] who reanalyzed data from 29 studies using generalized linear modeling and obtained a lifetime risk of completed suicide for schizophrenia of 4% compared to 6% for affective disorder and 7% for alcohol dependence.[8] The annual incidence of suicide in schizophrenic patients was estimated to be between 0.4 and 0.8%.[1–3,9,10] The estimated annual number of suicides in the US for schizophrenia is 3,200–4,000, some 12% of total suicides.[1–3] Suicide accounted for 52% and 35% of deaths among first-episode male and female schizophrenic patients, respectively, in a recent Danish study.[11] Suicide risk was particularly increased during the first year of follow-up. According to Harris and Barraclough,[12] the standardized mortality rate for schizophrenia based on worldwide reporting is 8–9% compared to 18–23% for major depression and 12–18% for bipolar disorder. Thus, by any standard, suicide in schizophrenia is a major public health problem and one that must be seen as a key issue in the treatment of this disorder. However, some clinicians underestimate the occurrence of suicide in this syndrome compared to their awareness of its importance in major depression.

RISK FACTORS FOR SUICIDE IN SCHIZOPHRENIA

There has been an extensive effort to identify factors that may predict suicide in schizophrenic patients. Risk factors for suicide in schizophrenia are: (1) previous suicide attempts; (2) depression; (3) hopelessness; (4) substance abuse; (5) male sex; (6) insight, that is, awareness of the effects of the illness on social and cognitive function and fear of a worsening condition; (7) recent discharge from the hospital without adequate treatment planning; (8) Caucasian race; (9) deteriorating health with high levels of premorbid functioning; and (10) adverse life events.[1–3,12–15] Kaplan and Harrow[16] have provided prospective evidence that the construct of poor overall function, a summation of the factors just noted with emphasis on poor social and work function and poor quality of life, is predictive of later suicide. Biological markers for suicide with requisite sensitivity or specificity have not yet been identified.

Previous suicide attempts and hopelessness appear to be the most important of these risk factors from a clinical perspective. In a long-term follow-up study of 61 patients between the ages of 14 and 18 years admitted to an adolescent psychiatric unit, eight patients with a diagnosis of schizophrenia committed suicide.[17] All but one of these patients had attempted suicide one to five times previously. A retrospective study examining the clinical characteristics of suicide victims with schizophrenia in the general population of Finland found that active illness (78%), depressive symptoms (64%), and a history of previous suicide attempts (71%) were highly prevalent immediately before suicide.[18]

Depression and Hopelessness

Persistent depressed mood, particularly feelings of hopelessness and psychomotor disturbances, were significantly associated with suicide in a prospective US study of 104 schizophrenic patients, 15 of whom subsequently committed suicide.[19] Similarly, in the study of Cohen *et al.*,[9] higher levels of self-reported subjective distress were described by the eight patients with schizophrenia, schizoaffective disorder, or schizotypal personality disorder who committed suicide compared with the 114 patients who did not. This study also found that self-reported subjective distress was consistently predicative of later suicide risk, whereas investigator-rated assessments were not. Results of a 5- to 10-year follow-up study of 207 patients hospitalized due to suicidal ideation led Beck *et al.*[20] to hypothesize that hopelessness may predict greater long-term suicide. Recent studies also found an association between depressive episodes or suicidal ideation during depression and suicide attempts. Gupta *et al.*[21] reported that of 336 patients with schizophrenia or schizoaffective disorder, the 98 patients with a history of suicide attempts had

TABLE 1. Suicide risk in treatment-responsive and treatment-resistant schizophrenic patients during prior and current episodes of suicidality (adapted from Meltzer and Okayli[22])

	No suicidal thoughts (%)	Suicidal thoughts, plans, or threats (%)	Suicide attempts	
			Low probability of success[a] (%)	High probability of success[b] (%)
Prior episodes (excluding current episode)				
Neuroleptic-responsive (n = 217)	49.8	18.4	23.0	8.8
Neuroleptic-resistant (n = 167)	48.5	12.0	25.7	13.8
Current episodes				
Neuroleptic-responsive (n = 237)	63.3	23.6	9.3	3.8
Neuroleptic-resistant (n = 165)	69.1	22.4	6.7	1.8

[a]Defined as high likelihood of a nonfatal outcome due to low inherent lethality of the method and likelihood of detection
[b]Defined as method of high lethality with little chance of detection.

experienced a significantly higher mean number of lifetime depressive episodes compared with the 238 patients who had no history of suicide attempts.

Patients who have treatment-resistant schizophrenia by conventional criteria, that is, persistent moderate-severe positive symptoms, might be expected to feel hopeless and be at particular risk of suicide. To evaluate this hypothesis, we compared prior episodes of suicidality in 237 treatment-resistant and 183 treatment-responsive patients.[22] There was no significant difference in suicidality between the treatment-resistant and the treatment-responsive schizophrenic patients, possibly reflecting the poor social and work function characteristic of both groups (TABLE 1). This reflects the fact that controlling positive symptoms is often insufficient to restore work and social function in patients with schizophrenia.

Cognition and Insight

We examined cognitive function in patients with schizophrenia who have a lifetime history of suicidality (n = 41) and those without (n = 54). A description of the patient population and the cognitive battery has been reported elsewhere.[23] Those with a history of suicide had better function on the Digit Symbol Substitution test, Auditory Consonants Trigram, Category Instance Generation test, Rey's Verbal List Learning, immediate and delayed recall, and Wisconsin Card Sorting, categories formed (Meltzer et al., in prepara-

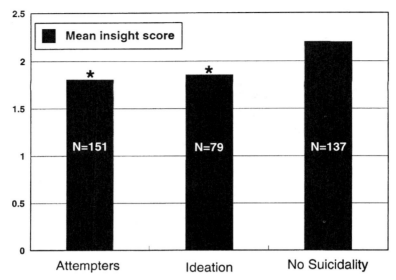

FIGURE 1. Mean insight score (lower score = greater insight) related to likelihood of suicide attempt, ideation, or no suicidality.

tion). Superior cognitive performance in the group of patients with sucidality may reflect some relation between cognition and other factors such as depression and hopelessness.

Insight, defined as having an awareness of one's mental disorder, particularly symptoms and functional condition, and awareness of the social consequences of schizophrenia and of the need for treatment, has been associated with suicidality in several studies.[24–28] We assessed insight in 367 patients with schizophrenia or schizoaffective disorder using the insight item from the Schedule for Affective Disorders and Schizophrenia.[29] This item defines insight as awareness of having a mental illness that is due to a biological process affecting the nervous system. We found that those with more insight were more likely to have attempted suicide or to have suicidal ideation than those who did not (FIG. 1). Insight and cognitive measures were in general not significantly correlated. There was a weak inverse relation between percent perseverative errors (rho = 0.16, $n = 163$, $p = 0.04$) in the Wisconsin Card Sorting test and the insight item just noted. No other significant correlations were noted. Awareness of illness and the limited benefits of treatment may lead to demoralization, depression, and concern about the potential for satisfaction in life. These results suggest the need for clinicians to be particularly alert to the potential for suicide in patients with insight when they have a feeling of hopelessness concerning their potential for meaningful recovery.

We carried out a logistic relationship to determine the ability of substance abuse status, insight, and cognitive measures to predict suicidality. Data were available from 146 patients (99 with a history of suicidality and 47 who were nonsuicidal). A history of substance abuse was the most significant predictor, followed by working memory performance and then by insight (Meltzer, in preparation).

EFFECT OF NEUROLEPTIC DRUGS, ANTIDEPRESSANTS, AND MOOD STABILIZERS

Evidence is inconclusive that typical neuroleptic drugs decrease the risk of suicide, although Palmer et al.[30] concluded that typical antipsychotic medications possibly have a weak effect, based on uncontrolled studies. Inadequate dosage and non-compliance complicate interpretation of their effect on the suicide rate.[31] The rate of suicide in schizophrenia after the introduction of neuroleptic drugs appears to be similar to that prior to their introduction.[32,33] However, it is risky to draw conclusions on this basis, because other factors may have served to enhance the tendency to suicide during the neuroleptic era, which might have counteracted some of the beneficial effects of these agents on suicidality.

Long-term treatment with conventional neuroleptics is associated with extrapyramidal side effects (EPS) such as akathisia. Case reports suggest an association between akathisia and suicide in schizophrenia.[34,35] Adjunctive treatment with antidepressant drugs and mood stabilizers may be useful in reducing depression, aggression, and impulsivity in some patients with schizophrenia. There are no conclusive data that they decrease the suicide rate, however.

SUICIDE RISK REDUCTION WITH ATYPICAL ANTIPSYCHOTIC DRUGS

There are various reasons for hope that atypical antipsychotic drugs such as clozapine, risperidone, olanzapine, quetiapine, ziprasidone, and iloperidone might reduce the risk of suicide in schizophrenia. As a group, these agents have superior efficacy in treating positive, disorganized, and negative symptoms in some but not all patients with schizophrenia compared to typical neuroleptic drugs.[36] They have also been found to improve cognitive dysfunction, which is a major factor in poor outcome with regard to work and social function.[37] There is also evidence that they have an antidepressant and mood-stabilizing action.[38] Some evidence, at least for clozapine, indicates that substance abuse is less in patients treated with these agents than with neuroleptics.[39] Finally, less EPS, especially less akathisia, would be expected to improve compliance and lead to fewer relapses. All of these factors address the key risk factors for suicide in schizophrenia just noted.

There are some data that are relevant to the risk of suicide in patients with schizophrenia or schizoaffective disorder treated with olanzapine. No differences in the rate of self-directed aggression in patients in randomized trials involving olanzapine, haloperidol, and placebo have been reported.[40] A reduction in suicide rate at the end of 1 year of olanzapine treatment compared to haloperidol has also been reported.[41] However, suicidal ideation decreased more on olanzapine than on haloperdiol.[41]

The most abundant evidence for an effect of an atypical antipsychotic on the suicide rate relates to clozapine, the prototypical atypical antipsychotic drug. Clozapine was initially introduced because of its low EPS profile.[42] It was subsequently found to not produce tardive dyskinesia and have greater efficacy in patients with neuroleptic-resistant schizophrenia than the typical neuroleptic drugs.[43] It has also been found to have antidepressant properties as well as mood-stabilizing properties.[38] We reported that it improved cognitive function, but not working memory,[23] and that it produced marked improvement in quality of life, including improved work and social function.[44] These results are generally confirmed in clinical practice. Were it not for its ability to produce agranulocytosis,[45] it would no doubt be a serious contender for first-line treatment of schizophrenia, but other side effects such as weight gain, sedation, increased risk of seizures, hypotension, tachycardia, and hypersalivation limit its tolerability for many patients.[42]

Clozapine was first reported to reduce the rate of suicide in schizophrenic patients by Meltzer and Okayli.[22] The purpose of this retrospective study was to determine if clozapine treatment decreased suicidality in neuroleptic-resistant patients diagnosed with chronic schizophrenia or schizoaffective disorder according to DSM-III-R criteria. In total, 183 neuroleptic-resistance patients were studied between 1986 and 1993. Most patients were male (69%) and Caucasian (89%). Thirty-three patients (18%) were diagnosed as having schizoaffective disorder. The mean duration of illness was 14 years.

Clozapine treatment (mean daily dose of 500 mg) was initiated in the hospital. Suicidality was assessed at weekly intervals during hospitalization and at 6 weeks, 3 and 6 months, and every 6 months thereafter for a mean follow-up period of 3.5 years. At the final visit, patients were reinterviewed for information on suicidality. Suicidality was recorded as: (1) no suicidal thoughts; (2) suicidal thoughts; (3) suicidal threats or plans; (4) unintentional self-harm; and (5) suicide attempts. The Hamilton Depression Rating Scale was used to assess depressive symptoms, including helplessness and hopelessness at baseline and at all scheduled follow-up visits. Of the 183 patients,

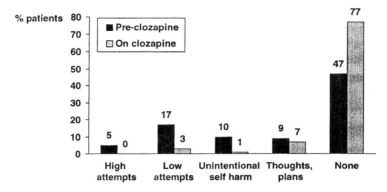

FIGURE 2. Suicidality in 88 treatment-resistant schizophrenic patients before and after 2 years of clozapine treatment. (Adapted from Meltzer and Okayli.[22])

88 (73 treatment-resistant schizophrenia and 15 schizoaffective) received clozapine for at least 6 months.

In this study, clozapine treatment was associated with markedly reduced suicidality The percentage of patients with no suicidality increased from 53% at baseline to 88% at follow-up. There were 22 suicide attempts in the 2 years prior to the initiation of clozapine therapy and only 3 suicide attempts with low probability for lethality in patients treated with clozapine over the 2 years of follow-up (FIG. 2). This is a decrease of 86% in suicide attempts in the first 2 years of clozapine therapy. There was also a dramatic reduction in the lethal potential of the suicide attempts. Before clozapine treatment the lethality of reported attempts was assessed as minimal to mild in 11 instances and moderate to severe in 11 attempts. All three suicide attempts after clozapine treatment were considered to have no substantial potential for lethality.

The decrease in suicidality among this cohort of patients was also associated with an improvement in hopelessness and depression. The Total Hamilton Depression Scale scores were significantly improved both after 6 weeks of treatment ($p = 0.002$) and at the final visit ($p = 0.009$) compared with baseline in the 22 patients who had made previous suicide attempts. Hamilton suicide ratings were also significantly improved ($p = 0.03$) at 6 weeks and the final visit compared with baseline. Possible explanations for these results include the effect of clozapine to reduce suicidality, the benefits of weekly clinical contact for the requisite blood monitoring, superior psychosocial treatment, poor psychopharmacological and psychosocial treatment prior to beginning clozapine, an interaction between clozapine and psychosocial treatment, and a cohort effect, that is, a generalized reduction in the suicide rate in schizophrenia during the period of clozapine treatment compared to prior periods.

Meltzer and Okali[22] also cited data from the US Clozaril® National Registry from 1989–1993 that indicated a reduced rate of completed suicide in patients receiving clozapine compared to the expected rate for all patients with schizophrenia.[22] Data from the US Clozaril National Registry from April 1991 to the end of 1993 showed an incidence of suicide of 0.039% and 0.22% per year for current and former users of clozapine, respectively.[40]

Walker et al.[47] undertook a retrospective evaluation of mortality and morbidity in current and former clozapine users on the US Clozaril National Registry (white blood count monitoring system for patients treated with Clozaril [clozapine]) from April 1991 until the end of 1993. In total, 67,072 patients were eligible for study. Deaths occurring in this cohort of patients were ascertained using the Social Security Administration Death Master Files and The National Death Index. In total, 859 deaths were found and the cause of death was ascertained for 790 patients. Of the 396 deaths in patients between 10 and 54 years of age, suicide accounted for 19%. The standard mortality ratio for the cohort compared with the US general population was 1.73. In patients aged 10 to 54 years, the overall standardized mortality ratio was reduced by 54% in current users of clozapine compared with former users (FIG. 3). This was primarily due to an 83% reduction in death by suicide among current clozapine users compared with past clozapine users. The suicide rates among current and former users of clozapine were 39 and 222 per 100,000 person-years, respectively.

Further Clozaril National Registry data were cited by Reid et al.[46] for the period from the beginning of 1990 to June 1996. The reported incidence of suicide in patients receiving clozapine was 0.0157% per year compared with the rate of 0.4–0.8% per year reported in previous studies with classical antipsychotics.[1,2] Although these data are subject to multiple interpretations, they are consistent with the possibility that clozapine treatment may be associated with a marked reduction in the risk for suicidality in schizophrenia.

The reduced risk of suicide among patients treated with clozapine has also been confirmed in a retrospective study of patients with schizophrenia or schizoaffective disorders in the Texas State Mental Health System.[46] This study examined the annual suicide rates in more than 82,000 severely and chronically mentally ill patients, including more than 30,000 patients with schizophrenia and schizoaffective disorder, and compared these rates with those in a subgroup of patients who had been treated with clozapine. The annual suicide rate for all psychiatric patients was 60.2 per 100,000 patients. Among patients with schizophrenia and schizoaffective disorder, the annual suicide rate in those treated with clozapine was 12.7 per 100,000 patients compared with 63.1 per 100,000 for all patients. This suicide rate for patients

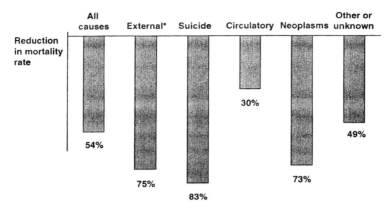

FIGURE 3. Reduction in mortality rate for current clozapine exposure compared with past exposure in subjects aged 10–54 years of age. Data from Walker *et al.*[47]

receiving clozapine in the Texas State Mental Health System study is comparable to that determined for the US Clozaril National Registry in June 1996, where the rate was 15.7 per 100,000 patients per year (Novartis, data on file).

Suicidality, impulsiveness, and aggressiveness were evaluated in 30 neuroleptic-resistant, chronic schizophrenic patients who had been maintained on clozapine for at least 1 year and were compared with symptoms in 30 chronic schizophrenic patients who had been treated with classical therapy for the same period.[48] Clozapine was associated with fewer suicidal attempts (p <0.05), less impulsiveness (p <0.05), and less aggressiveness (p <0.01) compared with chlorpromazine.

THE INTERSEPT STUDY

The International Suicide Prevention Trial (InterSePT) was initiated as a controlled trial of the effect of clozapine on suicidality. The InterSePT is a large-scale, prospective, randomized, open-label, single-blind, parallel-group study to compare the effectiveness of clozapine (300–900 mg/day) with olanzapine (10–20 mg/day) in reducing suicide and suicide-related events. The study is being conducted at 68 sites in 11 countries: US (31), France (6), UK (5), Hungary (5), Argentina (5), Italy (5), South Africa (3), Czech Republic (3), Canada (2), Croatia (2), and Chile (1). The large-scale, international nature of this study will enable evaluation of potential risk factors associated with suicidality, such as age, race, sex, genotype, associated psychiatric conditions, and the relationship to discharge in multiple countries and cultures

TABLE 2. Primary and secondary efficacy parameters of the InterSePT study

Primary	Secondary

Serious suicide attempts
  Hospitalization for imminent risk of suicide
  Clinical Global Impression — severity of
    suicide (CGI-SS) [change from baseline]
	Suicide
	  InterSePT Scale of Suicide Thinking
	    (ISST)
	  Number of rescue interventions
	Psychotic
	  Positive and Negative Syndrome Scale
	    (PANSS)
	  Clinical Global Impression -psychosis
	    (CGI-P)
	  Extrapyramidal Symptom Rating Scale
	    (ESRS)
	Mood
	  Calgary Depression Scale (CDS)
	  Covi Anxiety Scale
	  Pharmacoeconomic Scale of Function-
	    ing
	  Pharmacoeconomic forms

(TABLE 2). Both groups of patients will receive equal clinical contact with study personnel during the 2 years of observation.

Nine hundred eighty patients were entered into the study. The mean age was 37.1 (SD 10.3). Of these 609 (62.1%) were diagnosed as having schizophrenia and 371 (37.9%), were schizoaffective. Most were Caucasian (70.9%), with 15.3% of African descent. Most were male (61.4%). The mean number of suicide attempts was 3.4 (SD 6.2, range 0–120) The median number was 2. The mean number of hospitalizations to prevent a suicide attempt was 3.4 (SD 6.42) with more than three quarters of the patients having been hospitalised to prevent a suicide attempt within the 3 years prior to the study. The most common means of attempted suicide was overdosage (35.6%). Substance abuse or alcohol abuse was present in 49.2% of the sample. At the time of entry into the study, 23.6% were considered not at all suicidal, 27.6% were considered mildly suicidal, 35.8% were considered moderately suicidal, 10.7% were considered severely suicidal, and 0.8% had just attempted suicide, according to the admitting psychiatrist. The results of the treatment component of the study will be available by 2002, if not before.

TREATMENT OF SUICIDALITY IN SCHIZOPHRENIA

Reducing the risk of suicidality in schizophrenia requires, in the first instance, improving overall outcome. Controlling psychosis and depression, limiting substance abuse, preventing or reversing cognitive deterioriation, improving general health, facilitiating work and social function, and decreasing isolation from family and others are necessary to achieve a meaningful reduction in the suicide rate. Atypical antipsychotic drugs, utilized early in the course of illness, coupled with intensive psychosocial support in an outpatient setting, appear to be the best means to achieve these ambitious goals.

CONCLUSIONS

Suicide is the major cause of death in schizophrenia, accounting for the death of about 10% of schizophrenic patients. Multiple risk factors for suicide in schizophrenic patients have been identified including a history of suicide attempts, depression, feelings of hopelessness, male sex, social isolation, and deteriorating health. Insight coupled into a sense of hopelessness may be a risk factor. Conventional neuroleptics appear to have minimal effect to reduce the suicide rate among schizophrenic patients. Furthermore, the EPS associated with these agents may contribute to suicidality in certain cases.

Clozapine, the first atypical antipsychotic, has been reported to reduce the suicide rate by 75–85% in several uncontrolled clinical trials and an epidemiologic study linking medical examiner records with the Clozaril National Registry. The possible benefits of clozapine to reduce suicide risk may be due to improved symptom control, cognitive improvement, direct antidepressant and mood-stabilizing actions, reduced EPS, improved compliance, and improved insight coupled to a decrease in hopelessness.

The InterSePT study will provide data on the effect of clozapine and olanzapine, another atypical antipsychotic, on suicide rates in patients with schizophrenia and schizoaffective disorder.

REFERENCES

1. ALLEBECK, P. 1989. Schizophrenia: a life-shortening disease. Schizophr. Bull. **15:** 81–89.
2. CALDWELL, C.B. & I.I. GOTTESMAN. 1990. Schizophrenics kill themselves too: a review of risk factors for suicide. Schizophr. Bull. **16:** 571–589.
3. HEILA, H., E.T. ISOMETSA, M.M. HENRIKSSON, *et al.* 1997. Suicide and schizophrenia: a nationwide psychological autopsy study on age- and sex-specific clinical characteristics of 92 suicide victims with schizophrenia. Am. J. Psychiatry **154:** 1235–1242
4. BLEULER, E. 1950. Translated by J. Zinkin. Dementia praecox of the group of schizophrenias (1911). International Universities Press. New York.

5. WYATT, R.J., I. HENTER, M.C. LEARY, *et al.* 1995. An economic evaluation of schizophrenia: 1991. Soc. Psychiatry Psychiatr. Epidemiol. **30:** 196–205.

6. CALDWELL, C.B. & I.I. GOTTESMAN. 1992. Schizophrenia – a high-risk factor for suicide: clues to risk reduction. Suicide Life Threat. Behav. **22:** 479–493.

7. MILES, C.P. 1977. Conditions predisposing to suicide: a review. J. Nerv. Ment. Dis. **164:** 231–246.

8. INSKIP, H.M., E.C. HARRIS & B. BARRACLOUGH. 1998. Lifetime risk of suicide for affective disorder, alcoholism and schizophrenia. Br. J. Psychiatry **172:** 35–37.

9. COHEN, L.J., M.A. TEST & R.L. BROWN. 1990. Suicide and schizophrenia: data from a prospective community treatment study. Am. J. Psychiatry **147:** 602–607.

10. AXELSSON, R. & M. LAGERKVIST-BRIGGS. 1992. Factors predicting suicide in psychotic patients. Eur. Arch. Psychiatry Clin. Neurosci. **241:** 259–266.

11. MORTENSEN, P.B. & K. JUEL. 1993. Mortality and causes of death in first admitted schizophrenic patients. Br. J. Psychiatry **163:** 183–189.

12. HARRIS, E.C. & B. BARRACLOUGH. 1998. Excess mortality of mental disorder. Br. J. Psychiatry **173:**11–53.

13. HARKAVY-FRIEDMAN, J.M., K. RESTIFO, D. MALASPINA, *et al.* 1999. Suicide behavior in schizophrenia: charactertisitcs of individuals who had and had not attempted suicide. Am. J. Psychiatry **156:** 1276–1278.

14. HEILÄ, H., M.E. HEIKKINEN, E.T. ISOMETSA, *et al.* 1999. Life events and completed suicide in schizophrenia: a comparison of suicide victims with and without schizophrenia. Schizophr. Bull. **256:** 519–531.

15. ROSSAU, C.D. & P.B. MORENSEN. 1997. Risk factors for suicide in patients with schizophrenia: nested case-control study. Br. J. Psychiatry **171:** 355–359.

16. KAPLAN. K.J. & M. HARROW. 1996. Positive and negative symptoms as risk factors for later suicidal activity in schizophrenics vs depressives. Suicide Life Threat. Behav. **26:** 105–121.

17. KRAUSZ, M., T. MÜLLER-THOMSEN & C. HAASEN. 1995. Suicide among schizophrenic adolescents in the long-term course of illness. Psychopathology **28:** 95–103.

18. HEILA, H., E.T. ISOMETSA, M.M. HENRIKSSON, *et al.* 1997. Suicide and schizophrenia: a nationwide psychological sutopsy study on age- and sex-specific clinical characteristics of 92 suicide victims with schizophrenia. Am. J. Psychiatry **154:**1235–1242.

19. DRAKE, R.E., C. GATES & P.G. COTTON. 1986. Suicide among schizophrenics: a comparison of attempters and completed suicides. Br. J. Psychiatry **149:** 784–787.

20. BECK, A.T., R.A. STEER, M. KOVACS & B. GARRISON. 1985. Hopelessness and eventual suicide: a 10-year prospective study of patients hospitalized with suicidal ideation. Am. J. Psychiatry **142:** 559–563.

21. GUPTA, S., D.W. BLACK, S. ARNDT, *et al.* 1998. Factors associated with suicide attempts among patients with schizophrenia. Psychiatr. Serv. **49:**1353–1355.

22. MELTZER, H.Y. & G. OKAYLI. 1995. Reduction of suicidality during clozapine treatment of neuroleptic-resistant schizophrenia: impact on risk-benefit assessment. Am. J. Psychiatry **152:** 183–190.

23. HAGGER, C., P. BUCKLEY, J.T. KENNY, *et al.* 1993. Improvement in cognitive function and psychiatric symptoms in treatment-refractory schizophrenic patients receiving clozapine. Biol. Psychiatry **34:** 702–712.

24. SCHWARTZ, R.C. & S. PETERSEN. 1999. The relationship between insight and suicidality among patients with schizophrenia. J. Nerv. Ment. Dis. **187:** 376–378.
25. STEPHENS, J.H., P. RICHARD & P.R. McHUGH. 2000. Long-term follow-up of patients with a diagnosis of paranoid state and hospitalized, 1913 to 1940. J. Nerv. Ment. Dis. **188:** 202–208.
26. SCHWARTZ, R.C. 2000. Insight and suicidality in schizophrenia: a replication study. J. Nerv. Ment. Dis. **188:** 235–237.
27. AMADOR, X.F., J.H. FRIEDMAN, C. KASAPIS, et al. 1996. Suicidal behavior in schizophrenia and its relationship to awareness of illness. Am. J. Psychiatry **153:** 1185–1188.
28. AMADOR, X.F. & D.H. STRAUSS. 1993. Poor insight in schizophrenia. Psychiatr. Q. **64:** 305–318.
29. ENDICOTT, J. & R.L. SPITZER. 1978. A diagnostic interview: the schedule for affective disorders and schizophrenia. Arch. Gen. Psychiatry **35:** 837–844.
30. PALMER, D.D., I.D. HENTER & R.J. WYATT. 1999. Do antipsychotic medications decrease the risk of suicide in patients with schizophrenia? J. Clin. Psychiatry **60:** 100–103.
31. HEILÄ, H., E.T. ISOMETSÄ, M.M HENRIKSSON, et al. 1999. Suicide victims with schizophrenia in different treatment phases and adequacy of antipsychotic medication. J. Clin. Psychiatry **60:** 200–208.
32. CIOMPI, L. 1976. Late suicide in former mental patients. Psychiatr. Clin. (Basel) **9:** 59–63.
33. WINOKUR, G. & M. TSUANG. 1975. The Iowa 500: suicide in mania, depression and schizophrenia. Am. J. Psychiatry **132:** 650–651.
34. DRAKE, R.E. & J. EHRLICH. 1985. Suicide attempts associated with akathisia. Am. J. Psychiatry **142:** 499–501.
35. SHEAR, M.K., A. FRANCES & P. WEIDEN. 1983. Suicide associated with akathisia and depot fluphenazine treatment. Suicide **3:** 235–236.
36. THE COLLABORATIVE WORKING GROUP ON CLINICAL TRIAL EVALUATIONS; HERBERT Y. MELTZER, Chair. 1998. Measuring outcome in schizophrenia: differences among the atypical antipsychotics. J. Clin. Psychiatry **59:** 3–9.
37. THE COLLABORATIVE WORKING GROUP ON CLINICAL TRIAL EVALUATIONS; HERBERT Y. MELTZER, Chair. 1998. Evaluating the effects of antipsychotics on cognition in schizophrenia. J. Clin. Psychiatry **59:** 35–40.
38. THE COLLABORATIVE WORKING GROUP ON CLINICAL TRIAL EVALUATIONS; HERBERT Y. MELTZER, Chair. 1998. Atypical antipsychotics for treatment of depression in schizophrenia and affective disorders. J. Clin. Psychiatry **59:** 41–45.
39. BUCKLEY, P., P. THOMPSON, L. WAY & H.Y. MELTZER. 1994. Substance abuse among patients with treatment-resistant schizophrenia: characteristics and implications for clozapine therapy. Am. J. Psychiatry **151:** 385–389.
40. BEASLEY, C.M., M.E. SAYLER, G.M. KIESLER, et al. 1998. The influence of pharmacotherapy on self-directed and externally-directed aggression in schizophrenia [abstr]. Schizophr. Res. **29:** 28.
41. GLAZER, W. 1998. Formulary decisions and health economics. J. Clin. Psychiatry **59:** 23–29.
42. MELTZER, H.Y. 1997. Treatment-resistant schizophrenia: the role of clozapine. Curr. Med. Res. Opin. **14:** 1–20.

43. KANE, J., G. HONIGFELD, J. SINGER & H.Y. MELTZER. 1988. Clozapine for the treatment-resistant schizophrenic: a double-blind comparison with chlorpromazine. Arch. Gen. Psychiatry 45: 789–796.
44. MELTZER, H.Y., S. BURNETT, B. BASTANI & L.F. RAMIREZ. 1990. Effect of six months of clozapine treatment on quality of life of chronic schizophrenic patients. Hosp. Commun. Psychiatry 41: 892–897.
45. ALVIR, J.M.J., J.A. LIEBERMAN, A.Z. SAFFERMAN, et al. 1993. Clozapine-induced agranulocytosis. Incidence and risk factors in the United States. N. Engl. J. Med. 329: 162–167.
46. REID, W.H., M. MASON & T. HOGAN. 1998. Suicide prevention effects associated with clozapine therapy in schizophrenia and schizoaffective disorder. Psychiatr. Serv. 49: 1029–1033.
47. WALKER, A.M., L.L. LANAZA, F. ARELLANO & K.J. ROTHMAN. 1997. Mortality in current and former users of clozapine. Epidemiology 8: 671–677.
48. SPIVAK, B., R. MESTER, N. WITTENBERG, et al. 1997. Reduction of aggressiveness and impulsiveness during clozapine treatment in chronic neuroleptic-resistant schizophrenic patients. Clin. Neuropharmacol. 20: 442–446.

DISCUSSION

J. JOHN MANN *(Chairman)*: I think you have a better sense of what a critical and pioneering piece of research that has been in creating a new potential avenue for reducing suicidal behavior in both psychotic and mood disorders. A question for Dr. Meltzer. For the psychotic patient, in addition to atypical antipsychotics, what other kinds of psychosocial intervention or other types of strategy can you recommend to address cognitive dysfunction in schizophrenia?

HERBERT Y. MELTZER: The success that we have had in getting people with schizophrenia back to work involved medication and the support of a skilled nurse, building on the strengths of each patient relative to his or her goals. As I indicated, there's an overall cognitive deficit associated with schizophrenia. Every type of cognitive function is impaired in schizophrenia, with deficits ranging from 1–2.5 standard deviations below normal limits. However, 15% of patients are within normal in most of their functions. These never fall below the 5% lower limit of normal in any function. Thus, one must assess the specific type and severity of a cognitive deficit in each patient.

There appear to be some differences among the newer drugs in terms of the pattern of cognitive deficits that they can improve. For example, risperdone, among all the atypicals, seems most effective in improving working memory. I was asked to assess a college student who, prior to his first episode, had been a high school valedictorian. By the first episode, the illness had absolutely devastated his short-term working memory. He had a very dramatic improvement after beginning treatment with risperdone and was able to go back to college. I think job coaching and newer techniques such as cognitive rehabilitation therapy that have been useful in people with traumatic brain injuries and the like are being explored in conjunction with the newer drugs in schizophrenia. Previous attempts to use cognitive rehabilitation therapy for schizophrenia have all been in people receiving typical neuroleptic drugs, and the results have been uniformly disappointing. It's time for another round of investigation of this approach in order to take advantage of the synergy that the newer drugs might provide.

MANN: A question for Dr. Meltzer concerning clozapine as a model for antisuicidal pharmacotherapy in psychotic disorders. You mentioned cognitive deficits and insight, the clinical correlates of suicide risk. One question is that presumably clozapine improves insight, so are you assuming an antisuicidal effect despite an improvement in insight? Another questioner asks, what about the effects of clozapine and risperdal on cognitive functions? This question goes hand in hand with trying to figure out the answer to the first question.

MELTZER: I had the same thought as I was preparing for this lecture, and I have only had a little time to look at that issue. Did clozapine improve insight? I found no evidence in our data that it did. I was trying to think through what might be going on there. It might be that patients improved in so many other ways, they began to deny that they had a serious illness. Like many other people who improve, not just people with chronic illnesses, once people with schizophrenia partially recover, they are often less committed to the notion that some irreversible or even serious disease process is going on. Our preliminary analysis suggests a trend to more denial after treatment. This is actually not inconsistent with the benefits of clozapine. The broader construct leading to more denial of illness is better outcome, better work and social function, a feeling of hope, and less conflict with families, being part of a more enduring and supportive treatment environment. All those good things are what's leading to a decrease in suicide despite no apparent improvement in insight.

MANN: A question for Dr. Meltzer; actually several people have asked the same question. In terms of the psychotherapeutic component or educational component of the therapy of schizophrenia, what do you do with insight now?

MELTZER: Again, I don't think you can treat any of these things in isolation. We come back to the concept of what schizophrenia is. John Mann and I were talking about some of the great controversies in psychiatry. An example is the controversy concerning psychosocial treatment versus drugs for schizophrenia. Another, between Ted Lidtz, a professor of psychiatry at Yale, and Seymour Kety, was about the genetics of schizophrenia. Ted Lidtz was adamantly resistant to the evidence of a genetic defect in schizophrenia, in part because he thought that such a view was tantamount to treatment resistance and that was not the message he would endorse. My approach to explaining schizophrenia to a person with the illness, and do not hesitate to call it schizophrenia, is to say that it is a biological, genetically driven disorder, but that does not mean the outcome is doomed to be negative. We can treat it. Some day we may be able to prevent it. We don't yet have strong evidence for irreversible structural brain damage in schizophrenia. Clearly, some neuropathologic studies show cellular and even gross abnormalities, but their significance is unknown. The newer medications can produce significant improvement in combination with a psychotherapeutic approach. The future, with these medications combined with physiosocial approaches, is to try to identify in the prodromal period before the cognitive deficit develops and to try to prevent its development.

Borderline Personality Disorder

Suicidality and Self-Mutilation

JOHN G. GUNDERSON AND MARIA E. RIDOLFI

Department of Psychiatry, Harvard Medical School; and Psychosocial and Personality Research, McLean Hospital, Belmont, Massachusetts 02478, USA

ABSTRACT: Epidemiological and neurobiological perspectives about suicidality in borderline patients are described, highlighting how self-destructive and seemingly suicidal acts are their "behavioral specialty." Principles for management, including the need for a primary clinician to oversee safety, and the pros and cons of both "contracting for safety" and hospitalization are presented. Clinical material is used to illustrate an approach that involves minimal initiative to rescue by therapists, a readiness to comply with patients' wishes for protection (the principle of false submission), and very active interpretation. This approach is contrasted with those advocated by Linehan and Kernberg.

KEYWORDS: Borderline personality disorder; Personality disorders; Recurrent hospitalizations; Self-mutilation; Suicidality

INTRODUCTION

The DSM IV criterion "recurrent suicidal threats, gestures, or behaviors or self-mutilative behaviors" is the fifth of nine criteria for borderline personality disorders (BPDs). It is neither the most sensitive nor the most specific predictor of DSM diagnostic membership,[1] but recurrent suicidality is central to the borderline construct, is often the most central issue for treatment, and is certainly the most central source of conflict and anguish for involved clinicians or families. Recurrent suicidal threats, gestures, or behaviors or self-mutilation is the borderline patient's "behavioral specialty." Its presence is a clear signal to clinicians whose patients present with depression, anxiety, or eating or substance abuse disorders that an underlying borderline personality disorder is likely, a disorder that, if ignored, will complicate treatment of these Axis I disorders and can render their usual therapies harmful. Unfortu-

Address for correspondence: Dr. John G. Gunderson, Director, Psychosocial and Personality Research, McLean Hospital, 115 Mill Street, Belmont, MA 02478. Voice: 617-855-2293; fax: 617-855-3522.

gleasop@mcleanpo.mclean.org

nately, whether because of the pressures of managed care or the paradigm shift towards biology in psychiatry, evidence exists that it is now common for clinicians to underdiagnose the underlying BPD.[2]

EPIDEMIOLOGICAL PERSPECTIVE

The rate of suicide in clinical samples of BPD is about 9%,[3] although good epidemiological data applicable to the estimated 2–3% of the general population who have this disorder are not yet available. The 9% rate is about 400 times the rate of suicide in the general population and more than 800 times the rate in young females (the rate is 0.005% for women 15–34 years old).[4] Still, when contrasted with the estimated 60–70% of borderline patients who make suicide attempts[5] and the finding that this plurality usually make multiple attempts (average 3), the 9% figure actually reflects the high frequency with which borderline patients make suicide attempts that are unsuccessful.

Suicide threats or gestures occur far more often than suicide attempts. We estimate that these occur in 90% of borderline patients and usually occur repeatedly. One study found that 33% of an inpatient sample had current plans.[6] The most common form of self-mutilative behavior is cutting (80%), but bruising (24%), burning (20%), head banging (15%), or biting (7%) is not unusual.[7] Self-mutilation should usually be seen as distinct from suicidal behaviors per se, but such behavior doubles the risk of actual suicide.[8]

As a caveat to this discussion, we believe that the attention sometimes given to cutting as a social contagion akin to tattoos[9] underestimates the seriousness of this behavior. Obviously, not all teenage cutters have BPD, but anyone who cuts themselves needs attention and those who cut themselves repeatedly are likely to have BPD and be in need of significant and sustained familial support and psychiatric help.

NEUROBIOLOGICAL CORRELATES OF SUICIDAL AND SELF-MUTILATING BEHAVIORS

Numerous studies have attempted to delineate a biological substrate for the suicidal and self-mutilating behaviors of borderline patients. Decreased levels of serotonin (5-HT) and/or its metabolite 5-hydroxyindoleacetic acid (5-HIAA) were found in the brain stem of suicide victims.[10,11] Consistent with these findings, lower levels of cerebrospinal fluid (CSF) 5-HIAA have been found in suicide attempters, especially those using violent methods, compared to nonattempters.[11,12] Interestingly, lower levels of CSF 5-HIAA in

BPD patients are significantly associated with a history of suicide attempts but not with self-mutilation or violence.[13]

Coccaro et al.[14] showed decreased prolactin responses to fenfluramine hydrochloride, an agent that stimulates serotonin release and blocks serotonin reuptake, in patients with major affective disorder and/or personality disorder compared to normal controls. Decreased prolactin responses were correlated with a history of suicide attempts in patients with either disorder, but with impulsive aggression in patients with personality disorder only.

Gardner and Cowdry[15,16] hypothesized that self-injurious behavior (SIB) in BPD may be related to low thresholds of excitability in limbic structures due to subtle CNS injury or to kindling as a result of repeated emotional traumas during early development. This suggestion is based on the similarity of symptoms often associated with SIB in subjects with BPD (depersonalization, derealization, mood swings, déjà vu phenomena, and perceptual distortions) and those observed in subjects with partial complex seizures. Furthermore, BPD patients who experience partial complex seizure-like symptoms have a higher incidence of EEG abnormalities, particularly posterior sharp activity, when compared to depressed patients. The same investigators[16] found decreased severity of behavioral dyscontrol, including SIB, in 11 women with BPD treated with carbamazepine, an anticonvulsant with primary effects on subcortical limbic structures, when compared to placebo.

PSYCHOSOCIAL TRIGGERING CONTEXT

The functions of self-injuries are variable (TABLE 1).[17] A patient struggling with her impulse to cut wrote: "I want to cut. I want to see pain, for it is the most physical thing to show. You cannot show pain inside. I want to cut, cut, show, show. Get it out. What out? Just pain." Although cutting can bring relief of dysphoric states, that is not its usual purpose; more often, cutting is to punish oneself. In my experience, cutting often provides relief from a poorly articulated but intolerable state involving intense shame, remorse, and convictions of badness and alienation. Cutting, then, is akin to religious expiation of badness or atonement for sins, which is thereby followed by restitutive fantasies of forgiveness that account for the relief. Leibenluft et al.[18] documented that at least half the patients with self-harming behavior have reported the absence of pain during the self-injurious episode. This could be identified as a dissociative defense mechanism or a release of endogenous opioids when marked dysphoria is experienced.

Zanarini et al.[19] documented the intensely dysphoric inner states reported by borderline patients. The mean percentages of their patients' time spent ex-

TABLE 1. Functions of self-injurious behavior[a]

Feel pain	60%
Punish self	50%
Control feelings	40%
Exert control	22%
Express anger	22%
Feel	20%

[a]From Shearer et al.[17]

TABLE 2. Being borderline: percent time spent experiencing dysphoric affects*,[a]

	Affect	BPD	Other PDs
Common	Overwhelmed	62%	30%
	Worthless	60%	28%
	Very angry	53%	21%
	Empty	61%	27%
Specific	Abandoned	45%	17%
	Betrayed	36%	7%
	Furious or enraged	39%	11%

*pc ≤ 0.001 for all contrasts.
[a]Zanarini et al.[19]

periencing dysphoric feelings were all significantly greater than those in control patients with other personality disorders (p <0.001). TABLE 2 shows that a subset of feelings, while less often experienced, were quite specific for patients having BPD. A similar analysis was done of dysphoric cognitions. Of note in TABLE 3 is that borderline patients spend 44% of their time thinking about killing themselves. The range of dysphoric thoughts and feelings and the percentage of time spent experiencing them are so extraordinary that it is surprising that borderline patients do not spend an even higher percentage of their time thinking about killing themselves.

Consistent with Fairbairn[20] and subsequently Bowlby's[21] thesis that humans have an innate biological drive for attachment and central to the thesis that intolerance of aloneness is the core psychopathology of borderline patients is the formulation that suicidal and self-destructive ideas and behaviors need to be understood within an interpersonal context.[22] As shown in TABLE 4, when a person with BPD feels cared for, that is, "held," s/he appears like a depressed waif – easy to sympathize with, grateful for signs of care, and, like

TABLE 3. Being borderline: percent time spent experiencing dysphoric cognitions*,[a]

	Cognition	BPD	Other PDs
Common	Misunderstood	52%	25%
	No one cares	40%	20%
	I'm bad	46%	30%
Specific	Think about hurting myself	44%	9%
	Think about killing myself	40%	14%
	I'm evil	24%	4%
	I'm a small child	36%	7%
	I'm damaged	39%	11%

*pc ≤ 0.001 for all contrasts.
[a]Zanarini et al.[19]

TABLE 4. How BPD phenomenology relates to perceived attachment[a]

Interpersonal context	Phenomenology	Others' responses	Clinical implication
Held-idealizing	Empty Dysfunctional Symptomatic	Sympathetic	Collaborative Interpretations Needs expressive, involving therapies
Frustrating-rejecting	Angry Self-destructive Pleas for help	Scared, guilty, angry	Confrontations Needs social supports, behavioral change
Alone	Terrified Dissociative Paranoid Substance-abuse Promiscuity	Rescue, avoid	Words unimportant Needs containment, medications

[a]Adapted from Gunderson.[5]

healthier neurotic patients, receptive to interpretations. Symptoms such as depression, eating disorders, substance abuse, or posttraumatic stress disorder often become the focus. When this occurs, the clinician or any other persons whom the borderline patient feels dependent upon for care will be surprised when separations are imminent.

When the person with BPD is confronted with the loss of their significant other's caring or holding, a different set of clinical phenomena becomes evident. It is this interpersonal context that triggers the borderline patient's "hyperbolic" tendency to exaggerate his/her feelings for fear they will otherwise be ignored.[23] It is also in this context that borderline patients convey suicidal intentions or conduct suicidal gestures or self-mutilative behaviors to solicit a caring response from others (TABLE 4). Such "calls for help" are primarily communications to the person whose absence is threatened, but they can potentially be lethal. This, we think, is why the risk of suicide is heightened for borderline patients just after poorly prepared discharges from hospitals.[24] Often, this causes the other to not leave or otherwise rescue the person with BPD, but to feel manipulated. This sets in motion a characteristic hostile dependency wherein the "other" finds the prospect of staying distasteful, but feels hostage to the threat of suicide.

When the person with BPD feels him- or herself to be without a caring other, that is, without a holding environment, a third set of clinically significant phenomena becomes evident. Here, self-mutilation may be to feel alive – the pain is reassuring. In this context, suicidal behaviors may be very dangerous, indicating a readiness to die unless a saving intervention is made. Indeed, there is evidence that borderline patients are particularly likely to have experienced separations or losses in the week prior to suicide.[25]

PRINCIPLES OF MANAGING SUICIDALITY

Need for a Primary Clinician

Many clinicians who believe that the treatment of choice for borderline patients is individual psychodynamic psychotherapy make this modality their sole treatment – a plan that is welcome to these patients. Unfortunately, the need for supportive attention of borderline patients usually surpasses what individual therapies allow, and their need for structure and social rehabilitation usually exceeds that provided by the framework for psychodynamic therapies. This means that taking on responsibility for a borderline outpatient requires clinical management and that modalities other than psychotherapy are usually necessary (and almost always desirable).[26] Both of these implications underscore the need for borderline outpatients to have a primary clinician who assumes responsibility for the patient's care, including monitoring safety and implementing appropriate interventions. While traditionally this role has been assumed by someone who defines him- or herself as the patient's therapist, there are inherent problems in trying to administrate the selection and implementation of a therapeutic effort and retaining the noncontrolling, exploratory, and empathic stance required of those therapists who practice psychodynamic psychotherapy.

Contracting for Safety

"Contracting for safety" has become a popular practice by clinicians with administrative responsibilities for borderline patients. It involves asking patients to give explicit agreement not to harm themselves, sometimes even writing this "contract" out. This invokes the patient's "word of honor" as a deterrent to impulsive actions; more specifically, it is an interpersonal promise such that suicide becomes a betrayal to that clinician's trust and confidence. This is often helpful for short-term agreements with patients who value the clinician's opinion of them.

For most borderline patients, clinicians should expect that suicidal ideas and impulses will recur and that the ongoing risk to their safety is a dynamic process that therapists are often best positioned to assess and mitigate. Because involvement in safety interventions (e.g., phone calls, ER visits, family meetings, contracts, etc.) often is a source of failure for transference-focused psychotherapies, Kernberg's group[27,28] advocates a psychotherapy contract that specifically excludes the therapist from such involvement. The responsibility for safety is the patient's to work out with others who are usually less knowledgeable. I prefer a more pragmatic empirical approach, which takes up problems, including suicidality, as they arise and adjusts the treatment when suicidality recurs. To undertake a dynamic psychotherapy with a BPD patient who is or becomes suicidal would not mean that that therapy is the wrong modality; it would mean that other collaborating modalities offering more support or structure need to be added (e.g., medications, dialectical behavior therapy skills training, family sessions, etc.).

Principle of "Split Treatment"

As described elsewhere, the use of more than one modality in treating borderline outpatients offers many advantages, as long as the therapies are provided by able clinicians who are explicitly in collaboration.[26] Linehan's DBT combining individual and group modalities is a good example of this.[29] In usual practice, the combination of a psychopharmacologist with a psychotherapist is most common. Split treatments help patients contain their acting out, including self-destructively, in response to frustrations encountered within or outside the treatment. Having said this, the presence of a team still requires that the borderline patient know about the different roles and goals of the therapies and specifically who will be responsible when safety crises occur. The case is made in the APA's draft of Treatment Guidelines that this role is usually best served by the psychiatrist because of greater experience in management, familiarity with commitment procedures, and inevitable liability when treatments go poorly. Those reasons are sensible, but most important is that the clinician have experience and skill with BPD and regular ongoing contacts with the particular patient.

Guidelines to Managing Safety

When informed by a borderline patient that he/she has suicidal ideas, impulses, or plans, we should always respond. The critical issue is to leave the responsibility for communicating such ideas on the borderline patient's shoulders. This is unlike Linehan's DBT, where each session is proactively begun with inquiries about recent self-harm. These behaviors are the primary target of DBT. With more generic approaches, I think such a focus is a type of "therapy-interfering behavior"—symptomatic of avoiding discussions of the problems in living about which therapy can be helpful. For clinicians to become proactive in searching out suicidal ideas, behaviors, and the like reinforces this as a way to seek help and encourages the patient's aversion to self-care. Expressions of concern are usually helpful, but concern is often best conveyed by inquiries about why (i.e., "when did this start," etc.) rather than expressions of alarm or by becoming proactive in prevention. When a precipitating incident (almost always interpersonal) has been identified, careful review of its meaning and the patient's associated feelings will usually bring relief. I am hesitant to ask them for reassurances about their safety. Better to ask whether there is any way they think you can be helpful; keep the patient in charge of his/her own safety.

When the crisis is past, it is important to discuss it. Often this is not welcomed. This discussion should include the clinician's disclosure about how it affected them, for example, "it was very scary" or "I worried after you left." Of particular importance is to insist on examining what it was that provided relief.

Patient: (*irritably*) I'm sorry for troubling you, but it was a crisis. I guess you've never been through what I go through.

Therapist: (*sidestepping her anger*) When you began to talk about what was bothering you, that seemed to have helped.

Patient: Yes, it really did. I appreciated that you listened.

Therapist: That was most interesting to me. What seemed to help was just having someone listen. I didn't do anything. How can that be?

The patient discussed how rare it was to have someone listen to her. The therapist used this exchange to educate the patient, explaining that some people (those with a borderline personality disorder) get overwhelmingly panicked when they do not have someone available to offer comfort and that such people find aloneness intolerable. That led to a discussion of the patient's living situation and alternative sources of comfort. The therapist said that although he was glad to have proved useful, it was dangerous for her safety to depend upon his availability. Moreover, it wasn't a function that he could serve too often without disrupting his own life (thereby actively drawing attention to his own limits, as opposed to setting limits on the patient).

Recurrent Hospitalizations and the Principle of False Submission

Some of the most difficult encounters with borderline patients involve those who voice active suicidal intentions accompanied by histories of chronic suicidality and multiple attempts. Such histories make it hard for clinicians to judge the seriousness of the suicidal intent and create moral and ethical dilemmas for them.[30,31] The clinician will usually feel that questioning the seriousness of the patient's suicidal intentions could magnify the likelihood and lethality of an attempt. Beyond this the clinician will know that hospitalizations — the usual response to suicidality — can rarely address the underlying causes for the suicidality and may actually perpetuate the borderline patient's allegations of being suicidal (due to the secondary gains of being rescued, getting attention, and avoiding community-based problems).

Vignette

Helene is a 35-year-old disheveled, agitated, overweight single woman who appears for her first clinic appointment. She promptly states she is grateful to "now have a therapist" and that she's needed one for 3 years. Even as the evaluating clinician feels uneasy about the role assigned by the patient, she goes on to say that she feels very suicidal. In response to the clinician's inquiries, she reports that she has been suicidal "off and on for many years" and has already had 31 hospitalizations.

Clinician: What has caused you to become suicidal now?

Patient: I don't know; what difference does it make? (*is now becoming irritated and defensive*)

Clinician: Has anything happened in your life recently? (*skeptical about the patient's lethality and hoping to isolate specific events that can be addressed, but already feeling quite anxious about the patient's volatility and potential flight*)

Patient: All I know is that I visited my parents and became very upset and had to leave. No, I don't know why. No, they didn't say anything. Yes, it's happened before and last time I nearly killed myself.

Clinician: What happened?

Patient: I drank a quart of vodka, and then took any fucking pills I could find.... I would have been dead if my landlord hadn't noticed that the TV was on all night.

Clinician: (*now convinced that the patient is dangerous, but still feeling coerced into suggesting hospitalization*) Are you feeling that way again?

Patient: I just want to get control of myself. If I can't, I'm going to slash my neck. This time I don't want to fail.

Clinician: Would you like to go into the hospital?

Patient: Yes, I need to.

This vignette illustrates a not unusual situation, that is, a relatively unknown patient presents with agitation and suicidal ideation, and a not unusual intervention, that is, the patient gets hospitalized. This is done despite the clinician's doubt about the seriousness of the intention and despite an expectation that another hospitalization (in Helene's case, the 32nd!) is unlikely to help and may even be reinforcing a self-defeating pattern. The clinician will usually feel coerced, manipulated, and helpless. Still, in the absence of alternatives that can surely safeguard the patient, he is doing the right thing by suggesting hospitalization.

My own approach to this situation starts by making the dilemma explicit. I tell a patient, such as Helene, that hospitalization would be the safest option, but that it is not likely to be helpful and probably will be harmful to her longer-term welfare. I explain that hospitalization involves inviting others to assume control for her life and this can discourage her learning self-controls. Moreover, I say that for many patients such "rescues" become a way of feeling cared for and that being hospitalized feels like being adopted, although that it is actually not what it means. "To me, offering hospitalization to you represents primarily a way to avoid my being legally liable should you otherwise commit suicide. I actually believe the more 'caring' response would be to try to keep you out of the hospital despite the potential risk to me." I tell such patients that in my judgment the best way to proceed would be to take the time needed to see why she is recurrently suicidal and to develop a treatment plan that addresses those reasons. Patients will often be unsurprised by such statements, and the discourse moves away from medical necessity.

This is the "principle of false submission." By ostensibly giving the patient what she wants but disarming it of its meaning, the cycle of repeated admissions (so-called "frequent flyers") can be broken. This will not usually happen the first time, that is, the patient will almost always go into the hospital upon hearing this exchange, but being hospitalized has a different meaning when they do.

In Helene's case, I would want to involve the patient's family and her previous treatment providers in any decision about being hospitalized. For practical reasons, such as accessibility, these involvements may prove unfeasible, but the principle behind advocating this process is to underscore the clinician's wish to do the right thing and to encourage the patient to consider alternatives.

"Borderline" (Meaning Ambivalent) Suicidal Intentions

The high rate of unsuccessful attempts, I believe, reflects the fact that suicide attempts by borderline patients are usually ambivalent. It is not that the borderline patient wants necessarily to die; it is that s/he wants to die if no one is willing to accept the responsibility for their living. If someone convinces them that they are "loved" by overt saving/rescuing/reassuring responses, then they will want to live, however miserably. This essentially ambivalent attitude about life is captured in examples such as the following. The patient who overdoses in a public place, but is ignored by passers-by who assume she is asleep. The patient whose death by car fumes occurs in the garage because her husband came home late. The patient who, after cutting her wrists for the third time, fainted while walking and hit her head lethally on the marble counter. Such examples illustrate the real risk of suicide and the thin thread of luck that often determines outcome. After successful suicide by borderline patients, the ambiguity of their intentions often stimulates much speculation about their intentions and many opportunities to raise "if only" or "what if" questions.

SUMMARY

This paper offers a selective review of the epidemiology, neuroscience, psychosocial context, and management of borderline patients' recurring suicidality. Basic principles governing management include the following:

(a) Disruptions of the borderline patient's basic need for ongoing interpersonal involvement give rise to intolerable dysphoric states.

(b) The borderline patient's wish to live or die depends upon sustaining such interpersonal involvement.

(c) Clinicians should be hesitant about rescuing but proactive about interpreting the need for involvement behind suicidal ideas and threats.

(d) Clinicians should be explicit about how "safety interventions" that may be in their own interest (peace of mind, reduced liability) may not be in the long-term interest of the borderline patient.

ACKNOWLEDGMENTS

Parts of this paper were reprinted from *Borderline Personality Disorder: A Clinical Guide* by J. Gunderson[26] with permission from American Psychiatric Press, Inc.

REFERENCES

1. GUNDERSON, J.G., M.C. ZANARINI & C.L. KISIEL. 1996. Borderline Personality Disorder. Source Book, Sect IV, Vol 2: 725. APA Press. Washington, DC.
2. ZIMMERMAN, M. & J.I. MATTIA. 1999. Differences between clinical and research practices in diagnosing borderline personality disorder. Am. J. Psychiatry **156:** 1570–1574.
3. PERRY, J.C. 1993. Longitudinal studies of personality disorders. J. Pers. Disorders Suppl. **1:** 63–85.
4. U.S. CENSUS BUREAU. 1995. Statistical Abstracts of the United States. U.S. Government Printing Office. Washington, DC.
5. GUNDERSON, J.G. 1984. Borderline Personality Disorder. American Psychiatric Press. Washington, DC.
6. ZISOOK, S., A. GOFF, P. SLEDGE, *et al.* 1994. Reported suicidal behavior and current suicidal ideation in a psychiatric outpatient clinic. Ann. Clin. Psychiatry **6:** 27–31.
7. SHEARER, S.L. 1994. Phenomenology of self-injury among inpatient women with borderline personality disorder. J. Nerv. Ment. Dis. **182:** 524–526.
8. STONE, M.H. 1987. Psychotherapy of borderline patients in light of long-term follow-up. Bull. Menninger Clin. **51:** 231–247.
9. EGAN, J. 1997. Cutting: the thin read line. NY Times Magazine :21–25, 39–44, 48. July 27.
10. MANN, J.J., V. ARANGO, & M.D. UNDERWOOD. 1990. Serotonin and suicidal behavior. Ann. N.Y. Acad. Sci. **600:** 476–484.
11. MANN, J.J. & V. ARANGO. 1998. The neurobiology of suicidal behavior. *In* Guide to Suicide Assessment and Intervention. D.G. Jacobs, ed. Biol. :98–114. Ossey-Bass. San Francisco, CA.
12. LESTER, D. 1995. The concentration of neurotransmitter metabolites in the cerebrospinal fluid of suicidal individuals: a meta-analysis. Pharmacopsychiatry **28:** 45–50.
13. GARDNER, D.L., P.B. LUCAS & R.W. COWDRY. 1990. CSF metabolites in borderline personality disorder compared to normal controls. Biol. Psychiatry **28:** 247–254.
14. COCCARO, E.F., L.J. SIEVER, H.M. KLAR, *et al.* 1989. Serotonergic studies in patients with affective and personality disorders. Correlates with suicidal and impulsive aggressive behavior. Arch. Gen. Psychiatry **46:** 587–599.
15. GARDNER, D.L. & R.W. COWDRY. 1985. Suicidal and parasuicidal behavior in borderline personality disorder. Psychiatric Clin. North Am. **8:** 389–403.
16. GARDNER, D.L. & R.W. COWDRY. 1986. Positive effects of carbamazepine on behavioral dyscontrol in borderline personality disorder. Am. J. Psychiatry **143:** 519–522.

17. SHEARER, S.L., C.P. PETERS, M.S. QUAYTMAN, *et al.* 1988. Intent and lethality of suicide attempts among female borderline inpatients. Am. J. Psychiatry. **145:** 1424–1427.
18. LEIBENLUFT, E., D.L. GARDNER & R.W. COWDRY. 1987. The inner experience of the borderline self-mutilator. J. Pers. Disorders **1:** 317–324.
19. ZANARINI, M.C., F.R. FRANKENBURG, C.J. DELUCA, *et al.* 1998. The pain of being borderline: dysphoric states specific to borderline personality disorder. Harvard Rev. Psychiatry **6:** 201–207.
20. FAIRBAIRN, W.R.D. 1963. Synopsis of an object-relations theory of the personality. Int. J. Psychoanal. **44:** 224–225.
21. BOWLBY, J. 1988. A Secure Base: Parent-Child Attachment and Healthy Human Development. Basic Books. New York.
22. GUNDERSON, J.G. 1996. The borderline patient's intolerance of aloneness: insecure attachments and therapist availability. Am. J. Psychiatry **153:** 752–758.
23. ZANARINI, M.C. & F.R. FRANKENBURG. 1994. Emotional hypochondriasis, hyperbole, and the borderline patient. J. Psychother. Pract. Res. **3:** 25–36.
24. KULLGREN, G. 1988. Factors associated with completed suicides in borderline personality disorder. J. Nerv. Ment. Dis. **176:** 40–44.
25. HEIKENEN, M.E., M.M. HENRIKSSON, T. ERKKI, *et al.* 1997. Recent life events and suicide in personality disorders. J. Nerv. Ment. Dis. **185:** 373–381.
26. GUNDERSON, J.G. 2000. Borderline Personality Disorder: A Clinical Guide. American Psychiatric Press, Inc. Washington, DC. In press.
27. SELZER, M.A., H.W. KOENIGSBERG & O.F. KERNBERG. 1987. The initial contract in the treatment of borderline patients. Am. J. Psychiatry **144:** 927–930.
28. YEOMANS, F.E., M. SELZER & J.F. CLARKIN. 1992. Treating the Borderline Patient: A Contract Based Approach. Basic Books. New York.
29. LINEHAN, M.M., H.L. HEARD & H.E. ARMSTRONG. 1993. Naturalistic follow-up of a behavioral treatment for chronically parasuicidal borderline patients. Arch. Gen. Psychiatry **50:** 971–974.
30. FINE, M.A. & R.A. SANSONE. 1990. Dilemmas in the management of suicidal behavior in individuals with borderline personality disorder. Am. J. Psychother. **44:** 160–171.
31. FRANCES, A.J. & L.J. MILLER. 1989. Coordinating inpatient and outpatient treatment for a chronically suicidal woman. Hosp. Community Psychiatry **40:** 468–470.

DISCUSSION

J. JOHN MANN (*Chairman*): Dr. Meltzer, are clinicians interested in the relative significance in terms of risk for suicidality in psychotic disorders between schizoaffective disorders and schizophrenia itself?

HERBERT Y. MELTZER: I haven't seen any good data on that. I would imagine that there is much ambiguity in making the diagnosis of schizoaffective disorder, and many people who probably have bipolar disease could easily be misdiagnosed as schizoaffective. My personal view on the whole issue from bipolar disorder to schizophrenia, with schizoaffective disorder in the middle, is that we have a continuum. The data from Ross Baldessarini showed that the overall suicide rate is much higher in the bipolar group. I would assume that if we had a rigorously defined schizoaffective disorder group, we would probably find that the suicide rate is intermediate between the 1.2% in bipolar disease and the approximately 0.5% that you saw in our data from schizophrenia.

MANN: A question for Dr. Gunderson. How does the problem of comorbid substance abuse with borderline personality disorder impact on treatment?

JOHN G. GUNDERSON: It increases the risk of suicide. If a substance abuser with borderline personality stops the substance abuse, the prognosis is particularly good. Involvement in substance abuse programs and especially self-help programs is a tremendous alliance. Even for borderline patients who are not substance abusing, such programs are a great social network, are free, and have built-in, round-the-clock coverage.

MANN: Dr. Meltzer, in addition to atypical antipsychotics in the psychotic patient, what other kinds of psychosocial intervention or types of strategy can you recommend to address cognitive dysfunction in schizophrenia?

MELTZER: The success we had in getting people back to work involved close interaction with a skilled therapist who looked at the particular strengths of a person relative to their goals. As I indicated, there's an overall cognitive deficit in schizophrenia. In our group as a whole, every function was impaired, ranging from 1–2.5 standard deviations, but actually 15% of patients are in the lowest quartile in most functions; they never hit the bottom 5%. Therefore, assess what the deficit is in a particular patient. There are differences among drugs in the pattern of cognitive deficits that they can handle. For example, Risperdal, among all the atypical drugs, seems most effective in improving working memory. I assessed a college student who, prior to his first episode, had been valedictorian, but the illness had absolutely devastated his short-term working memory. On Risperdal, improvement was so dramatic that he was able to return to college. The more typical patient is very treatment resistant. Job coaching, newer techniques such as cognitive rehabilitation therapy that have been useful in people with traumatic brain injuries, and the like are just being explored in conjunction with the newer drugs. Previous attempts to use that kind of methodology for schizophrenia have all been in people receiving typical neuroleptic drugs, and the results were uniformly disappointing. It is clearly time for another round of investigation to take advantage of the synergy that the newer drugs might present.

MANN: A crossover question for Dr. Gunderson. What role do the atypical antipsychotic versus the typical antipsychotic drugs play in the pharmacotherapy of borderline personality disorder?

GUNDERSON: The pharmacotherapy studies for borderline patients are woefully inadequate. The typical antipsychotics have been researched more than the atypical ones, and they have established a role for themselves empirically whereas the atypicals have not. They are good as antidepressants and they are very good for sedating agitated borderline patients. You can often take borderline patients off them after a period of weeks without much harm. So they're good for crisis management. The atypicals have more hope for sustained value, and clinically my experience has been positive. The downside relates to the obesity issue. Borderline patients are not well disciplined, and many of them become obese. That becomes a further social handicap for young women, for whom it is often problematic. What we need are more sustained trials with atypical drugs and then their gradual withdrawal, but that has not yet been done.

MELTZER: There is a spectrum of weight gain associated with the atypicals. Of the currently available ones, Risperdal produces the least, next comes clotiapine, and finally clozapine and olanzapine. Zeldox, zaprazidone, the Pfizer compound that may be available in about 6–12 months, has not been associated with weight gain, so that may be useful.

MANN: Dr. Meltzer, concerning clozapine as a model for antisuicidal pharmacotherapy in psychotic disorders, you mentioned the cognitive deficits and the insight, clinical correlates, as it were, of suicide risk. If clozapine presumably improves insight, are you assuming an antisuicidal effect despite improvement in insight. What about the effects of clozapine and Risperdal on cognitive function? I guess this goes hand in hand with the answer to the first question.

MELTZER: I had the same thought as I was preparing for this lecture, and I only had a little time to look at that issue. Did clozapine improve insight? I found no evidence in our data that it did. I was trying to think through what goes on there. It might be that as patients improved in so many other ways, they began to deny that they had a serious illness. Like many other people who improve, and not just people with serious mental illnesses, once they recover, they are not so entrenched or committed to the notion that there is something serious going on. So, to the extent that we have looked at it, and this is preliminary, if anything, I saw a trend to more denial. It was not actually inconsistent, but the broader, more important construct is better outcome, better work and social function, a feeling of hope, less conflict with families, and being part of a more enduring and supportive treatment environment. All of these good things are what is leading to a decrease in suicide despite no apparent improvement in insight.

GUNDERSON: I was interested in your report. It contrasts with borderline patients who generally, when they are told that they have this disorder and then accept it, feel relieved. Most of them felt that their problems were not understandable, and they were secretly alienated. The sense that there is a body of knowledge that can be brought to bear on their treatment and that there are other people who have the same problems are actually a big source of relief.

MELTZER: What we are talking about is the enormous stigmatization that occurs with the diagnosis of schizophrenia. For many patients and their families, when they hear that word, it's tantamount to hopelessness.

GUNDERSON: With borderline personality disorders, the stigma is within the mental health field more than anything.

MANN: Yes, I think that's true. I've been surprised by many patients who tell me that they have been diagnosed as having borderline personality disorder, and it is obviously a source of great comfort to them. Perhaps some of us who see how terrible this condition can be are alarmed at this diagnosis.

A question for Dr. Gunderson. There is an overlap, particularly in self-mutilation and suicidal behavior, between borderline personality disorder and antisocial personality disorder. Do some of the suggestions you made, not to dwell on these morbid fascinations, compulsions, and thoughts and feelings of the patients, extend to people with antisocial personality disorder, and how do you deal with self-destructive crises in that type of personality disorder?

GUNDERSON: First, there are about 25% or less borderline cases that meet the criteria for antisocial behavior and vice versa. The presence of any kind of ongoing self-destructiveness tips it towards a borderline diagnosis. If antisocial people are using self-destructiveness, it is to manipulate the social situation, often for secondary gain or to avoid repercussions from something else. That would not be typical for borderline patients.

MANN: Dr. Meltzer, in the psychotherapeutic component or educational component of the therapy of schizophrenia, what do you do with insight now?

MELTZER: Again, you cannot treat any of these things in isolation. We come back to the perception of what schizophrenia is. John and I were discussing some of the great controversies in psychiatry, such as psychosocial treatment versus drugs and the genetics of mental illness. My approach to explaining schizophrenia to a person with the illness, and I have no hesitation to use the word, is to say that yes, it is a disorder, but it isn't necessarily hopeless. We can treat it. My own view, and I may be in somewhat of a minority at this point, is that we don't have great evidence for irreversible structural brain damage in schizophrenia. Clearly, new neuropathology studies show some changes, but their significance and whether through medication we can produce significant improvement and my own observations with atypicals in combination with a psychotherapeutic approach have led to some very dramatic improvements. I want to echo Charlie Nemeroff's remark about prevention. The future of these medications and many other approaches rests in catching people in the prodrome of this illness, before cognitive deficits develop, and in trying to prevent it. If I am sharing my view that the person has this illness, that is, has an organic basis and consequences, I'm also saying that it is not equivalent to assigning him or her to a terrible outcome. With that message of hope, people can accept the insight message. They don't have to deny it all. They have a basis for a working relationship with me and the rest of the staff and some hope for going forward.

MANN: Dr. Gunderson, what role does validation play in the management of safety in borderline personality disorder? Perhaps you should explain what validation is.

GUNDERSON: Validation generally refers to some affirmation that you can understand or appreciate a patient's point of view on an issue or a feeling state that he or she is in. It's critically important. Ironically, it is as important in DBT treatment as it is in self-psychology within psychoanalytic theory. Both of them give heavy weight to that and rightly so. With respect to self-destructiveness, it's very important not to question the borderline patient's intentions because that would be taken as a challenge to his perspective and reality. It's always best to assume that what the person says is the case. This doesn't mean that you should respond by getting interventive. You should respond by indicating that you understand how desperate he is and how bad he feels and you should convey that by your manner as well as your words.

Treating the Substance-Abusing Suicidal Patient

JACK R. CORNELIUS, IHSAN M. SALLOUM, KEVIN LYNCH,
DUNCAN B. CLARK, AND J. JOHN MANN[a]

*University of Pittsburgh School of Medicine, Pittsburgh,
Pennsylvania 15213, USA*

[a]*Department of Psychiatry, Columbia University, New York,
New York 10032, USA*

ABSTRACT: Studies concerning the treatment of substance-abusing suicidal
patients are scarce despite the frequent presence of suicidal behavior
among this population. Indeed, suicidality (ideation or behavior) is generally an exclusion criterion for participation in treatment studies of subjects
with alcohol or drug abuse. Consequently, to date, little is known about the
optimal treatment of this population. The first study involving substance-
abusing suicidal patients was an open-label trial conducted in the early
1990s. This study involved 12 patients, all of whom demonstrated recent
suicidal ideations and had made a lifetime suicide attempt. The results of
that open-label study demonstrated significant within-group improvement
in both depressive symptoms (including suicidal ideations) and level of
drinking. However, substantial residual depressive symptoms and drinking persisted at the end of the trial. Also, because no placebo control group
was utilized, the authors of that study could not rule out the possibility that
the apparent therapeutic effect from fluoxetine was the result of the placebo effect. To date, only one double-blind, placebo-controlled study of subjects with alcohol or substance abuse has included substantial numbers of
suicidal patients. The study involved 51 subjects, of whom 20 (39%) had
made a suicide attempt in the current depressive episode, 31 (61%) had
made a suicide attempt in their lifetime, and 46 (90%) had reported suicidal ideations in the week before hospitalization. The results of that double-
blind, placebo-controlled study suggest that fluoxetine was effective in
decreasing but not eliminating both the depressive symptoms (including
suicidal ideations) and the level of alcohol consumption among a study
group of subjects with comorbid major depressive disorder and alcohol dependence, many of whom displayed suicidal ideations. A secondary data
analysis from that study suggested that cigarette smoking is also significantly decreased by fluoxetine, but the magnitude of the decrease is limited
and few of these patients totally quit smoking with fluoxetine treatment
alone. Another secondary data analysis from that study suggested that

Address for correspondence: Jack R. Cornelius, MD, MPH, 3811 O'Hara Street, PAARC
Suite, Pittsburgh, PA 15213, USA. Voice: 412-624-2636; fax: 412-624-0850.
jcornel@pitt.edu

78

marijuana smoking was also significantly decreased in a subgroup of subjects who demonstrated cannabis abuse and that the magnitude of this improvement was robust. A third secondary data analysis from that study suggested that cocaine abuse acts as a predictor of poor outcome for both depressive symptoms (including suicidality) and level of alcohol use in this population. The results of a 1-year naturalistic follow-up study involving the patients from that study suggest that the benefits of fluoxetine in decreasing depressive symptoms and level of drinking persist 1 year after entering the treatment program. To date, no other double-blind, placebo-controlled studies involving substantial numbers of substance-abusing suicidal patients have been reported to either confirm or refute these findings. Further studies are clearly warranted to evaluate the efficacy of various pharmacotherapeutic agents and various psychotherapies in the treatment of substance-abusing suicidal patients.

KEYWORDS: Alcohol dependence; Antidepressants; Depression; Fluoxetine; Mood disorders; Substance abuse; Suicidal behavior; Suicide and substance abuse

PREVALENCE OF SUICIDAL BEHAVIOR AMONG SUBSTANCE-ABUSING PATIENTS

Major depression and alcohol dependence are the most commonly diagnosed psychopathologic disorders among persons who commit suicide.[1-6] For example, Barraclough *et al.*[1] found that 85% of the 100 completed suicides that they studied involved individuals who had either depression, alcoholism, or both. The prevalence of substance abuse among persons attempting suicide is not unexpected, inasmuch as data from the National Comorbidity Survey (NCS) demonstrate that many more Americans have been affected by dependence on alcohol and other psychoactive substances than by any other psychiatric disturbance.[7] Comorbidity of substance use disorders and mood disorders is common among those completing suicide,[8,9] which may reflect the fact that comorbidity is very common in community samples.[10-13] Indeed, Lesage *et al.*[14] reported that comorbidity is the rule rather than the exception among those completing suicide. This strong association between completed suicide and comorbidity may in part reflect the fact that more than one third (37%) of alcoholics demonstrate a comorbid psychiatric disorder, as shown in the Epidemiologic Catchment Area (ECA) Study.[11] Indeed, Weissman and colleagues[15] found that the higher rate of suicide attempts in alcoholics was accounted for entirely by alcoholics having at least one psychiatric diagnosis other than alcoholism. The most common comorbid pattern among those completing suicide involved major depression in combination with a substance use disorder.[1,6]

CLINICAL PRESENTATION OF SUBSTANCE-ABUSING PATIENTS EXHIBITING SUICIDAL BEHAVIOR

Substance-abusing patients who complete suicide demonstrate different clinical features from those of substance-abusing patients who do not complete suicide. For example, alcoholics who later complete suicide have a higher rate of depressive symptoms than do alcoholics who do not eventually complete suicide.[16] Alcoholics who complete suicide are characterized by continued drinking,[17] consumption of a greater amount of alcohol,[18] a recent alcohol binge,[19] and alcohol consumption shortly before a suicide attempt or as part of a suicide attempt.[20] Suicide attempts among patients with alcohol and drug dependence are typically impulsive in nature, involving little, if any, planning.[19] The clinical presentation of suicidal behavior and other depressive symptoms among substance-abusing patients is influenced by factors such as gender, age, socioeconomic status, comorbid major depression, and ethnicity.[21-27] Alcohol consumption is also associated with suicidal ideation.[28,29] Trimorbidity, such as that involving major depression, alcoholism, and substance abuse, appears to be particularly associated with suicidal behavior.[18,30-32]

Onset and Clinical Course of Substance-Abusing Patients Exhibiting Suicidality

Early onset of alcohol or substance use appears to further increase the risk of suicide, because patients who started abusing alcohol in their teens were shown to be four times as likely to attempt suicide as those who started abusing alcohol later in life.[33] A diagnosis of current major depression at entry into an inpatient treatment program for alcohol dependence (which is often associated with suicidal ideation, as noted above) has been shown to predict shorter times to first drink and relapse of alcoholism.[34] Similarly, depressed or anxious mood is the reason most frequently given for relapse into pathologic alcohol use among alcohol abusers.[35] The presence of comorbid major depression among alcoholics has been associated with poorer treatment outcome, regardless of the presence or absence of suicidality.[36] These findings suggest that patients with comorbid disorders, who often demonstrate elevated levels of suicidal behavior, generally have a particularly difficult clinical course and a poorer response to treatment.

PHARMACOTHERAPY OF SUICIDAL SUBSTANCE-ABUSING PATIENTS

Treatment efforts addressing substance use disorders and psychiatric conditions such as suicidality and depression have developed in parallel, with little integration.[37] Information concerning treatment of substance-abusing patients with suicidal ideation or a suicide attempt is particularly rare despite the prevalence of this condition, because few studies involving subjects with comorbid substance abuse and serious psychiatric disorders associated with suicidality have been conducted. Furthermore, those few studies that have been conducted involving subjects with serious psychiatric illnesses and substance abuse have generally systematically excluded subjects with significant suicidal ideation or suicidal behavior. Consequently, little is known about treatment response in substance-abusing patients who display suicidal behavior or suicidal ideation.[38]

To date, only two pharmacotherapy studies involving a significant number of suicidal substance-abusing patients have been conducted. These two studies include one small pilot study, in which all of the patients exhibited suicidal behavior, and a larger double-blind, placebo-controlled study, which included a majority of subjects with recent suicidal ideations and a lifetime history of having made a suicide attempt. Neither study was initially designed to primarily focus on suicidality, however. These two studies are described in further detail.

Open-Label Fluoxetine Study in Suicidal, Depressed Alcoholics

The results of this study, conducted in 1990 and 1991, were published in 1993.[39] Patients diagnosed with comorbid major depression and alcohol dependence who had been admitted to an inpatient dual diagnosis unit were recruited into the study. The presence or absence of suicidal ideation or suicidal behavior was neither an inclusion criterion nor an exclusion criterion for participation. Thus, although the study was not designed to be a study of suicidal patients, it happened that all of the patients who entered the study exhibited a history of suicidal behavior and recent suicidal ideations.

Detoxification and a subsequent 1-week washout period were completed prior to entry into the study. All patients were treated with fluoxetine for 8 weeks in an open-label manner with weekly ratings of symptoms. The initial 20-mg oral daily dose was increased to 40 mg after 2 weeks if substantial depressive symptoms persisted in the judgment of the treating psychiatrist. No patient required a dose greater than 40 mg. Seven patients remained on the 20-mg daily dose throughout the course of the trial; five patients required the larger dose. Weekly ratings of symptoms were performed for 8 weeks. The first two ratings were performed while the patient was still in the hospital, and the remaining 6 weekly ratings sessions were conducted on an outpatient basis.

Twelve patients, seven women and five men, participated in this study. Six of the patients were African American and 6 were Caucasian. Their mean age was 33 years, with a range of 19–49. Two of the patients were married, two were divorced, two were separated, and six were single. All 12 patients reported suicidal behavior at some point in their lifetime. All 12 exhibited suicidal ideation during the week prior to admission to the hospital for their index admission. Six of the patients had made a serious suicide attempt shortly before admission to the hospital, five by overdose and one by carbon monoxide poisoning. In addition, one patient had pointed a loaded gun to his head shortly before admission, whereas another had stabbed his wife with a knife shortly before admission. Eight of the 12 patients had been involuntarily committed to the hospital by court order for their recent suicidal or homicidal behavior. Nine of the 12 patients had made at least one serious suicide attempt prior to their current depressive episode, with a mean of 2.1 prior suicide attempts (range 1–5). Ten patients had been admitted to a psychiatric hospital for treatment of depression at least once before their current episode, with a mean of 2.3 prior psychiatric hospitalizations. Six of the patients were legally drunk on admission to the hospital, with an average blood alcohol level of 220 mg/dl, which is more than twice the legal limit for driving. Mean alcohol consumption in the week preceding admission was 38.8 drinks, as measured on the Timeline Follow-Back scale.

Prominent depressive severity on admission to the hospital was demonstrated on the Beck Depression Inventory (BDI), with a mean score of 26, and on the Hamilton Depression Rating Scale (HAM-D-24), with a mean score of 33. Following detoxification and a subsequent 1-week washout period, a moderate level of depressive symptoms persisted, as shown on the BDI (mean = 16) and the HAM-D-24 (mean = 17). Suicidal ideation decreased during detoxification and the subsequent 1-week washout to at most a mild level of severity, as rated on item 3 of the HAM-D-24.

During the fluoxetine trial, statistically significant improvements in depressive symptoms were measured on the BDI and the HAM-D-24. A great statistically significant decrease in alcohol consumption was also noted during the medication trial. No patient made a suicide attempt during the study. These findings were interpreted as suggesting promise for fluoxetine in treating both the depressive symptoms and the drinking behavior of suicidal patients with comorbid major depressive disorders and alcohol dependence.[39]

Double-Blind, Placebo-Controlled Study of Fluoxetine in Depressed Alcoholics, Most of Whom Demonstrated Suicidal Ideation and a History of Suicidal Behavior

In this study,[38] 51 patients diagnosed as having comorbid major depressive disorder and alcohol dependence were randomized to receive fluoxetine ($n = 25$) or placebo ($n = 26$) in a 12-week, double-blind, parallel-group trial.

Weekly ratings of depression and alcohol consumption were obtained throughout the 12-week course. Detoxification and a subsequent 1-week washout period were completed prior to entry into the study. The first two ratings were performed while the patient was still in the hospital, and the remaining 10 weekly ratings sessions were conducted on an outpatient basis. All subjects were initially given one capsule (20 mg fluoxetine or placebo), which could be increased to two capsules after 2 weeks if substantial residual depressive symptoms persisted.

The subjects in this study included 26 men and 25 women with a mean age of 35 ± 10 years. Twenty-seven of the patients were African American and 24 were Caucasian. Twenty (39%) of the 51 patients had made a suicide attempt in the current episode, 18 (35% of the total sample) in the week before admission to the hospital. Thirty-one (61%) patients had made a suicide attempt in their lifetime. Forty-six (90%) reported suicidal ideations in the week before hospitalization. Thus, this sample showed a high level of current and past suicidal behavior and of current suicidal ideation.

Improvement in depressive symptoms during the medication trial was significantly greater in the fluoxetine group than in the placebo group. Total alcohol consumption during the trial was significantly lower in the fluoxetine group than in the placebo group. The investigators concluded that fluoxetine is effective in reducing both the depressive symptoms and the alcohol consumption of patients with comorbid major depressive disorder and alcohol dependence, most of whom demonstrated current suicidal ideations and at least one suicide attempt during their lifetime. None of the patients in either treatment group made a suicide attempt during the course of the treatment study. The findings of this study were published in the *Archives of General Psychiatry*.[38]

One-Year Naturalistic Follow-Up Study

A 1-year naturalistic (open-label) follow-up study was conducted involving the patients from the double-blind placebo-controlled study just described. This 1-year follow-up evaluation was conducted to evaluate the long-term efficacy of fluoxetine in decreasing the depressive symptoms and alcohol use of patients with comorbid major depressive disorder and alcohol dependence. Most of these patients had demonstrated suicidal ideations on initial recruitment into the acute phase of the study, and most had made a lifetime suicide attempt, as described. Most had chosen to continue with their original treatment medication assignment during the follow-up period. Thus, most of those who had originally been assigned to fluoxetine treatment remained on it, whereas most who had originally been randomized to placebo chose not to start active medication. No patient in either treatment group made a suicide attempt during the follow-up phase. The authors of that study concluded that the results of the 1-year follow-up evaluation suggested persistent efficacy of fluoxetine in treating the depressive symptoms and excessive alcohol consumption of patients with comorbid major depression and alcohol dependence.[40]

Studies Involving Selective Serotonergic Antidepressants in Nonsuicidal Depressed Alcoholics

One published study to date[41] assessed the efficacy of the selective serotonergic (SSRI) medication sertraline in 36 depressed alcoholics, who remained in an intensive day program throughout the study. These 36 depressed, recently abstinent alcoholics were randomized in a 6-week double-blind placebo-controlled trial of sertraline 100 mg daily. The results demonstrated a significant group by time interaction for both the Hamilton Depression Rating Scale (HDRS) and the BDI. Patients receiving sertraline had significantly lower mean posttreatment HDRS and BDI scores than did patients receiving placebo. Furthermore, significantly more patients receiving sertraline obtained a Clinical Global Impression rating of "very much improved." However, the effects of sertraline on drinking in this population could not be assessed, because their treatment setting precluded them from drinking. Also, it is unclear to what extent the results of this study involving nonsuicidal patients can be generalized to the treatment of suicidal depressed alcoholics. However, the results of this study are consistent with the results of Cornelius et al.,[38] whose study did involve suicidal patients.

Kranzler et al.[42] conducted a randomized, double-blind, placebo-controlled study of fluoxetine to prevent alcohol relapse in 101 alcoholics, 14 of whom demonstrated current major depression. The study demonstrated that fluoxetine is not of use in preventing alcoholism relapse in patients with mild to moderate alcohol dependence and no comorbid depression. However, fluoxetine reduced HDRS scores more than did placebo treatment among the 14 subjects with current major depression. The effect of fluoxetine on drinking among the 14 depressed alcoholics was unclear, because of limited sample size. The authors concluded that fluoxetine is not of use for relapse prevention in alcoholics with mild to moderate alcohol dependence and no comorbid depression. These findings by Kranzler et al.[42] do not confirm the earlier reports by Naranjo et al.,[43] which suggested at least partial efficacy for fluoxetine in decreasing drinking in nondepressed alcohol abusers. However, the findings of Kranzler et al.[42] suggest that in alcoholics with major depression, fluoxetine may reduce depressive symptoms. Thus, the findings of this study are consistent with those of Roy[41] and of Cornelius et al.,[38] which were just described. Taken together, these studies strongly suggest that fluoxetine is of benefit in reducing the depressive symptoms of alcoholics with comorbid major depression, including those with suicidal ideations or a history of suicidal behavior. The effect of fluoxetine in reducing alcohol use in this population is less clear, because only one of these three studies adequately assessed this outcome measure among depressed alcoholics. However, the data from that study[38] suggest that drinking behavior is also decreased by treatment with fluoxetine in that population.

Studies of Tricyclic Antidepressants in Nonsuicidal Depressed Alcoholics

A few recent well-controlled studies have been conducted to evaluate the efficacy of tricyclic antidepressants in individuals with comorbid alcohol use disorders and major depressive disorder. McGrath *et al.*[44] studied the tricyclic antidepressant imipramine versus placebo in 69 alcoholics with primary depression and found that imipramine improved depression, but had no overall effect on drinking. A study of nortriptyline by Powell *et al.*[45] showed no significant improvement versus placebo in either depressive symptoms or drinking behavior of depressed alcoholics. Mason *et al.*[46] conducted a study of 71 patients with primary alcohol dependence, 28 of whom had major depression secondary to alcoholism. They found that final HAM-D scores of desipramine patients were significantly decreased relative to those of placebo patients, with baseline HAM-D as the covariate. Survival curves demonstrated a significant difference between placebo and desipramine in time to relapse, favoring the desipramine group. There were more relapses on placebo than on desipramine among depressed patients (40% vs. 8%) and among nondepressed patients (27% vs. 14%), but the rates did not reach statistical significance. These findings were interpreted by those investigators as suggesting that desipramine is efficacious in treating the depressive symptoms of alcoholics with secondary major depression and that a statistically significant increase in length of abstinence is noted among those with comorbid depression; however, the use of desipramine to reduce alcohol relapse was not supported. These investigators also suggested that in this population SSRI antidepressants might have certain advantages over tricyclic antidepressants, such as greater tolerability and lower toxicity in overdose.

The results of these studies involving tricyclic antidepressants are consistent with those involving SSRI antidepressants, as just described, in suggesting efficacy for antidepressant medications in treating the depressive symptoms of alcoholics with comorbid major depression. However, evidence from these studies is mixed concerning the efficacy for tricyclic antidepressants in treating the drinking behavior of this dual-diagnosis population, which again is consistent with the results from studies involving SSRI antidepressants described above. It should be reemphasized that none of the studies involving tricyclic antidepressants included suicidal patients, inasmuch as no studies involving tricyclic antidepressants in suicidal depressed alcoholics have been conducted. Thus, it is unclear to what extent the results of these studies can be generalized to treatment of suicidal, depressed alcoholics. Indeed, as Mason et al.[46] pointed out, SSRI antidepressants demonstrate a greater tolerability and lower toxicity in overdose than do tricyclic antidepressants in depressed alcoholics; therefore, SSRI antidepressants may be safer than tricyclic antidepressants in treating suicidal, depressed alcoholics.

Antidepressant Medication Studies Involving Suicidal Substance Abusers Other Than Alcoholics

Antidepressant medication studies involving substance abusers other than alcoholics are scarce, and double-blind studies of these populations are virtually nonexistent. Double-blind, placebo-controlled studies of suicidal substance abusers other than alcoholics have not yet been conducted. Consequently, the only data that are currently available regarding pharmacotherapy in this population are from pilot studies or secondary analyses of studies that focused primarily on the treatment of alcoholics. Data from small pilot studies[47,48] and from secondary analysis of a study involving alcoholics[49] suggest, at best, limited efficacy for fluoxetine in the treatment of cocaine abuse. Data from secondary analysis of depressed alcoholics also suggest limited efficacy for fluoxetine in decreasing cigarette use in depressed alcoholics.[50] Indeed, to date, there is no empirically proven pharmacotherapeutic agent of choice in the treatment of cocaine abuse either alone or in combination with major depression (with or without accompanying suicidality). In contrast, results of a secondary data analysis of a study involving alcoholics[51] provide preliminary evidence that fluoxetine decreases marijuana use and depressive symptoms in alcoholics with comorbid marijuana abuse and major depression. These findings suggest that among those with major depression, various substance abuse disorders may respond differently to antidepressant medication, with marijuana abuse being more responsive than cocaine abuse. However, these data should be considered preliminary. Also, these studies generally did not focus on suicidal patients; therefore, the extent to which these preliminary findings can be generalized to include suicidal patients is unclear.

Psychotherapy of the Substance-Abusing Suicidal Patient

Psychosocial treatments are generally considered to be powerful interventions for both substance use and psychiatric disorders.[52-54] However, to date, there have been no reported studies evaluating any psychotherapy for any substance-abusing suicidal group of patients. Further work is needed to develop therapies that are specifically intended to treat individuals with comorbid affective and substance use disorders, because these are generally the substance-abusing patients who periodically exhibit suicidal symptoms.

CONCLUSIONS

Few studies have evaluated the efficacy of various treatment agents in suicidal, substance-abusing patients. Data from studies to date suggest that SSRI antidepressants such as fluoxetine appear to decrease depressive symptoms and alcohol consumption in patients with comorbid major depressive disorder and alcohol dependence. Tricyclic antidepressants also are effective in decreasing the depressive symptoms of depressed alcoholics, although their efficacy in decreasing alcohol consumption is less clear, and they tend to be associated with greater side effects and greater toxicity in overdose. Antidepressant medication studies of nonalcoholic substance-abusing patients are particularly scarce, so little is known about the treatment response of this population, particularly those with suicidal ideation or a history of suicidal behavior. Further studies are warranted: to evaluate the efficacy of various pharmacologic agents in the treatment of substance abuse, substance abuse comorbid with major depression, and suicidal substance abusers; to assess the predictors of treatment response among substance-abusing suicidal patients;[54,55] to determine whether the addition of medications such as naltrexone or acamprosate provide additional benefit in suicidal substance-abusing patients;[56,57] to assess the efficacy of various psychotherapies and other psychosocial interventions in this population; and to assess the optimal combination of psychotherapy with various pharmacologic agents to provide the most efficacious treatment in this population.

ACKNOWLEDGMENTS

This work was supported in part by grants from the National Institute on Alcohol Abuse and Alcoholism (P50 AA08746 and K02 AA00291), the National Institute on Drug Abuse (P60 DA05605), the Veterans Administration (MIRECC to VISN 4, Stars and Stripes Network), and the National Institute on Mental Health (MH46745).

REFERENCES

1. BARRACLOUGH, B., J. BUNCH, B. NELSON, *et al.* 1974. A hundred cases of suicide: clinical aspects. Br. J. Psychiatry **125:** 355–373.
2. ROY, A. & M. LINNOILA. 1986. Alcoholism and suicide. Suicide Life Threatening Behav. **16:** 244–273.
3. WINOKUR, G. & D.W. BLACK. 1987. Psychiatric and medical diagnoses as risk factors for mortality in psychiatric patients: a case-control study. Am. J. Psychiatry **144:** 208–211.

4. HESSELBROCK, M., V. HESSELBROCK, K. SYZMANSKI, *et al.* 1988. Suicide attempts and alcoholism. J. Stud. Alcohol **49:** 436–442.
5. HENRIKSSON, M.M., H.M. ARO, M.J. MARTTUNEN, *et al.* 1993. Mental disorders and comorbidity in suicide. Am. J. Psychiatry **150:** 935–940.
6. CHENG, A.T.A. 1995. Mental illness and suicide: a case-control study in East Taiwan. Arch. Gen. Psychiatry **52:** 594–603.
7. ANTHONY, J.C., L.A. WARNER & R.C. KESSLER. 1994. Comparative epidemiology of dependence on tobacco, alcohol, and controlled substances and inhalants: basic findings from the National Comorbidity Study. Exp. Clin. Psychopharmacol. **2:** 244–268.
8. BEAUTRAIS, A.L., P.R. JOYCE, R.T. MULDER, *et al.* 1996. Prevalence and comorbidity of mental disorders in persons making serious suicide attempts: a case-control study. Am. J. Psychiatry **153:** 1009–1014.
9. CONWELL, Y., P.R. DUBERSTEIN, C. COX, *et al.* 1996. Relationships of age and axis I diagnoses in victims of completed suicide. Am. J. Psychiatry **153:** 1001–1008.
10. HELZER, J.E. & T.R. PRYZBECK. 1988. The co-occurrence of alcoholism and other psychiatric disorders in the general population and its impact on treatment. J. Stud. Alcohol **49:** 219–244.
11. REGIER, D.A., M.E. FARMER, D.E. RAE, *et al.* 1990. Comorbidity of mental disorders with alcohol and other drug abuse: results from the Epidemiologic Catchment Area (ECA) study. JAMA **264:** 2511–2518.
12. KESSLER, R.C., K.A. MCGONAGLE, S. ZHAO, *et al.* 1994. Lifetime and 12-month prevalence of DSM-III-R psychiatric disorders in the United States. Results from the National Comorbidity Survey. Arch. Gen. Psychiatry **51:** 8–19.
13. KESSLER, R.C., R.M. CRUM, L.A. WARNER, *et al.* 1997. Lifetime co-occurrence of DSM-III-R alcohol abuse and dependence with other psychiatric disorders in the National Comorbidity Survey. Arch. Gen. Psychiatry **54:** 313–321.
14. LESAGE, A.D., R. BOYER, F. GRUNBERG, *et al.* 1994. Suicide and mental disorders: a case-control study of young men. Am. J. Psychiatry **151:** 1063–1068.
15. WEISSMAN, M.M., J.K. MYERS & P.S. HARDING. 1980. Prevalence and psychiatric heterogeneity of alcoholism in a United States urban community. J. Stud. Alcohol **41:** 672–681.
16. BERGLUND, M. 1984. Suicide in alcoholism: a prospective study of 88 suicides. I. The multidimensional diagnosis at first admission. Arch. Gen. Psychiatry **41:** 888–891.
17. MURPHY, G.E., R.D. WETZEL, E. ROBINS, *et al.* 1992. Multiple risk factors predict suicide in alcoholism. Arch. Gen. Psychiatry **49:** 459–463.
18. ROY, A., D. LAMPARSKI, J. DEJONG, *et al.* 1990. Characteristics of alcoholics who attempt suicide. Am. J. Psychiatry **147:** 761–765.
19. CORNELIUS, J.R., I.M. SALLOUM, M.D. CORNELIUS, *et al.* 1996. Patterns of suicidality and alcohol use in alcoholics with major depression. Alcohol. Clin. Exp. Res. **20:** 1451–1455.
20. HAWTON, K., J. FAGG & S.P. MCKEOUN. 1989. Alcoholism, alcohol, and attempted suicide. Alcohol Alcohol. **24:** 3–9.
21. FABREGA, H., R. ULRICH & J. CORNELIUS. 1993. Sociocultural and clinical characteristics of patients with comorbid depressions: a comparison of substance abuse and non-substance abuse diagnoses. Compr. Psychiatry **34:** 312–321.

22. CORNELIUS, J.R., I.M. SALLOUM, J.E. MEZZICH, *et al.* 1995. Disproportionate suicidality in patients presenting with comorbid major depression and alcoholism. Am. J. Psychiatry **152**: 358–364.
23. CORNELIUS, J.R., P.J. JARRETT, M.E. THASE, *et al.* 1995. Gender effects on the clinical presentation of alcoholics at a psychiatric hospital. Compr. Psychiatry **36**: 435–440.
24. SALLOUM, I.M., J.E. MEZZICH, J.R. CORNELIUS, *et al.* 1995. Clinical profile of comorbid major depression and alcohol use disorders in an initial psychiatric evaluation. Compr. Psychiatry **32**: 260–266.
25. CORNELIUS, J.R., I.M. SALLOUM, D.C. DALEY, *et al.* 1996. Clinical profile and evaluation of comorbid major depression and alcoholism. *In* Treating Substance Abuse, Part II. J. Lonsdale, ed. :119–137. Hatherleigh Press. New York, NY.
26. CORNELIUS, J.R., H. FABREGA, M.D. CORNELIUS, *et al.* 1996. Racial effects on the clinical presentation of alcoholics at a psychiatric hospital. Compr. Psychiatry **37**: 102–108.
27. CORNELIUS, J.R., I.M. SALLOUM, J.G. EHLER, *et al.* 1997. Double-blind fluoxetine in depressed alcoholic smokers. Psychopharmacol. Bull. **33**: 165–170.
28. KING, C.A., E.M. HILL, M. NAYLOR, *et al.* 1993. Alcohol consumption in relation to other predictors of suicidality among adolescent inpatient girls. J. Am. Acad. Child Adolesc. Psychiatry **32**: 82–88.
29. GRANT, B.F. & D.S. HASIN. 1999. Suicidal ideation among the United States drinking population: results from the National Longitudinal Alcohol Epidemiology Survey. J. Stud. Alcohol **60**: 422–429.
30. SCHUCKIT, M.A. 1986. Primary men alcoholics with histories of suicide attempts. J. Stud. Alcohol **47**: 78–81.
31. PETRONIS, K.R., J.F. SAMUELS, E.K. MOSCICKI, *et al.* 1990. An epidemiologic investigation of potential risk factors. Soc. Psychiatry Psychiatr. Epidemiol. **25**: 193–199.
32. CORNELIUS, J.R., M.E. THASE, I.M. SALLOUM *et al.* 1998. Cocaine use associated with increased suicidal behavior in depressed alcoholics. Addict. Behav. **23**: 119–121.
33. BUYDENS-BRANCHEY, L., M.H. BRANCHEY & D. NOUMAIR. 1989. Age of alcoholism onset. I. Relationship to psychopathology. Arch. Gen. Psychiatry **46**: 255–230.
34. GREENFIELD, S.F., R.D. WEISS, L.R. MUENZ, *et al.* 1998. The effect of depression on return to drinking. Arch. Gen. Psychiatry **55**: 259–265.
35. PICKENS, R.W., D.K. HATSUKAMI, J.W. SPICER, *et al.* 1985. Relapse by alcohol abusers. Alcohol. Clin. Exp. Res. **9**: 244–247.
36. ROUNSAVILLE, B.J., Z.S. DOLINSKY, T.F. BABOR, *et al.* 1987. Psychopathology as a predictor of treatment outcome in alcoholics. Arch. Gen. Psychiatry **44**: 505–513.
37. BRADY, K.T., P. HALLIGAN & R.J. MALCOLM. 1999. Dual diagnosis. *In* Textbook of Substance Abuse Treatment, 2nd Ed. M. Galanter & H.D. Kleber, eds. : 475–483. The American Psychiatric Press. Washington, DC.
38. CORNELIUS, J.R., I.M. SALLOUM, J.G. EHLER, *et al.* 1997. Fluoxetine in depressed alcoholics: a double-blind, placebo-controlled trial. Arch. Gen. Psychiatry **54**: 700–705.
39. CORNELIUS, J.R., I.M. SALLOUM, M.D. CORNELIUS, *et al.* 1993. Fluoxetine trial in suicidal depressed alcoholics. Psychopharmacol. Bull. **29**: 195–199.

40. CORNELIUS, J.R., I.M. SALLOUM, R.F. HASKETT, et al. 2000. Fluoxetine versus placebo in depressed alcoholics: a one-year follow-up study. Addict. Behav. **25:** 307–310.
41. ROY, A. 1998. Placebo-controlled study of sertraline in depressed recently abstinent alcoholics. Biol. Psychiatry **44:** 633–637.
42. KRANZLER, H.R., J.A. BURLESON, P. KORNER, et al. 1995. Placebo-controlled trial of fluoxetine as an adjunct to relapse prevention in alcoholics. Am. J. Psychiatry **152:** 391–397.
43. NARANJO, C.A., K.E. KADLEC, P. SANHUEZA, et al. 1990. Fluoxetine differentially alters alcohol intake and other consummatory behaviors in problem drinkers. Clin. Pharmacol. Ther. **47:** 490–498.
44. MCGRATH, P.J., E.V. NUNES, J.W. STEWART, et al. 1996. Imipramine treatment of alcoholics with major depression: a placebo-controlled clinical trial. Arch. Gen. Psychiatry **53:** 232–240.
45. POWELL, B.J., J.L. CAMPBELL, J.F. LANDON, et al. 1995. A double-blind placebo-controlled study of nortriptyline and bromocriptine in male alcoholics subtyped by comorbid psychiatric disorders. Alcohol. Clin. Exp. Res. **19:** 462–468.
46. MASON, B.J., J H.. KOCSIS, C.E. RITVO, et al. 1996. A double-blind, placebo-controlled trial of desipramine for primary alcohol dependence stratified on the presence or absence of major depression. JAMA **275:** 761–767.
47. POLLACK, M.H. & J.F. ROSENBAUM. 1991. Fluoxetine treatment of cocaine abuse in heroin addicts. J. Clin. Psychiatry **52:** 31–33.
48. RIGGS, P.D., S.K. MIKULICH, L.M. COFFMAN, et al. 1997. Fluoxetine in drug-dependent delinquents with major depression: an open trial. J. Child Adolesc. Psychopharmacol. **7:**87–95.
49. CORNELIUS, J.R., I.M. SALLOUM, M.E. THASE, et al. 1998. Fluoxetine versus placebo in depressed alcoholic cocaine abusers. Psychopharmacol. Bull. **34:** 117–121.
50. CORNELIUS, J.R., K.A. PERKINS, I.M. SALLOUM, et al. 1999. Fluoxetine versus placebo to decrease the smoking of depressed alcoholics. J. Clin. Psychopharmacol. **19:** 183–184.
51. CORNELIUS, J.R., I.M. SALLOUM, R.F. HASKETT, et al. 1999. Fluoxetine versus placebo for the marijuana use of depressed alcoholics. Addict. Behav. **24:** 111–114.
52. O'MALLEY, S.S. & K.M. CARROLL. 1996. Psychotherapeutic considerations in pharmacological trials. Alcohol. Clin. Exp. Res. **20:** 17A–22A.
53. PROJECT MATCH RESEARCH GROUP. 1998. Matching alcoholism treatments to client heterogeneity: Project MATCH three-year drinking outcomes. Alcohol. Clin. Exp. Res. **22:** 1300–1311.
54. MCLELLAN, A.T., L. LUBORSKY, G.E. WOODY, et al. 1983. Predicting response to alcohol and drug abuse treatments. Arch. Gen. Psychiatry **40:** 620–625.
55. NUNES, E.V., P.F. MCGRATH, F.M. QUITKIN, et al. 1996. Predictors of antidepressant response in depressed alcoholic patients. Am. J. Addict. **5:** 308–312.
56. SALLOUM, I.M., J.R. CORNELIUS, M.E. THASE, et al. 1998. Naltrexone utility in depressed alcoholics. Psychopharmacol. Bull. **34:** 111–115.
57. PAILLE, F.M., J.D. GUELFI, A.C. PERKINS, et al. 1995. Double-blind randomized multicenter trial of acamprosate in maintaining abstinence from alcohol. Alcohol Alcohol. **30:** 239–247.

DISCUSSION

J. JOHN MANN *(Chairman)*: Do you think that medications such as fluoxetine or SSRIs work for alcohol abuse or dependence in individuals who are not depressed?

JACK R. CORNELIUS: There has been work in that area by Naranjo in Canada. He actually did that work at least 10 or 15 years ago, before the work I did with dual-diagnosis patients. He studied people with the alcohol diagnosis alone without comorbid depression and did show some level of improvement in terms of decreased drinking, but the improvement was small, was often barely statistically significant, and was of questionable clinical significance. So, in terms of whether you would see a clinically significant improvement in a nondepressed population, probably in most of them you would not. It has been relatively disappointing in less seriously depressed nonsuicidal patients.

MANN: What concerns are there about patients who continue to abuse substances such as alcohol and cocaine while taking fluoxetine? Is there any downside to that?

CORNELIUS: If you read what the pharmaceutical companies say about any of these medications, you should not have people taking these medicines if they are also using drugs or alcohol. They would say that about practically any medicine. Would they encourage people to drink heavily with antibiotics? Of course not; so on some level using those two together is not a good idea. There have been studies of whether there is an interactive effect, for example, to see if various SSRIs have markedly more side effects if someone is drinking or if drunkenness is a much more serious problem if someone is on SSRIs, as a counterexample. Really not much has been found there, so neither I nor anyone else would encourage people to drink if they're taking these medications, and certainly the standard wisdom is that you should not and you should encourage your patients not to. On the other hand, you need to keep the other side in mind as well and kind of balance that. Actually, most people occasionally do use a little alcohol, and if they use it only rarely and not very much (I must admit having seen many hundreds of those examples over the last 15 or 20 years), it doesn't seem to make a lot of difference.

MANN: There are many individuals who are engaged in substance abuse of different types who have a mood disorder and are self-medicating, but not all of them use alcohol. Some use benzodiazepines, for example. If you tried an agent such as an SSRI, would you begin it before withdrawal of the benzodiazepines or at the same time?

CORNELIUS: Clearly it's preferable to detoxify subjects before you try to treat them with any psychiatric medication. For someone who is regularly getting either drunk or stoned, you wouldn't be able to detect good therapeutic effects from any psychotropic medication. If possible, I always try to detoxify people first. It doesn't mean that they will never drink again or have a little bit on the side, but if they are drinking very heavily on a daily basis or using drugs, the likelihood that they will get much benefit from any medicine you give them is pretty slim. Usually, they need to have basically detoxed at least to a point where they are using little or none at all, or it's likely that any additional treatments you have won't be of any good to them.

MANN: Someone wants to know what is naltrexone and someone else wants to discuss using SSRIs in persons who are taking methodone.

CORNELIUS: Let me start with methodone. Methodone originally was used to treat opium addiction. More recently, in the last 10 years, a couple of studies, one or maybe both of which were published in the *Archives of General Psychiatry,* looked at naltrexone in patients with alcohol dependence. Those studies, even though relatively few in number, were sufficiently convincing to the FDA to approve an indication for the use of that medication in the treatment of alcohol dependence. It was the first medication approved by the FDA for that indication, I think, in 40 or 50 years, since disulfuram, or Anabuse, was approved. In my personal experience, the effect associated with naltrexone in alcoholism is relatively limited. It does appear, at least in some people, to help cut down on drinking. On the other hand, many people don't get much of a response at all; in those who do, it's not necessarily a large response; and a fair number of people don't get any good effect but they do get side effects, such as nausea. Therefore, I don't want to portray naltrexone as a wonder drug. In some people, as an adjunct, it might be helpful, especially at a dose of 50 mg, at which it's somewhat less likely to have side effects, such as increases in liver function test results, noted in the higher dose range. As for SSRIs and methodone patients, I must admit that it is one patient population that I have not looked at much, so I can't discuss a particular study I have done. I have clinically treated people who are on methodone or who have used various opiates and who also were depressed and whom I treated with SSRIs. In my own clinical experience with that group, if they were relatively stable, for example, on methodone or whatever and also were depressed, they often would respond to an SSRI such as fluoxetine. I have not found that to be a particular problem, and in my personal experience it seems to work reasonably well. However, I don't have any empirical data to support that theory, so you should take it with a large grain of salt.

MANN: Someone asked about the role of dopamine in managing substance abuse and how it would interact with suicide risk. I assume they are referring to the fact that enhancing dopaminergic activity in the mesolimbic system may have something to do with substance dependence in alcoholism.

CORNELIUS: Certainly many basic scientific findings suggest that, indeed, that is correct. On the other hand, most studies to date that involve most substances of abuse and pharmacotherapeutic agents for those have been somewhat disappointing. Some pharmacotherapeutic agents have been tried for different kinds of substance abuse disorders in people without comorbid depression. A number of them initially started with open-label studies and those open-label studies often looked promising. They were followed by a double-blind, placebo-controlled study, and the double-blind, placebo-controlled study would not be positive. So, whether or not the dopamine angle, as described here, is particularly helpful clinically in deciding what treatment to use, only time will tell.

Treating Impulsivity and Anxiety in the Suicidal Patient

JAN FAWCETT

Department of Psychiatry, Rush Institute for Mental Well-Being, Chicago, Illinois 60612-3824, USA

ABSTRACT: It has been found that while over 90% of people who commit suicide have a psychiatric illness at the time, over 50% are under active psychiatric or mental health care. How can suicide risk be detected and preventive treatment provided? Both communication of suicidal ideation or intent and prior suicide attempts have been shown to be risk factors, which should be assessed in patients with psychiatric illness. Research shows that suicidal ideation is often not communicated to professionals or is denied by patients just prior to suicide and, when present, is often useful not as an immediate risk factor, but as a chronic risk factor. Suicide attempts predict a 10–30% occurrence of suicide over 10 years, but often do not indicate immediate risk. Recent research has shown that impulsiveness and severe anxiety, panic attacks, and agitation comorbid with depression are often immediate suicide risk factors that are potentially modifiable if recognized and treated urgently with effective medications and watchful support.

KEYWORDS: Anxiety; Impulsivity; Suicide

INTRODUCTION

The public health problem of suicide, which is the eighth overall cause of death as well as the third most common cause of death in persons in the 15–35-year-old range, breaks down into two parts. First are the approximately 40–50% of patients who commit suicide every year who are undiagnosed and have never had access to clinical assessment or treatment. Retrospective studies, such as the classic study of Robins and colleagues,[1] found that well over 94% of people who committed suicide in St. Louis in the mid-1950s would have been diagnosed with a major psychiatric illness and most often with depression, schizophrenia, or alcoholism. This is a public health problem that we need to do something about if more people are to be assessed and treated for depression and suicide risk.

Address for correspondence: Dr. Jan Fawcett, Department of Psychiatry, Rush Institute for Mental Well-Being, 1725 West Harrison Street, Suite 955, Chicago, IL 60612-3824. Voice: 312-942-5372.

Let us consider the second part of the suicide problem. Over 50% of patients who commit suicide have been seen by a mental health clinician or physician, and many were under their care when they committed suicide. What percentage of suicides occur while a patient is in active treatment? Robins found that 51% had care within 1 month of their suicide, and 75% were seen clinically within 1 year of their suicide. Barraclough and associates[2] in the late 1970s found that 70% of patients who completed suicide had been seen within 1 month. We do not know what proportion were seen by a general physician or a psychiatrist in this sample.

The problem to be addressed is the high rate of suicide among patients who complete suicide while they are in active treatment. How can we reduce the suicide rate of patients receiving treatment for psychiatric disorders? First, we have to achieve more accurate detection of acute high suicide risk. Acute risk can be differentiated from chronic suicide risk by the immediacy of the risk of a completed suicide, requiring immediate therapeutic intervention. Probably a third to a half the patients we treat are at chronic risk for suicide at some time in the future. (They have a major mental disorder and/or had suicidal thoughts or made a prior suicide attempt, have a history of impulsivity, or have comorbid alcohol/drug abuse.) A much smaller proportion at any given time are in an acute high risk state. It is clear, even from the limited data we have, that this acute high risk state is often not noted or detected by treating clinicians. Our problem is to be able to make the assessment that a patient has become an acute risk, so that we can intervene to reduce the immediate risk. This requires that we make assessments with the question in mind of whether a particular patient is at acute suicide risk, chronic suicide risk, or low risk.

How do we detect acute risk? What helps us make this assessment and what can mislead us? Inquiring as to the presence of suicidal ideation is standard for assessing suicide risk (*DSM IV, APA Guidelines for Major Depression*[3]). Suicidal thoughts, impulses, or plans are important if communicated and taken seriously. Robins, in his classic study of 134 suicides, found that suicidal ideation was communicated within a year of suicide in 69% of the cases he reviewed. The suicidal communication was made to spouses in 60% of cases and in 50% of the cases to friends or coworkers within a year of the suicide, to an average of three people for each case. What should be carefully noted is that the suicidal communication was made to helping professionals in only 18% of cases. The patients told their spouses and friends about their suicidal ideas, but less than a fifth of the patients revealed suicidal thoughts to a physician or therapist, even when an inquiry was made. That is an important finding to keep in mind. The lesson is to ask significant others and to take seriously what significant others report, even if denied by the patient. I have reviewed many cases of completed suicide in which the significant others had told a psychiatrist that the patient had recently made suicide threats, and the patient denied current suicidal intent, only to complete suicide hours or days later. The psychiatrist should not readily accept the patient's claim that he or she is not presently suicidal in the presence of a history of recent suicidal ideation or an attempt reported by a loved one. Suicidal ideation is important if present, but a denial can be misleading. It is clear that a denial of suicidal risk should not be reassuring in the presence of other data to the contrary, which should be pursued in a careful clinical assessment. Denial of suicidal impulses or intent can be misleading in the presence of other clinical factors. Merely asking a person if they have suicidal ideation is clearly not an adequate suicide assessment.

In the National Institute of Mental Health (NIMH) Collaborative Depression Study, 13 suicides occurred in the first year after the patients were discharged from the hospital. Most of the patients were hospitalized patients when they were brought into the study. The patients who committed suicide where compared with the majority who survived. The majority, 929 patients, who did not commit suicide, expressed suicidal ideation with a greater absolute frequency (not significant) than did the 13 patients who completed suicide within a year of clinical assessment. In other words, the presence of suicidal ideation at baseline assessment by a trained professional interviewer did not predict suicide within 1 year of follow-up.

In another study of suicide among 76 inpatients, we looked at the chart notes of patients who committed suicide in the hospital. We found that 77% of those patients had a note conveying a patient's denial of suicidal intent recorded by the nurse within the week before the patient completed suicide in the hospital. Twenty-eight percent of those patients had either made verbal or signed no-harm contracts with the staff before they killed themselves. These records were obtained from hospitals across the country. Most were from community hospitals; a quarter of the cases were from university medical centers.

How useful is a history of prior suicide attempts as a clinical risk factor? We know from two studies, one over 50 years ago and another published last year, that between 7.7 and 12% of patients who make suicide attempts kill themselves within 10 years. Roughly 1 of 10 patients who make a suicide attempt will kill themselves within 10 years. The question is, are suicide attempts a good predictor of acute suicide risk? In the Robins study, only 10% of those who committed suicide made an attempt within the year before they killed themselves. Isometsa,[5] in a recent study of 1,397 suicides, found that 38% of attempts by females occurred within 1 year before their suicide and the figure was 19% for males. We know that women make more attempts than men, so this report suggests that attempts may mean a little more in females than in males in terms of acute risk of suicide. Experience reviewing these cases tends to show that recent violent or highly lethal attempts are often associated with a completed suicide within days. Recent suicide attempts in patients with comorbid borderline disorder and major depressive disorder may also signify a high risk of a dangerous repeat attempt.

Data from the NIMH Collaborative Study showed that prior suicide attempts (past or recent) were no more frequent in patients who completed suicide within 1 year of follow-up than they were in the survivors. Suicide attempts did not differentiate between those who committed suicide and the majority who did not within 1 year of their original assessment. In this prospectively studied sample, suicide attempts were not potent predictors of subsequent completed suicide within 1 year after baseline assessment. The history of a suicide attempt came close to being a significant association with subsequent completed suicide over 2–10 years of follow-up, indicating a chronic high risk factor. A history of prior and especially recent suicide attempts can be important if the attempt was violent or highly lethal, but generally prior attempts are not potent acute risk factors. The difficult truth clinicians must face is that most suicides occur in individuals who have no history of prior attempts and deny suicidal ideation in their last communication with a physician or therapist.

How much do our standard risk factors actually help us to prevent suicide? Suicidal ideation is often denied by patients who then subsequently complete suicide within hours or days. We should talk to the patients' families. We should actually seek them out, get permission to talk to them, and find out what the patient has been saying. If we do not, we are overlooking a valuable assessment tool. A history of attempts is important, but it may not be useful in assessing acute risk except when a recent attempt has been violent or highly lethal.

What other risk factors can we rely on to indicate high acute risk? In our analyses of the NIMH Collaborative Depression Study, we found several anxiety symptoms present to a severe level in individuals who completed suicide within 1 year of assessment. It is important to note that one third of the suicides within a 10-year follow-up occurred within the year after hospital discharge. The time of highest risk for hospitalized patients is within 6 months to 1 year after they are discharged from the hospital.

This study found that the presence of panic attacks discriminated between suicides occurring within days up until a year from assessment (62 vs. 28%). Severe psychic anxiety was present in a highly significant number of patients who completed suicide compared to patients who survived. This requires careful clinical assessment for the presence of severe anxiety symptoms. The severity discrimination is key, since we have previously reported that 70% of patients with major depression manifest at least moderate levels of anxiety as rated by SADS-C (Fawcett and Kravitz[4]). This is illustrated in a recent study by Placidi et al., which rated levels of psychic anxiety across 269 inpatients with depression, 143 of whom had made a suicide attempt. Patients who had made a suicide attempt were less anxious and agitated as a group than those without a history of a suicide attempt. The severity, as rated on a Hamilton Depression Scale psychic anxiety mean rating, was under 2.0 (mild anxiety) for both groups and a mean 1.0 (mild = 1) for the agitation item in this sample. The severity scale is from 0–4 for psychic anxiety and 0–3 for agitation severity on the Hamilton scale. A severe psychic anxiety rating on this scale would be 3–4, and severe levels of agitation would merit a rating of 2–3 . We observed severe levels of anxiety and agitation (with a SADS-C rating of 4–5) in a group of 13 patients who subsequently completed suicide within weeks to 1 year after assessment.

Recurrent, severe ruminative anxiety that consumes most other thoughts, panic attacks, and agitation is particularly important to assess. It is important to inquire how much of the time the patient experiences his or her anxiety (as is done with the SADS-C ratings) as well as the intensity of the anxiety to establish a clinical estimate of severity.

Global insomnia, which implies that patients have trouble falling asleep and staying asleep and that they are up early in the morning (essentially they are hardly sleeping), is commonly associated with acute high suicide risk. Recent onset of moderate alcohol abuse is also associated with acute suicide risk, and this does not necessarily imply a chronic history of substance abuse, which is a chronic risk factor. In such cases, people begin by abusing alcohol to a moderate degree. It is clinical speculation that they use alcohol as ineffective self-treatment of anxiety and global insomnia. These factors were all significantly associated with suicide within days to 1 year of clinical assessment.

In a separate study of 14 inpatient chart records of patients who had committed suicide, we found corroborating findings (Busch and Fawcett[6]). Seventy-nine percent of the patients who killed themselves within 1 week were ranked as having either severe anxiety or severe agitation on the SADS-C rating scale. That was the most outstanding symptom evident in these patients' chart notes over the 7 days before their suicide in the hospital. All these data lead to the conclusion that severe anxiety/agitation symptoms and severe recurrent ruminative anxiety in depressed patients are a high-risk suicide factor and an acute suicide risk factor in many patients.

Is the association of severe anxiety symptoms and suicidal behavior in depressed patients supported by other studies? Hall[7] reported a study of 100 severe suicide attempts by persons who presented in the emergency room. Severe suicide attempts were defined as severe enough to require admission to the hospital. These patients were interviewed shortly after admission. Ninety percent of them described severe anxiety before their attempt, and

80% had had panic attacks. Schnyder[8] also published 30 consecutive ER suicide attempts. The staff assessed these patients for what they felt was their predominant state and assessed them as hopeless, but when the patients were asked to report what bothered them most just prior to their suicide attempt, they reported that they were very anxious and felt dissociated. Apter *et al.*[9] reported high anxiety and impulsivity in their suicidal patients in Israel. This suggests the likelihood that severe anxiety triggers impulsiveness in individuals with this trait. Ohring and Stein[10] reported adolescent suicidal cases in which they found high state and trait anxiety.

Impulsivity is a very important risk factor for suicide, both chronic as well as acute. When a person who is highly impulsive by history is stressed, sustains a loss, or becomes anxious, his impulsivity increases, leading to suicide attempts, often of a violent type. This trait is commonly associated with a history of alcohol or substance abuse and is activated by these behaviors.

Evidence indicates that lithium, besides ameliorating the course of bipolar disorder, is also effective in reducing suicide attempts in patients with both bipolar and unipolar major depression by a factor of 7–9, according to some European studies,[11] only one of which was a prospective random assignment study. Most of these studies are follow-ups of treated samples who remained in treatment. Earlier data showed that lithium reduced impulsive aggression in prison inmates. This is the kind of aggression that is expressed from explosive, nonpremeditated aggression. That lithium does reduce this type of impulsivity suggests that it may act otherwise than by reducing mood swings. The reduction of impulsivity in patients with bipolar or unipolar disorders may account for some of its putative antisuicidal effect.

A hypothetical four-pathway model of suicide can be conceptualized from studies that we have reviewed. If a person has bipolar disorder or unipolar depression, what pathways take that person to suicide? One of two clinical-biological pathways is anxiety/agitation. It is hypothesized that evidence of hypothalamic-pituitary-adrenal hyperfunction such as high cortisol secretion or elevated CRH, as reported by Nemeroff and colleagues,[12] is related to clinically manifested anxiety/agitation as one pathway leading to suicide. CRH also agonizes the locus ceruleus, releasing noradrenaline, which may promote further anxiety in these patients. CRH may be a major culprit, because increasing evidence indicates that it is a major modulator of the stress system in the brain. When CRH blockers are developed, it will be interesting to use them to reduce acute suicidal anxiety and agitation. On the other hand, we believe that impulsivity is related to low serotonin function in the brain and that it may be increased by anxiety.

Beck and associates[13] showed that hopelessness is a common correlate of suicide. Their studies do not specifically address time to suicide. We did find it to be a strong chronic, but not an acute, risk factor in our studies. We (Young et al.[14]) also found that hopelessness is trait-like; in other words, some patients experience more hopelessness per unit of depression severity and some patients manifest hopelessness even when they are not in an episode of depression.

Anhedonia also seems to be a chronic trait that becomes very severe prior to suicide. In the prospective Collaborative Study, it was significantly worse in suicidal patients than in depressed ones who did not attempt suicide. These "pathways to suicide" are proposed as a hypothetical model, a heuristic model, a way to direct clinical thinking when patients are being evaluated for acute suicide risk.

The question then arises as to whether suicide is related to specific psychiatric illness or if it is a separate heritable behavior triggered by psychiatric illness. In other words, does the suicidal dimension of behavior run across diagnosis? Do some people have it and some people do not, no matter their diagnosis, or is it related to the severity of their illness? Some studies are beginning to support the notion that it might be a separate dimension, and several investigators have noted that suicide runs in specific families independent of any specific disorder. Brent noted this in adolescents, Egland found it in Amish groups, and Tsuang found it in large clinical samples. In addition, Brent presented evidence that impulsivity runs in families. Therefore, these factors that lead to high-risk suicide may be heritable. A family history then becomes so important, because it might tell you something about your patient when doing a complete assessment of risk.

Are there specific treatments for acute suicidal risk? Clinical experience suggests that suicidal risk can be reduced by treating high-risk features such as panic, anxiety, and agitation aggressively with benzodiazepines or other anxiolytic agents. The possibility of benzodiazepine dependency does not pose a greater risk than the risk of suicide, especially with acute treatment. This treatment is sustained for days or weeks, maybe months, but not years. In borderline patients, behavioral disinhibition is a possibility with benzodiazepines and should be considered. Alternatively, anticonvulsant medication such as divalproex can be used to reduce agitation. Schatzberg and associates[15] reported on a patient who made a serious suicide attempt after her agitation persisted after ECT. The atypical neuroleptics, such as olanzapine or quetaipine, seem to produce anxiolytic and antiagitation effects in some patients. Studies have shown that the atypical antipsychotic medication clozapine substantially reduces suicide attempts in schizophrenic patients (including schizoaffective patients), and olanzepine is more effective than haloperidol in reducing suicide attempts. These treatments in a depressed patient can be lifesaving in the short term, when anxiety is severe. A case vignette might illustrate this point.

A 33-year-old male patient came to the ER after calling to say that he was so anxious he was jumping out of his skin and could not talk, admitting that he had stopped taking the divalproex that he had been prescribed for bipolar II disorder. The patient took one dose just before coming to the ER as he was ordered to do when he called, but he was still very anxious. He was given 2.0 mg of lorazepam by mouth, and in 45 minutes he appeared much improved. Both patient and parents agreed that he was over the incident. The patient, who refused admission and was not certifiable, was allowed to go home accompanied by his parents. The patient had been treated for substance abuse in the past and did not want to take medications such as divalproex because he had been told not to take 'drugs' in the course of his successful treatment for severe substance abuse and dependence 2 years before. He went home, appearing very relaxed, and retired for the night. During the night the patient jumped to his death from a bedroom window on the twelfth story of the family's condominium building.

What went wrong in this case? Lorazepam appeared to address the patient's anxiety and agitation, but how long did its effect last? Lorazepam has an intermediate (8–12-hour) half-life, with a clinical effect rarely lasting longer than 3–4 hours. Lorazepam took the agitation completely away when the patient was in the ER, but its effect wore off after several hours, probably allowing the patient's anxiety to recur, reawakening his suicidal impulse. The sustained, closely supervised management of severe anxiety/agitation can be lifesaving.

The bottom line is the importance of detecting acute suicide risk factors and treating severe anxiety and agitation with a proactive and sustained approach and with appreciation of the danger involved. Obviously most patients at acute high-risk of suicide must be hospitalized until the crisis is resolved, but it is not enough to hospitalize them, because they can also kill themselves in the hospital if not supervised one to one. In our study of the inpatient hospital sample quoted above, 42% of the patients studied were on 15-minute checks when they hanged themselves. One-to-one supervision is necessary when managing an acute high-risk inpatient.

The decision of who is at acute risk must be made. Treatment should be very aggressive, and both anxiety and agitation must be treated. This may not address all acute suicidal patients, but it will enable an increased percentage of suicidal patients to be successfully treated.

It is impossible to predict suicide in an individual patient at our current state of knowledge, and because of the difficulty in accurately predicting "rare" events, this may never be attained. We can assess for high or low acute versus chronic risk groups and sort them out by careful clinical examination. We can proactively treat high-risk patients. We need more reliable, empirically derived risk factors from research. The practicing clinician needs the benefit of more clinical research to become more effective in preventing suicide.

REFERENCES

1. ROBINS *et al.* 1981. The Final Months. Oxford University Press. Cambridge.
2. BARRACLOUGH, B., J. BUNCH, B. NELSON & P. SAINSBURY. 1974. A hundred cases of suicide: clinical aspects. Br. J. Psychiatry **125:** 355–373.
3. APA GUIDELINES FOR MAJOR DEPRESSION. 1998. APA Press.
4. FAWCETT, J., W. SCHEFTNER, L. FOGG, *et al.* 1990. Time-related predictors of suicide in major affective disorder. Am. J. Psychiatry **147**(9): 1189–1194.
5. ISOMETSA, E.T. & J.K. LONNQVIST. 1998. Suicide attempts preceding completed suicide. Br. J. Psychiatry **173:** 531–535.
6. BUSCH, K.A., D.C. CLARK, J. FAWCETT & H.M. KRAVITZ. 1993. Clinical features of inpatient suicide. Psychiatr. Ann. **23**(5): 256–262.
7. HALL, R.C., D.E. PLATT & R.C. HALL. 1999. Suicide risk assessment: a review of risk factors for suicide in 100 patients who made severe suicide attempts. Evaluation of suicide risk in a time of managed care. Psychosomatics **40**(1): 18–27.
8. SCHNYDER, U., L. VALACH, K. BICHSEL & L. MICHEL. 1999. Attempted suicide. Do we understand the patients' reasons? Gen. Hosp. Psychiatry **21**(1): 62–69.
9. APTER, A., N. LAUFER, M. BAR-SEVER, *et al.* 1999. Serum cholesterol, suicidal tendencies, impulsivity, aggression, and depression in adolescent psychiatric inpatients. Biol. Psychiatry **46**(4): 532–541.
10. OHRING, R., A. APTER, G. RATZONI, *et al.* 1996. State and trait anxiety in adolescent suicide attempters. J. Am. Acad. Child Adolesc. Psychiatry **35**(2): 154–157.
11. TONDO, L. & R.J. BALDESSARINI. 2000. Reduced suicide risk during lithium maintenance treatment. J. Clin. Psychiatry **61**(suppl 9): 97–104.
12. NEMEROFF, C.B., E. WIDERLOV, G. BISSETTE, *et al.* 1984. Elevated concentrations of CRF corticotropin-releasing factor-like immunoreactivity in depressed patients. Science **226:** 1342–1344.
13. BECK, A.T., R.A. STEER, M. KOVACS & B. GARRISON. 1985. Hopelessness and eventual suicide. Am. J. Psychiatry **142:** 559-563.
14. YOUNG, M.A., L.F. FOGG, W. SCHEFTNER, *et al.* 1996. Stable trait components of hopelessness: baseline and sensitivity to depression. J. Abnorm. Psychiatry **105**(2): 155–165.
15. SCHATZBERG, A.F. & C. DEBATTISTA. 1999. Phenomenology and treatment of agitation. J. Clin. Psychiatry **60**(suppl 15): 17–20.

DISCUSSION

J. JOHN MANN (CHAIRMAN): What is the role of early adoption on suicide risk? What is the impact of adverse rearing experiences on suicide risk?

JAN FAWCETT: There are studies of suicide at an early age in adopted infants, and it is important to mention that suicide follows the biological parents rather than the raising parents. Also, identical twins have a higher rate of suicide than dizygotic twins, indicating probably a genetic factor. As for adverse rearing circumstances, more research is being done. Dr. Nemeroff is studying the effect of adverse rearing circumstances on the stress system, which has to do with CRH, as I discussed. The response seems to be in the patient, entrained at a very early age, and it often lasts. Dr. Nemeroff is studying and teaching us some mechanisms by which early rearing translates into clinical events, specifically suicide. I do not know of any studies that specifically focus on suicide except studies of early abuse relating to suicide attempts. There is a correlation.

MANN: How useful is platelet serotonin reuptake as a marker?

FAWCETT: This is "Dr. Serotonin." I think you should answer that.

MANN: You're thinking about recent studies of platelet 5Ht-2A receptors, which were touted as a tremendous breakthrough in trying to determine who is at risk. The short answer is that this is not the way to find out who is at risk, but it is part of the process of trying to get the answer. Some people are working on blood tests, some with promising and others with not so promising results. We have a way to go with that. An important question is, if the patient starts out with chronic anxiety disorder and perhaps panic attacks and subsequently becomes depressed, how important is that as an indicator of risk?

FAWCETT: I don't have data on that cohort of patients. We do know that many people who develop depressive disorders have a history of anxiety disorders, particularly in childhood. I regard anxiety, severe anxiety, and severe recurrent anxiety as symptoms to be pursued aggressively, particularly in a depressed patient. It as a very dangerous symptom. The combination of unremitting recurrent anxiety and depression wears a patient down. With depression you get hopelessness. With anxiety you get psychic pain. If you have both hopelessness and psychic pain, it's like being in a jail and being tortured every day with no escape. Suicide seems a rational way out if you have nothing but pain. Just a word of caution. Some of these cases scare me, because the anxiety isn't that dramatic in outpatients, but it is there and it is recurrent. The patient goes on and suddenly commits suicide. Everybody wonders why it happened. I think it is the untreated anxiety and depression.

MANN: Given that the greatest risk for suicide is shortly after discharge from the hospital and with the limitations of insurance and health coverage, what suggestions do you have for providing more intensive transitional care in stepping people down from an inpatient stay?

FAWCETT: You can see them more frequently. If someone objects, cite the high- risk period for suicide and the need to see these persons more frequently after discharge. There is nothing better than close outpatient follow-up. If someone tries to get in the way, you have to cite the facts and tell them that you don't want to put this patient at risk. Ask them if they do.

MANN: What about the anxiety that patients experience when they undergo benzodiazepine withdrawal, if they have perhaps been using it in the context of a mood disorder?

FAWCETT: I've seen five patients admitted to the hospital who were taking high doses of benzodiazepines. When the clinician decided that they were abusing benzodiazepines, he withdrew them and the patients hanged themselves. I would not do it that way. If a patient is taking high levels of benzodiazepines, usually it's because they're very anxious. The benzodiazepines might not be adequate. It's up to you to find something adequate while you are treating their depression. Then you withdraw them from the benzodiazepine after their depression is treated, not while they are depressed. I'm not answering the question you asked. The danger of benzodiazepine withdrawal is nonexistent if the benzodiazepines are withdrawn slowly. I'm not talking about patients who have been on them for 6 months or a year; I'm talking about patients who have been on them for weeks or maybe a couple of months. They are not a problem. You do it gradually; you withdraw lithium and all CNS drugs gradually, and I don't see that as a problem. I do see a problem when patients are taken off benzodiazepines when they are depressed and anxious. That's asking for suicide.

MANN: You didn't mention ECT among your short-term life-saving treatments.

FAWCETT: ECT is certainly a very useful treatment. You have to get the person's consent to take ECT, for one; a lot of people won't give it. If they do, you also have to realize that ECT doesn't work in a day or two and that there have been suicides in patients getting ECT. ECT does not suicide-proof a patient. Also, if with ECT you get a successful outcome, remember that there is a very high recurrence rate within a year, up to 50%. If the patient is on maintenance medication, it may be only 20 or 25%, but ECT is an important acute treatment. I don't minimize its effectiveness, but it does not solve your whole problem.

MANN: What about the unnatural calm, like the calm before the storm. Some patients are agitated, then they become calm, and that is actually the state they are in just before they kill themselves.

FAWCETT: Yes. There is the calm and the euphoria people who have been very anxious and agitated sometimes feel before they kill themselves. If you have ever talked to a patient who tried to kill him- or herself and woke up in the ICU instead, frequently they will tell you how wonderful they felt once they had made the decision to take their life. Many of them will be angry with you for interfering, and of course they are still highly suicidal. A certain portion of patients look abruptly better before they suicide, and that's what we're talking about. Usually, they have made a decision at that point, and all the criticism and all the anxiety are relieved; there's nothing to be anxious about if you're not going to be alive. However, most patients with depression who commit suicide do not suddenly get better; they suddenly get worse. For no good reason they get more anxious and more agitated, and I don't know why. I don't know what is happening, but I do know it is a very dangerous time. Any abrupt change, either positive or negative, in a depressed patient is very clinically significant.

Assessment and Treatment of the Youthful Suicidal Patient

DAVID A. BRENT

Division of Child and Adolescent Psychiatry, Western Psychiatric Institute and Clinic, Pittsburgh, Pennsylvania 15213, USA

ABSTRACT: In this review, a framework for the assessment of suicidal risk in the adolescent is described, based on existing epidemiological and clinical studies. The assessment of risk can then be used to determine the immediate disposition, intensity of treatment, and level of care. Furthermore, the assessment of psychiatric and psychological characteristics of the individual and family, as well as the motivation and precipitants for the suicidal episode, can be used to target areas of vulnerability and thereby help the patient reduce the risk of recurrent suicidal behavior. The approach to treatment, guided by the assessment, uses a model of suicidal behavior that is based on our clinical experience and the few extant clinical trials of the treatment of suicidal behavior. Recommended interventions involve treatment of psychopathology; amelioration of cognitive distortion and difficulties with social skills, problem-solving, and affect regulation; and family psychoeducation and intervention. Given the chronic and recurrent nature of the conditions associated with adolescent suicide attempts, a long-term care plan involving both continuation and maintenance treatment is advocated. Further research is necessary to identify the most effective approaches to the treatment of adolescent suicide attempters.

KEYWORDS: Adolescent suicide; Suicide in adolescents

INTRODUCTION

The assessment and treatment of the youthful suicidal patient is one of the most common and, at the same time, demanding emergencies in child and adolescent mental health practice. This article aims to guide the practitioner in this effort by reviewing the descriptive epidemiology of suicidality among youth, discussing the assessment of suicidal risk, and then outlining treatment approaches that target these risk factors to reduce the risk for subsequent suicidal behavior.

Address for correspondence: Dr. David Brent, Western Psychiatric Institute & Clinic, 3811 O'Hara Street, Pittsburgh, PA 15213. Voice: 412-624-5172; fax: 412-624-7997.
brentca@msx.upmc.edu

DESCRIPTIVE EPIDEMIOLOGY

Suicidal ideation is common in adolescence, approaching a point prevalence of 20%, although more specific suicidal ideation with intent or with a plan is substantially less frequent.[1] The point prevalence of suicide attempts in the United States ranges from 1.3–3.8% in males and 1.5–10.1% in females, with a relatively lower prevalence (1–3%) for medically serious attempts.[1,2] There is a substantial risk for recurrence of suicidal behavior ranging between 5 and 15% per year, and there is also a substantially increased risk for completed suicide of 0.5–1.0% per year.[3–7] It is the latter association, that of a 10–60-fold increased risk for suicide among suicide attempters, that makes the proper assessment and treatment of suicidal youth so critical.[8,9]

ASSESSMENT

Assessment of the Suicidal Youth

There are five domains critical to the assessment of the suicidal youth: (1) characteristics of the suicidality (ideation or attempt); (2) current and lifetime psychopathology; (3) psychological characteristics; (4) family and environmental factors; and (5) availability of lethal agents (such as firearms and medication).

Characteristics of the Suicidality

Suicidal youth most often present in emergent situations after having made an attempt. Since the assessment of suicide attempters involves assessment of their current ideation, the approach to the ideator who has not attempted will also be discussed. Four characteristics of the suicide attempt should be assessed: (1) suicidal intent and current suicidal ideation; (2) medical lethality; (3) precipitant for the attempt; and (4) motivation for the attempt.

Assess What Is Observable. Because suicidal individuals are often ambivalent about getting help, they may provide information that may cause the assessor to underestimate suicidal risk. Therefore, it is vital to gather as much information as possible about observable behavior, which can be more objectively assessed and has been shown to be predictive of future recurrences of suicidality.

Suicidal Intent. Suicidal intent is the extent to which the suicide attempter wished to die,[10] and it relies on a combination of the attempter's self-report and the actual suicidal behavior of the attempter. Suicidal intent consists of four components: (1) belief about intent (i.e., the extent to which the individual wished to die); (2) preparatory behavior (e.g., making a will, saying goodbye, giving away prized possessions, saving up pills for overdose); (3) prevention of discovery (planning the attempt so that rescue is unlikely); and (4) communication of suicidal intent.[11] "Completers" are more likely than "attempters" to show high suicidal intent, specifically, evidence of planning, timing the attempt so as to avoid detection, confiding suicidal plans ahead of time, and expressing a wish to die.[12] In fact, prospective studies show that high suicidal intent is associated with recurrent suicide attempts and with suicide completion.[6,13]

Current Suicidal Ideation and Past Suicidal Behavior. The severity and pervasiveness of current suicidal ideation give important and proximal clues to the assessment of suicidal risk, even in those not presenting with an actual suicide attempt. Severity refers to the intent conveyed by the ideation—from passive thoughts of death, to ideation with a wish to die, and, most seriously, to ideation with an active plan and a wish to carry out that plan. Pervasiveness refers to the frequency and intensity of ideation—from its most mild, fleeting form, to ideation that is constant and preoccupying. Longitudinal studies have shown that the more severe and pervasive the suicidal ideation, the more likely such ideation is to eventuate in an attempt.[1] In addition, those who have engaged in suicide attempts in the past, especially in light of current ideation, are more likely to reattempt.[1,3,7,14,15]

Lethality. Suicide attempts of high medical lethality, using methods such as hanging, shooting, carbon monoxide poisoning, or jumping, are more likely to show evidence of high suicidal intent. Individuals who make such attempts are at extremely high risk of completing suicide.[12,16,17] However, the converse is not necessarily true, that is, an attempt of low lethality does not necessarily mean that suicidal intent is low. This is especially true in the preadolescent or early adolescent child. In younger patients, cognitive immaturity may make it difficult for a suicidal young person to formulate and execute a lethal suicidal plan. Therefore, younger individuals may engage in suicidal behavior that they *believe* to be quite dangerous.[8,18] Thus, lethality should always be assessed in the context of suicidal intent. Moreover, in an impulsive individual for whom a lethal agent is available, an attempt with relatively low intent may result in a medically serious and even fatal attempt.[8,18-20]

Nonsuicidal Self-Harm. It is important to differentiate nonsuicidal self-harm from actual suicide attempts. Nonsuicidal self-harm most commonly involves self-cutting in a repetitive and stereotypical manner, usually to relieve distress rather than to attempt suicide. Such behavior may be precipitated by an interpersonal crisis and may be accompanied by anxiety, a feeling of emptiness, or depersonalization. Prior abuse may be a risk factor for such behavior.[21] Often patients will engage in both nonsuicidal self-harm and suicide attempts, so that the presence of the former should heighten the clinician's vigilance about the possibility of the latter.

Precipitant. The characterization of the precipitant for suicidal behavior is helpful both in the assessment of suicidal risk and also for the purpose of treatment planning. With regard to assessment of risk, if the precipitant is part of a chronic and ongoing problem, such as family discord or abuse, the likelihood of recurrence of suicidal behavior is increased. The most common precipitants for adolescent suicidal behavior are interpersonal conflict or interpersonal loss, usually involving either a parent (in adolescents aged <16 years) or a romantic attachment (in adolescents aged ≥16 years).[8] Ongoing physical or sexual abuse is a particularly ominous precipitant, because if the child is not removed from the abusive situation, the suicidal behavior is likely to recur and may even eventuate in completed suicide.[4,8] Legal and disciplinary problems are also common precipitants for suicidal behavior and suicide, particularly in youths with conduct disorder and substance abuse problems.[8,22,23] With regard to treatment, clarification of the precipitant allows the clinician to help the patient make explicit the chain of external and internal events that led from the precipitant to the suicidal act. If the precipitant is a commonly occurring stressor, such as parent-child discord, then helping the family and patient to utilize alternative means of handling this stress may be a critical initial intervention.[24,25]

Motivation. Motivation is the reason given by the patient and family for the suicidal act and flows naturally from the clarification of the precipitant. For the one third of attempters with the highest suicidal intent, their motivation is to die or to permanently escape a psychologically painful situation.[26,27] Those attempters who wish to die or to escape a painful situation (e.g., an abusive home)[4] are at highest risk for recurrent suicide attempts. For most suicide attempters, a major motivation for suicidal behavior is to influence others or to communicate a feeling (i.e., make someone feel guilty or sorry, gain sympathy or attention, express hostility).[26,27] Understanding the motivation of suicide-attempting patients is critical to the formulation of the treatment plan. For example, often patients engage in a suicide attempt to express hostility or to gain attention. Helping these patients to identify those needs more explicitly and to find more efficient and less dangerous ways to get those needs met may help such patients avoid suicidal behavior when confronted with similar stressors in the future.

CURRENT AND LIFETIME PSYCHOPATHOLOGY

The vast majority of suicide attempters in both community and clinical samples have evidence of serious psychopathology; the most common conditions are mood, anxiety, disruptive, or substance abuse disorders, often seen

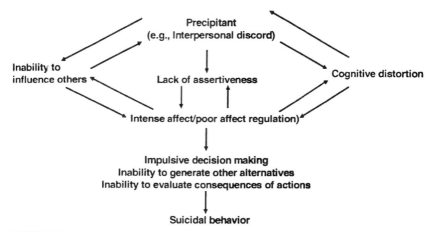

FIGURE 1. Pathways to suicidal behavior: prescriptions for psychosocial interventions. Adapted from Brent, D.A. 1999, J. Child. Psychol. Psychiatry 38: 277-286.

in combination.[1,28] Mood disorders are most closely associated with suicide attempt, and as the number of comorbid conditions increases, so does the risk for suicide attempt.[28–30] Chronicity of disorder also increases the risk for both attempted and completed suicide,[9,12,31,32] although some psychological autopsy and longitudinal studies indicate that suicide is often a relatively early complication of mood disorder.[31,33] Conditions that are labile and relatively treatment refractory, such as bipolar disorder, chronic depression, comorbid mood and substance abuse, psychosis, and eating disorders, are associated with increased suicide risk.[34]

Psychological Characteristics

Hopelessness. While hopelessness is often correlated with depressed mood, it is a stronger correlate of suicidal intent even after controlling for depression, and it predicts risk for reattempt and completion of suicide beyond psychopathological characteristics.[6,28,35,36] Hopelessness may be more common in mood-disordered than in impulsive suicide attempts.[18] Hopelessness is a critical domain to target in treatment, not only because of its strong relationship to suicidal risk, but also because hopeless patients are more likely to drop out of treatment.[37] Therefore, the restoration of hope is a critical first step to the development of a treatment alliance and further intervention.

Impulsivity, Affective Regulation, and Poor Problem-Solving Skills. Adolescent suicide attempters are frequently impulsive and carry out their attempts with relatively little planning or consideration about the consequences. Such youths often lack the requisite skills to generate alternative solutions, evaluate the relative merits of these alternatives, take a course of action, and reevaluate.[38] Moreover, many suicide attempters have difficulties not only with mood disorders, but also with affective regulation (i.e., considerable reactivity of mood to stressful circumstances).[24] Consequently, many affectively dysregulated attempters may be successfully treated for depression and yet, under stress, may re-attempt suicide because their impulsivity, mood lability, and problem-solving ability have not been assessed or addressed in treatment.

Social Skills Deficits. Many suicide attempters engage in suicidal behavior in order to express hostility, get attention, or influence other people. These motivations for engaging in self-destructive behavior indicate difficulties with social skills and interpersonal effectiveness. For example, an attempter who makes an attempt in order to express hostility or request attention should be taught more direct (and less dangerous) methods of communicating feelings and needs. By improving communication skills, assertiveness, and self-efficacy, a more direct route to getting one's needs met is opened up, and suicidal behavior can then become a less desirable option.

Hostility and Aggression. This domain overlaps with that of impulsivity and affect regulation. Hostility and tendency to impulsive aggression and cluster B (impulsive-aggressive) personality disorder are associated with suicidal behavior and completed suicide among youth as well as being predictive of repeated suicide attempts.[39–42] The tendency to impulsive aggression or the tendency to respond with hostility or aggression in response to frustration or provocation is a trait closely related to alteration in central serotonin.[43]

Homosexuality/Bisexuality. Evidence is accumulating from population-based studies that homosexual or bisexual behavior is associated with a markedly increased risk for attempted suicide.[44] In some studies, homosexual or bisexual males are at particularly increased risk.[45,46] The relationship between homosexuality and suicide attempt may be mediated by gender nonconformity, early awareness of homosexuality, parental or peer rejection, victimization, the increased risk for depression and substance abuse among some adolescents involved in the "coming-out" process, or other, yet to be determined mechanisms.[44] However, these findings underscore the importance of inquiry about sexual orientation and any associated turmoil.

Family Factors

Parental Psychiatric Illness. The parents of suicide attempters and completers consistently show much higher than expected rates of mood disorder, substance abuse, aggressive behavior, and suicidal behavior.[12,16,47–50] In fact, parental depression may contribute to suicidal risk even after adjusting for the increased risk for depression in the offspring, suggesting an environmental as well as a genetic mechanism.[47]

Discord, Neglect, and Abuse. Parent-child and parent-parent discord, unsupportive interactions, lack of parental monitoring, and both physical and sexual abuse are related to risk for suicide attempt and completion.[8,15,28,29,47,51–54] Youths who are runaways or homeless also appear to be at increased risk.[9,55]

Availability of Lethal Agents

The convergent evidence from epidemiological, case-control, quasiexperimental, and prospective studies shows that a gun in the home is a risk factor for completed suicide. Moreover, the risk for suicide is greater if the gun in the home is a handgun rather than a long gun, stored loaded rather than unloaded, and stored unlocked rather than locked.[20] Therefore, removal of guns from the homes of all at-risk youth is a reasonable intervention. However, many parents will be unwilling to remove guns, but would be willing to secure them.[56,57] Therefore, it may be helpful to explore other alternatives to removal such as storing guns locked, unloaded, and/or disassembled.

With regard to medication, there may be evidence that providing drugs in a blister pack with relatively limited quantities may reduce the risk of serious overdose.[58] With regard to the choice of medication for treatment of depression, it is important to keep in mind that tricyclic antidepressants convey a much higher risk of completed suicide than do selective serotonin reuptake inhibitors (SSRIs).[59,60] Moreover, in adolescents, SSRIs may be more efficacious than tricyclic antidepressants (TCAs) at any rate.[61] Therefore, we should always consider the overdose potential of any medication that is being prescribed for a suicidal individual in the context of an overall risk-benefit analysis.

TREATMENT

Initial Treatment Approach to the Suicidal Patient

Several generic steps in the initial approach to the suicidal patient should be taken regardless of the specific modalities of treatment implemented. These include: (1) establishing a no-suicide contract; (2) taking steps to increase the likelihood of compliance with treatment; and (3) determining the level and intensity of treatment required.

TABLE 1. No-suicide contract[a]

• Promise to avoid self-harm
• Promise to contact parent or clinician in event of suicidal impulse
• Need for 24-hour back-up
• Probe of alliance and personal and family resources (emotional regulation, "truces")

[a]Adapted from Drye *et al.* 1973. Am. J. Psychiatry **130**: 171-174.

No-Suicide Contract. In the no-suicide contract (TABLE 1), the patient, in the presence of family and clinician, promises not to engage in suicidal behavior and to notify the clinician, parent, or responsible adult when faced with the recurrence of suicidal thoughts.[62] The ability to implement such a contract depends on having 24-hour availability of a trained clinician to respond to any potential crisis. In at least one study, the 24-hour availability of a physician for suicide-attempting patients has been shown to result in fewer suicide attempts and threats on follow-up than did ordinary care.[63]

The no-suicide contract helps to commit the patient and family to pursue strategies inconsistent with suicide. Furthermore, the manner in which the patient and family respond to the development of such a contract provides the clinician with valuable information about the patient's suicidal risk, the coping skills of the patient and family, and family supports and resources.[24] In the formulation of a no-suicide contract, the clinician and family review alternative methods of coping with the stressors that led to the suicidal crisis. Through this exercise, the clinician learns about the family's ability to respond adaptively and to adhere to the terms of the contract. For example, if parent-child discord was a precipitant for the suicidal event, then the clinician would attempt to negotiate a truce and suggest that the family avoid focusing on certain controversial topics until more effective family communication styles can be developed through treatment. The review of the no-suicide contract and current suicidality should be part of every treatment session and can be explored in the context of how the patient is coping with ongoing and intermittent stressors.

Steps to Increase Compliance with Treatment. Adolescent suicide attempters can be notoriously noncompliant with treatment recommendations.[25,64–66] Noncompliance is of particular concern in this population, given that the correlates of noncompliance are also associated with a higher risk for attempted and completed suicide (e.g., hopelessness, higher suicidal intent, and more severe psychopathology).[25,37,65,67-71] Therefore, certain steps should be taken that are well known to increase compliance in a variety of outpatient settings[72] (TABLE 2). In addition, it has been shown that both psychoeducation about mental health treatment and the provision of a mechanism for contacting the responsible clinician on a 24-hour basis can improve both compliance and outcome.[25,63]

TABLE 2. Steps to maintain compliance with outpatient treatment[a]

- Patient given a definite appointment for follow-up at the time of intake
- Patient scheduled in a timely fashion
- Patient reminded of the appointment by telephone
- 24-hour clinical back-up available for crises
- No-shows pursued by phone calls and letters
- Explicit contract between patient, family, and therapist about the type of treatment that is developed
- Involvement of family members and other significant adults in treatment (e.g., teachers, physicians)

[a]Adapted from Brent & Kolko. 1990. Psychiat. Disord. Child. Adoles.: 372–391.

TABLE 3. Indicators of a need for a more intensive level of care[a]

Characteristics of the attempt/current suicidality
   Active suicidal ideation (with plan and intent)
   High intent or lethality attempt
   Motivation to die or to escape a painful situation or affect

Psychopathology
   Depression— severe or comorbid
   Bipolar illness
   Substance abuse
   Psychosis
   Multiple diagnoses

Past history
   Previous noncompliance or failure with outpatient treatment
   Past attempt

Psychological characteristics
   Hopelessness
   Aggression / hostility

Family problems
   Abuse
   Severe parental psychiatric illness
   Parents unable / unwilling to protect or monitor patient

[a]Adapted from Brent & Kolko. 1990. Psychiat. Disord. Child. Adoles.: 372–391.

Determine Level of Care Required. There are wide variations in the availability of more restrictive levels of care as a function of both geography and insurance. However, as a general principle, the greater the suicidal risk, the more intensive and restrictive the recommended treatment. Psychiatric hospitalization is recommended for those patients whose safety can be assured only by 24-hour monitoring in a hospital setting. Partial hospitalization or intensive outpatient treatment is indicated for patients whose safety can be assured but whose level of function is very impaired. TABLE 3 lists indicators of a need for more intensive treatment.

Previous Studies of the Treatment of Suicidal Adults and Youths

Hawton and colleagues[73] recently reviewed the literature on the impact of specialized psychosocial and pharmacological treatments on repetition of suicidal behavior in adult suicide attempters, which is summarized in TABLE 4. Problem-solving therapy, intensive aftercare, and provision of an emergency card explaining how to access services on a 24-hour basis were each contrasted with treatment as usual, and while the odds of repetition were somewhat lower in the experimental treatment, meta-analyses indicated that these differences did not reach statistical significance. Two types of studies have shown more promise. First, Linehan et al.[74] showed that dialectical behavior therapy (DBT) was more efficacious than treatment as usual in reducing the number and lethality of suicide attempts in chronically suicidal female borderline adults, despite no differential treatment effect between the two groups on suicidal ideation, depression, or hopelessness. This reduced rate of suicide attempts was sustained upon 1-year follow-up.[75] Second, in a placebo-controlled trial of chronically and recurrently parasuicidal adults, a depot neuroleptic (flupenthixol) was much more effective than placebo in preventing the repetition of the suicide attempt.[76] One study published subsequent to Hawton et al.'s meta-analyses examined adult attempters who were randomized to either paroxetine or placebo for up to 52 weeks.[77] Although there was no significant effect on depression, hopelessness, or anger, there was a significant reduction in recurrent suicide attempts in the subgroup of attempters who did not have cluster B characteristics and who had made fewer than five previous attempts. This appears in contrast to Coccaro et al.'s[78] promising placebo-controlled study, in which impulsive aggression was reduced in personality-disordered patients by treatment with fluoxetine.

Relatively few studies focus exclusively on young suicidal individuals. Lerner and Clum[79] randomized young suicidal depressed college student volunteers to either a problem-solving group or a supportive therapy group. The problem-solving group was superior to the control treatment with regard to

TABLE 4. Review of treatment studies of adult suicide attempters[a]

Type of treatment	Comparison	Odds of repetition (95% CI)
Problem-solving therapy	Usual aftercare	0.73 (0.45–1.18)
Intensive aftercare	Usual aftercare	0.83 (0.61–1.14)
Emergency card	Usual aftercare	0.45 (0.19–1.07)
Dialectical behavior therapy	*Usual care*	*0.24 (0.06–0.93)*
Antidepressant	Placebo	1.19 (0.53–2.67)
Flupenthixol	*Placebo*	*0.09 (0.02–0.50)*

[a]Adapted from Hawton et al., 1998. Brit. Med. J. **317**: 441–447.

depression, hopelessness, and problem-solving, but the two treatments had no differential effect on suicidal ideation.

Brent *et al.* randomized 107 depressed adolescents to either cognitive behavior treatment (CBT), family therapy, or supportive treatment. Across the three treatments, 35.1–40.0% had significant suicidality (suicidal ideation with a plan or a recent attempt) at intake. Although a substantial reduction in ideation occurred across the three treatments, there was no differential reduction by treatment, despite one treatment (CBT) being significantly more efficacious for the treatment of depression.

Rotheram-Borus *et al.*[25] randomized 140 Latina adolescent suicide attempters to a brief cognitive behavioral family therapy either alone or in combination with a specialized emergency room intervention designed to increase compliance. The combination of the emergency room and family intervention resulted in improved compliance, lower maternal depression, improved family interaction, and lower adolescent depression and suicidality than did the family intervention alone.

Harrington *et al.*[80] compared a brief, home-based family intervention to routine care for adolescents who took an overdose. There were no overall differences between the two treatments with regard to hopelessness, suicidal ideation, rate of subsequent suicide attempts, or changes in the family environment. Post-hoc analyses indicated a significant reduction in suicidal ideation in the nondepressed group only.

While more definitive treatment studies in young suicide attempters are clearly needed, a few general principles can be derived from the aforementioned studies. Several studies show a dissociation between the impact of treatment on depression and its impact on suicidality. Two experimental treatments were superior to comparison treatments for depression, but had no differential effect on suicidality.[67,79] Conversely, several studies showed a reduction in suicidality, but without any differential effect on depression or hopelessness.[74,77,80] This suggests that treatment of depression may not be necessary or sufficient to reduce suicidal risk in some high-risk populations.

Treatment Approach to the Youthful Suicidal Patient

In summary, the studies performed thus far suggest that treatments characterized by more aggressive outreach and psychoeducation and a greater focus on improving interpersonal efficacy, problem-solving ability, and emotional regulation are more likely to result in reductions in subsequent suicidal behavior. Such interventions also result in improved problem-solving, social skills, and functional status. The aforementioned risk factor research, along with research in treatment outcomes, suggests the need to target three domains: (1) treatment of current psychopathology; (2) remediation of social, problem-solving, and affect regulation deficits; and (3) family psychoeducation and intervention.

Treatment of Current Psychiatric Illness. Most adolescent suicide attempters are suffering from some type of major mood disorder. For those with unipolar mood disorder, both cognitive behavior therapy and selective serotonin reuptake inhibitors have been efficacious.[61,67,81,82] For those with chronic or double depression, on the basis of studies with adults, the combination of psychosocial and pharmacological treatment is likely to be more efficacious than either monotherapy alone.[37,83,84] While it is true that treatment of depression may not be sufficient to completely reduce the risk for recurrent suicidal behavior, among those who made an initial suicide attempt, lack of relief of depression predicted re-attempt.[3]

Comorbidity, especially with substance abuse, anxiety, or disruptive disorder, can increase the risk for continued depression, which in turn is a risk factor for recurrent suicidal behavior.[3,8,83,85–87] Therefore, it is important to address comorbid conditions, in addition to depression, to bring about symptomatic relief, restore function, and reduce suicidal risk. Careful monitoring and aggressive treatment of substance use is very important, insofar as the combination of mood and substance abuse disorder conveys a markedly increased risk for suicide among male adolescents.[8,9]

Mood disorders in youth tend to be chronic and recurrent, so that the treatment should be of sufficient duration (6–8 months) to avoid relapse.[83,86,88,89] Specifically, treatment duration with an SSRI that was at least 6 months after initial symptomatic recovery was optimal in terms of preventing relapse.[86] Similarly, high rates of relapse after CBT treatment are observed unless monthly booster sessions are offered after the initial recovery.[82,83,88,89]

Suicidal behavior is quite common in those with bipolar spectrum mood disorders[90] and appears to be associated with the severity of depressive symptoms, regardless of the degree of mania.[91] A mixed state conveys a particularly high risk for completed suicide.[12,31] Therefore, a combination of mood stabilization with either lithium or valproate (or both), along with treatment of the depression with an antidepressant, is key to the prevention of recurrent suicidal behavior in this high-risk group. Patients with prepubertal onset may be relatively lithium resistant compared to those with adolescent onset.[92] In adolescent-onset cases, lithium may be helpful for mood stabilization and prophylaxis even in those who are concurrently abusing substances.[93] Long-term stabilization requires long-term compliance and may be facilitated by family-based psychoeducation and psychotherapy.[94] Long-term compliance with mood stabilizers may prevent suicide and suicidal behavior in bipolar patients.[95]

Hopelessness. As just noted, hopelessness is a strong correlate of suicidal intent, repetition, and completion of suicide. In addition, hopeless patients are more likely to drop out of treatment.[37] For these two reasons, it is vital to target hopelessness early in treatment, especially hopelessness about treatment. The patient's attitudes towards treatment and previous experience should be carefully explored, with a specific goal to identify elements of treatment that would increase the patient's hopefulness about recovery. For example, a patient may have a previous, unsuccessful experience with treatment, which helps to reinforce a hopeless view of recovery. By identifying specific elements in the proposed treatment that may be more likely to promote recovery, it may be possible to partially reverse demoralization about treatment. Because hopelessness is often part of a global cognitive style, it is best to help the patient set clear, short-term goals that will be easily achievable, which in turn will help build confidence in the efficacy of treatment. Cognitive therapy has specific techniques for dealing with the issue of hopelessness[96]; however, one comparison of cognitive therapy and antidepressant medication showed a significant, but comparable decrement in hopelessness in both types of treatment.[97]

Other Cognitive Distortions. The most common precipitant for adolescent suicide attempts are interpersonal discord and/or loss.[12,51] In younger adolescents, these difficulties most often involve parents, whereas in older adolescents, the interpersonal difficulty is most often with a girl- or boy-friend.[8] An understanding of the precipitants and concomitant motivation for suicidal behavior can shed light on other cognitive distortions that, unless remedied, can lead to recurrent suicidal behavior. For example, a patient may make a suicide attempt after a break-up with a girlfriend, thinking, "without her, I'm nothing." This can provide a theme for focal cognitive therapy that explores the erroneous assumption that one's self-esteem and happiness are entirely dependent on another person. A fight with a parent may also serve as the precipitant for an attempt, with the patient reporting, "We always fight; therefore, I must be a bad person and unlovable."

Social and Problem-Solving Skills. A review of the motivations for suicidal behavior will often provide guidance as to social and problem-solving skills that need to be addressed. Common motivations for suicide attempts are to express hostility, induce guilt, or gain attention. It is clear that engaging in suicidal behavior is an inefficient and risky means for achieving these interpersonal goals. The reason suicide attempters tend to use suicidal behavior as their means of communication is that they often lack the ability to be assertive and direct and thereby find it difficult to effectively negotiate differences directly.[38] Therefore, to prevent the recurrence of suicidal behavior, it is helpful to teach adolescent attempters how to listen to others with whom they have significant differences through role playing and guided practice in sessions and at home. A related issue is that adolescent attempters often have difficulty sizing up a problem, formulating a number of alternatives, choosing among them, and evaluating how well they have done.[38] Therefore, enhancing the attempter's ability to identify problems and generate and evaluate solutions is an important component of treatment, particularly for impulsive suicide attempters.[98] On the basis of Hawton et al.'s[73] meta-analysis, problem-solving training is likely to be helpful, but it is not sufficient to effectively prevent recurrent suicidal behavior. In contrast, Linehan et al.'s[74,75] approach, DBT, integrates elements of problem-solving, social skills and interpersonal effectiveness training, and affect regulation (see below). There is evidence that DBT can be adapted to adolescent populations, although clinical trials have not yet been conducted.[99]

Affect Regulation. Based on the results of Linehan et al.,[74,75] it is likely that the teaching of affect regulation is another important component in helping impulsive suicide attempters. It is important to note that affect dysregulation is different from a mood disorder per se, but there may be some shared diatheses. However, clinically we frequently observed patients who experienced remission from their mood disorder symptoms, and yet, under stress, were still plagued by suicidal behavior. The empirical evidence to support this is the relative dissociation between the effective treatment of depression and the prevention of suicidal behavior.[67,74,77,79,80]

Kienhorst et al.[27] noted that escalation in tension and frustration is reported to be associated with "crossing the bridge" between thinking about and actually attempting suicide. For many of these adolescents, as they feel increasingly under stress, they become more affectively labile and much less dispassionate and rational. Therefore, an appropriate initial approach for these patients is to try to help them avoid these situations through the use of a feeling thermometer, as recommended by Rotheram.[24] With this technique, which often is initially taught as part of the no-suicide contract, the adolescent creates a scale from 0–100, where 0 is totally in control and calm and 100 is totally out of control, agitated, and upset. The psychological and physiological markers are mapped for each 10-point increment. The adolescent is asked to identify where on his or her scale is the point of no return (e.g., "60"), that is, where things will be likely to escalate to an explosion or outburst. The adolescent is then asked to identify where on the scale he or she can still recognize that things may be likely to get out of control, but still may have the wherewithal to deal with stress effectively (e.g., "40"). The adolescent and parents are taught to recognize the psychological, physiological, and behavioral markers of this critical inflection point and to develop agreed-upon tactics on how to de-escalate.

Linehan et al.[74,75] have developed extensive and intensive techniques as part of DBT to aid the parasuicidal borderline patient in managing negative affect. These approaches involve self-monitoring of negative affect with a goal to develop increased ability to tolerate and cope with negative affect by integrating cognitive, self-talk, relaxation, self-soothing, and meditative techniques. It is important to note that Linehan's successful results came from much more intensive interventions (one individual and one group session per week for a year) than the less efficacious and also briefer interventions typically conducted in the literature.[73] Therefore, it is possible that for recurrently and severely suicidal individuals, much longer and more intense treatment is required, although this has not been put to an empirical test. As already noted, Miller *et al.*[99] have adapted DBT to adolescents by integrating parent-child work into the skills groups.

Family Involvement. Family involvement is a key element in the treatment of adolescent suicide attempters. Family interventions need to encompass at least three aspects of family life: knowledge and understanding about suicide and psychiatric illness, dysfunctional family interactions, and parental psychopathology.

To teach family members about the nature of, course of, and treatment approaches to suicide attempts and related psychiatric illnesses, we embark on a didactic intervention with parents, referred to as family psychoeducation.[100] In our clinic, we had the experience that parents often felt that the adolescent patients were "faking" their symptoms or were simply being manipulative. We have developed a psychoeducational manual and a group educational program that have helped parents to understand better the problems of their adolescent.[101] The goals of such education are to increase compliance with treatment, promote a partnership with the parents so that they can monitor the patient with regard to treatment response and recurrences, and to help the family learn how to cope with a child with a psychiatric illness. Initial evaluation and satisfaction with this program by parents appear promising.[100] In a clinical trial of 107 depressed adolescents and their families who were exposed to this psychoeducational intervention, our dropout rate was 10%.[67] Psychoeducation is also an important component of DBT.

Dysfunctional family processes, particularly parent-child discord, are among the most common precipitants for suicidal behavior[6,12,28,52–54] and may also be related to increased risk of dropout.[65] Often, it is possible to get a "truce" while one helps the adolescent patient not to be so reactive to every "potential argument." In addition, sessions with the family that aim at teaching conflict resolution and communication skills may attenuate the level of conflict. Models for family treatment of suicide-attempting adolescents have been elaborated and show promise.[25,102] There is accumulated evidence that parent-child discord is related to slower recovery from depression and greater propensity to experience depressive relapse or recurrence in patients treated with either CBT or fluoxetine.[86,88] Therefore, it is important to address par-

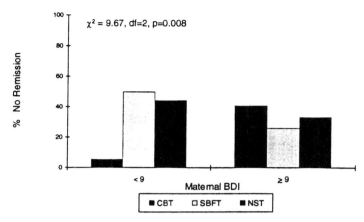

FIGURE 2. Failure to achieve remission as a function of self-reported maternal depression (BDI). Adapted from Brent et al.[37]

ent-child discord, because it lessens the short- and long-term efficacy of even proven effective treatments for depression such as CBT and fluoxetine.

In an attempter with past or current physical or sexual abuse, family involvement is critical. If the perpetrator is a relative, the family may be disbelieving or rejecting of the adolescent, and if the perpetrator is a parent or stepparent, these conflicts are even more intense and may lead to the adolescent's removal from the home. Clinical and epidemiological studies suggest that sexual abuse leaves long-lasting effects with regard to poor self-esteem, helplessness, poor choice of partner, and greater likelihood to enter into abusive relationships, all of which must be the target of individual and family treatment.[103,104]

Parents of suicide-attempting adolescents have much higher rates of affective illness, substance abuse, and antisocial disorder than do psychiatric, medical, or community controls.[16,47,50,51] Patients whose parents are psychiatrically ill may be more likely to drop out,[65] to have more impairment and a more prolonged course,[37,105] and to be more likely to have depressive recurrences.[105] Moreover, parental affective illness may have a significant influence on family climate, namely, increased parent-child and marital discord and decreased family cohesion.[106] Therefore, identification and treatment of parental psychopathology is a key component of family treatment. In fact, in one clinical trial, maternal depression wiped out the otherwise substantial efficacy of CBT in the treatment of adolescent depression[37] (FIG. 2).

Duration of Treatment and Follow-Up. Most clinical trials for depressed and/or suicidal individuals have been relatively brief, that is, 10–20 weeks in duration. The brevity of these interventions may be a mismatch for what is often a chronic and recurrent condition. For example, in the treatment of adolescent depression, two studies comparing CBT to other psychosocial treatments reported superior short-term efficacy for CBT, but high rates of relapse and recurrence, meaning, in essence, no long-term beneficial effects.[67,82,88] The provision of six monthly CBT booster sessions after acute treatment markedly reduces the relapse rate.[89] Similar patterns exist in the short- and long-term treatment with fluoxetine. Whereas there was marked superiority of fluoxetine to placebo in depressed children and adolescents, the proportion who remitted continued to increase markedly after the 8-week period of the trial, and the rate of relapse was much higher for those who (naturalistically) discontinued their medication.[81,86] Therefore, as in the treatment of adults with mood disorders, it is vital to have an acute phase followed by a continuation phase of 6–12 months in order to prevent the relapses that are otherwise likely to occur.

Less is known about the optimal duration of treatment required for suicidal individuals. Most studies have been of relatively brief duration and have also been negative, whereas the most promising results, with DBT, involve a twice-a-week, year-long intervention. Therefore, in more chronic and impairing conditions, it is logical to consider more intense and longer interventions. For example, it is known that suicide-attempting depressed adolescents are more likely to have chronic depression, comorbid anxiety, comorbid personality disorders, and parental psychopathology, all factors that make recovery from a depressive episode slower.[3,32,37,40,41,86–88] In our naturalistic studies of those youths with double depression (depression comorbid with dysthymia), treatment lasted around at least 1 year, and time from intake to recovery was around 11 months.[83]

ACKNOWLEDGMENTS

This work was supported by William T. Grant Foundation Grant 1063-85, National Institute of Mental Health (NIMH) grants MH46500 and MH55123, and Services for Teens at Risk (STAR), an appropriation from the Commonwealth of Pennsylvania. The development of this approach to suicidal patients was aided by Mary Beth Boylan, MA, Carl Bonner, PhD, David Kolko, PhD, and Kim Poling, LSW. The expert assistance of Beverly Sughrue in the preparation of this manuscript is gratefully acknowledged.

This work is in part an updated version of Brent, D.A. 1997. Practitioner Review: The aftercase of adolescents with deliberate self-harm. J. Child Psychol. & Psychiatry 38: 277–286. Reprinted with permission from Cambridge University Press.

REFERENCES

1. LEWINSOHN, P.M., P. ROHDE & J.R. SEELEY. 1996. Adolescent suicidal ideation and attempts: prevalence, risk factors, and clinical implications. Clin. Psychol. Sci. Pract. **3**: 25–46.

2. CENTERS FOR DISEASE CONTROL. 1991. Attempted suicide among high school students: United States, 1990. Morbid. Mortal. Weekly Rep. **40**: 633–635.

3. BRENT, D.A., D.J. KOLKO, M.E. WARTELLA, et al. 1993. Adolescent psychiatric inpatients' risk of suicide attempt at 6-month follow-up. J. Am. Acad. Child Adolesc. Psychiatry **32**: 95–105.

4. COHEN-SANDLER, R., A.L. BERMAN & R.A. KING. 1982. A follow-up study of hospitalized suicidal children. J. Am. Acad. Child Adolesc. Psychiatry **21**: 398–403.

5. HAWTON, K. & J. CATALAN. 1987. Attempted Suicide: A Practical Guide To Its Nature and Management, 2nd Ed. Oxford University Press. New York.

6. HAWTON, K. & M. GOLDACRE. 1982. Hospital admissions for adverse effects of medicinal agents (mainly self-poisoning) among adolescents in the Oxford region. Br. J. Psychiatry **141**: 166–170.

7. PFEFFER, C.R., KLERMAN, G.L., HURT, S.W., et al. 1991. Suicidal children grow up: demographic and clinical risk factors for adolescent suicide attempts. J. Am. Acad. Child Adolesc. Psychiatry **30**: 609–616.

8. BRENT, D.A., M. BAUGHER, J. BRIDGE, et al. 1999. Age and sex-related risk factors for adolescent suicide. J. Am. Acad. Child Adolesc. Psychiatry **38**: 1497–1505.

9. SHAFFER, D., M.S. GOULD, P. FISHER, et al. 1996. Psychiatric diagnosis in child and adolescent suicide. Arch. Gen. Psychiatry **53**: 339–348.

10. BECK, A.T., D. SCHUYLER & I. HERMAN. 1974. Development of suicidal intent scales. In The Prediction of Suicide. A.T. Beck, D.J. Lettieri & H.L.P. Resnick, eds. :45–55. Charles Press. Bowie, MD.

11. KINGSBURY, S.J. 1993. Clinical components of suicidal intent in adolescent overdose. J. Am. Acad. Child Adolesc. Psychiatry **32**: 518–520.

12. BRENT, D.A., J.A. PERPER, C.E. GOLDSTEIN, et al. 1988. Risk factors for adolescent suicide: a comparison of adolescent suicide victims with suicidal inpatients. Arch. Gen. Psychiatry **45**: 581–588.

13. PIERCE, D.W. 1981. The predictive validation of a suicide intent scale: a five year follow-up. Br J. Psychiatry **139**: 391–396.

14. GOLDSTON, D.B., S.S. DANIEL, D.M. REBOUSSIN, et al. 1999. Suicide attempts among formerly hospitalized adolescents: a prospective naturalistic study of risk during the first 5 years after discharge. J. Am. Acad. Child Adolesc. Psychiatry **38**: 660–671.

15. REINHERZ, H.Z., GIACONIA, R.M., SILVERMAN, A.B., et al. 1995. Early psychosocial risks for adolescent suicidal ideation and attempts. J. Am. Acad. Child Adolesc. Psychiatry **34**: 599–611.

16. GARFINKEL, B.D., A. FROESE & J. HOOD. 1982. Suicide attempts in children and adolescents. Am. J. Psychiatry **139**: 1257–1261.

17. OTTO, U. 1972. Suicidal acts by children and adolescents: a follow-up study. Acta Psychiatr. Scand. Suppl. 233.

18. BRENT, D.A. 1987. Correlates of the medical lethality of suicide attempts in children and adolescents. J. Am. Acad. Child Adolesc. Psychiatry **26:** 87–89.
19. BRENT, D.A., J. PERPER, G. MORITZ, *et al.* 1993. Suicide in adolescents with no apparent psychopathology. J. Am. Acad. Child Adolesc. Psychiatry **32:** 494–500.
20. BRENT, D.A., J.A. PERPER, G. MORITZ, *et al.* 1993. Firearms and adolescent suicide: a community case-control study. Am. J. Dis. Children **147:** 1066–1071.
21. VAN DER KOLK, B.A., J.C. PERRY & J.L. HERMAN. 1991. Childhood origins of self-destructive behavior. Am. J. Psychiatry **148:** 1665–1671.
22. BRENT, D.A., J.A. PERPER, G. MORITZ, *et al.* 1993. Stressful life events, psychopathology, and adolescent suicide: a case control study. Suicide Life Threatening Behav. **23:** 179–187.
23. SHAFFER, D. 1974. Suicide in childhood and early adolescence. J. Child Psychol. Psychiatry **15:** 275–291.
24. ROTHERAM, M.J. 1987. Evaluation of imminent danger for suicide among youth. Am. J. Orthopsychiatry **57:** 102–110.
25. ROTHERAM-BORUS, M.J., J. PIACENTINI, R. VAN ROSSEM, *et al.* 1996. Enhancing treatment adherence with a specialized emergency room program for adolescent suicide attempters. J. Am. Acad. Child Adolesc. Psychiatry **35:** 654–663.
26. HAWTON, K., D. COLE, J. O'GRADY & M. OSBORN. 1982. Motivational aspects of deliberate self-poisoning in adolescents. Br. J. Psychiatry **141:** 286–291.
27. KIENHORST, I., E.J. DE WILDE, F.W. DIEKSTRA & W. WOLTERS. 1995. Adolescents' image of their suicide attempt. J. Am. Acad. Child Psychiatry **34:** 623–628.
28. KERFOOT, M., E. DYER, V. HARRINGTON, *et al.* 1996. Correlates and short-term course of self-poisoning in adolescents. Br. J. Psychiatry **168:** 38–42.
29. FERGUSSON, D.M. & M.T. LYNSKEY. 1995. Suicide attempts and suicidal ideation in a birth cohort of 16-year-old New Zealanders. J. Am. Acad. Child Adolesc. Psychiatry **34:** 1308–1317.
30. LEWINSOHN, P.M., P. ROHDE & J.R. SEELEY. 1994. Psychosocial risk factors for future adolescent suicide attempts. J. Consult. Clin. Psychol. **62:** 297–305.
31. BRENT, D.A., J.A. PERPER, G. MORITZ, *et al.* 1993. Psychiatric risk factors of adolescent suicide: a case control study. J. Am. Acad. Child Adolesc. Psychiatry **32:** 521–529.
32. RYAN, N.D., J. PUIG-ANTICH, P. AMBROSINI, *et al.* 1987. The clinical picture of major depression in children and adolescents. Arch. Gen. Psychiatry **44:** 854–861.
33. GUZE, S.B. & E. ROBINS. 1970. Suicide and primary affective disorders. Br. J. Psychiatry **117:** 437–438.
34. BRENT, D.A. 1995. Risk factors for adolescent suicide and suicidal behavior: mental and substance abuse disorders, family environmental factors, and life stress. Suicide Life Threatening Behav. **25:** 52–63.
35. BECK, A.T., A. WEISSMAN, D. LESTER & L. TREXLER. 1974. The measurement of pessimism: the Hopelessness Scale. J. Consult. Clin. Psychol. **42:** 861–865.
36. BECK, A.T., R.A. STEER, M. KOVACS & B. GARRISON. 1985. Hopelessness and eventual suicide: a 10-year prospective study of patients hospitalized with suicidal ideation. Am. J. Psychiatry **142:** 559–563.
37. BRENT, D.A., D. KOLKO, B. BIRMAHER, *et al.* 1998. Predictors of treatment efficacy in a clinical trial of three psychosocial treatments for adolescent depression. J. Am. Acad. Child Adolesc. Psychiatry **37:** 906–914.

38. MCLEAVEY, B.C., R.J. DALY, C.M. MURRAY & M. TAYLOR. 1987. Interpersonal problem-solving deficits in self-poisoning patients. Suicide Life Threatening Behav. **17:** 33–49.
39. APTER, A., A. BLEICH, R. PLUTCHIK, et al. 1988. Suicidal behavior, depression, and conduct disorder in hospitalized adolescents. J. Am. Acad. Child Adolesc. Psychiatry **27:** 69–699.
40. BRENT, D.A., B. JOHNSON, S. BARTLE, et al. 1993. Personality disorder, tendency to impulsive violence, and suicidal behavior in adolescents. J. Am. Acad. Child Adolesc. Psychiatry **32:** 69–75.
41. BRENT, D.A., B.A. JOHNSON, J. PERPER, et al. 1994. Personality disorder, personality traits, impulsive violence, and completed suicide in adolescents. J. Am. Acad. Child Adolesc. Psychiatry **33:** 1080–1086.
42. GISPERT, M., M.S. DAVIS, L. MARSH & K. WHEELER. 1987. Predictive factors in repeated suicide attempts by adolescents. Hosp. Commun. Psychiatry **38:** 390–393.
43. COCCARO, E., L. SIEVER, H.M. KLAR, et al. 1989. Serotonergic studies in patients with affective and personality disorders. Arch. Gen. Psychiatry **46:** 587–599.
44. REMAFEDI, G. 1999. Commentary: suicide and sexual orientation: nearing the end of the controversy? Arch. Gen. Psychiatry **56:** 885–886.
45. GAROFALO, R., C. WOLF, L.S. WISSOW, et al. 1999. Sexual orientation and risk of suicide attempts among a representative sample of youth. Arch. Pediatr. Adolesc. Med. **153:** 487–493.
46. REMAFEDI, G., S. FRENCH, M. STORY, et al. 1998. The relationship between suicide risk and sexual orientation: results of a population-based study. Am. J. Public Health 88, 57–60.
47. BRENT, D.A., J.A. PERPER, G. MORITZ, et al. 1994. Familial risk factors for adolescent suicide: a case-control study. Acta Psychiatr. Scand. **89:** 52–58.
48. BRENT, D.A., J. BRIDGE, B.A. JOHNSON & J. CONNOLLY. 1996. Suicidal behavior runs in families: a controlled family study of adolescent suicide victims. Arch. Gen. Psychiatry **53:** 1145–1152.
49. JOHNSON, B.A., D.A. BRENT, J. BRIDGE, et al. 1998. The familial aggregation of adolescent suicide attempts. Acta Psychiatr. Scand. **97:** 18–24.
50. PFEFFER, C.R., L. NORMANDIN & K. TATSUYUKI. 1994. Suicidal children grow up: suicidal behavior and psychiatric disorders among relatives. J. Am. Acad. Child Adolesc. Psychiatry **33:** 1087–1097.
51. GOULD, M.S., P. FISHER, M. PARIDES, et al. 1996. Psychosocial risk factors of child and adolescent completed suicide. Arch. Gen. Psychiatry **53:** 1155–1162.
52. KAPLAN, S.J., D. PELCOVITZ, S. SALZINGER, et al. 1997. Adolescent physical abuse and suicide attempts. J. Am. Acad. Child Adolesc. Psychiatry **36:** 799–808.
53. KOSKY, R., S. SILBURN & S.R. ZUBRICK. 1990. Are children and adolescents who have suicidal thoughts different from those who attempt suicide? J. Nerv. Mental Disorders **178:** 38–43.
54. TAYLOR, E.A. & S.A. STANSFELD. 1984. Children who poison themselves. I. A clinical comparison with psychiatric controls. Br. J. Psychiatry **145:** 127–132.
55. ROTHERAM-BORUS, M.J. 1993. Suicidal behavior and risk factors among runaway youths. Am. J. Psychiatry **150:** 103–107.

56. BRENT, D.A., M. BAUGHER, B. BIRMAHER, et al. 2000. Compliance with recommendations to remove firearms by families participating in a clinical trial for adolescent depression. J. Am. Acad. Child Adolesc. Psychiatry **39:** 1220–1226.

57. WEBSTER, D.W., M.E.H. WILSON, A.K. DUGGAN & L.C. PAKULA. 1992. Parents' beliefs about preventing gun injuries to children. Pediatrics **89:** 908–914.

58. HAWTON, K., C. WARE, H. MISTRY, et al. 1996. Paracetamol self-poisoning: characteristics, prevention and harm reduction. Br. J. Psychiatry **168:** 43–48.

59. KAPUR, S., T. MIECZKOWSKI & J. MANN. 1992. Antidepressant medications and the relative risk of suicide attempt and suicide. J. Am. Med. Assoc. **268:** 3441–3445.

60. MANN, J.J. & S. KAPUR. 1991. The emergence of suicidal ideation and behavior during antidepressant pharmacotherapy. Arch. Gen. Psychiatry **48:** 1027–1033.

61. KELLER, M.B., N.D. RYAN, B. BIRMAHER, et al. 1998. Paroxetine and imipramine in the treatment of adolescent depression [Abstr.]. New Research Program Abstracts, Annual Meeting of the American Psychiatric Association.

62. DRYE, R., R. GOULDING & M.E. GOULDING. 1973. No-suicide decisions: patient monitoring of suicide risk. Am. J. Psychiatry **130:** 171–174.

63. MORGAN, H.G., E.M. JONES & J.H. OWEN. 1993. Secondary prevention of nonfatal deliberate self-harm: the green card study. Br. J. Psychiatry **163:** 111–112.

64. HAWTON, K., M. OSBORN, J. O'GRADY & D. COLE. 1982. Classification of adolescents who take overdoses. Br. J. Psychiatry **140:** 124–131.

65. TAYLOR, E.A. & S.A. STANSFELD. 1984. Children who poison themselves. II. Prediction of attendance for treatment. Br. J. Psychiatry **145:** 132–135.

66. TRAUTMAN, P.D., N. STEWART & A. MORISHIMA. 1993. Are adolescent suicide attempters noncompliant with outpatient care? J. Am. Acad. Child Adolesc. Psychiatry **32:** 89–94.

67. BRENT, D.A. 1997. Practitioner review: the aftercare of adolescents with deliberate self-harm. J. Child Psychol. Psychiatry **38:** 277–286.

68. GREER, S. & C.R. BAGLEY. 1971. Effect of psychiatric intervention in attempted suicide: a controlled study. Br. Med. J. **1:** 310–312.

69. KENNEDY, P. 1972. Efficacy of a regional poisoning treatment centre in preventing further suicidal behaviour. Br. Med. J. **4:** 255–257.

70. MOTTO, J.A. 1976. Suicide prevention for high-risk persons who refuse treatment. Suicide Life Threatening Behav. **6:** 223–230.

71. WELU, T.C. 1977. A follow-up program for suicide attempters: evaluation of effectiveness. Suicide Life Threatening Behav. **7:** 17–30.

72. BAEKELAND, F. & L. LUNDWALL. 1975. Dropping out of treatment: a critical review. Psychol. Bull. **82:** 738–783.

73. HAWTON, K., ARENSMAN, E., TOWNSEND, E., et al. 1998. Deliberate self harm: systematic review of efficacy of psychosocial and pharmacological treatments in preventing repetition. Br. Med. J. **317:** 441–447.

74. LINEHAN, M.M., H.E. ARMSTRONG, A. SUAREZ, et al. 1991. Cognitive-behavioral treatment of chronically parasuicidal borderline patients. Arch. Gen. Psychiatry **48:** 1060–1064.

75. LINEHAN, M.M., H.L. HEARD & H.E. ARMSTRONG. 1993. Naturalistic follow-up of a behavioral treatment for chronically parasuicidal borderline patients. Arch. Gen. Psychiatry **50:** 971–974.

76. MONTGOMERY, S.A., D.B. MONTGOMERY, S. JAVANTHI-RANI, et al. 1979. Maintenance therapy in repeat suicidal behavior: a placebo controlled trial. *In*

Proceedings of the 10th Intervention. Anonymous. :227–229. Ottawa, Ontario.

77. VERKES, R.J., R.C. VAN DER MAST, M.W. HENGEVELD, *et al.* 1998. Reduction by paroxetine of suicidal behavior in patients with repeated suicide attempts but not major depression. Am. J. Psychiatry **155:** 543–547.

78. COCCARO, E.F. & R.J. KAVOUSSI. 1997. Fluoxetine and impulsive aggressive behavior in personality-disordered subjects. Arch. Gen. Psychiatry **54:** 1081–1088.

79. LERNER, M.S. & G.A. CLUM. 1990. Treatment of suicide ideators: a problem-solving approach. Behav. Ther. **21:** 403–411.

80. HARRINGTON, R., KERFOOT, M., DYER, E., *et al.* 1998. Randomized trial of a home-based family intervention for children who have deliberately poisoned themselves. J. Am. Acad. Child Adolesc. Psychiatry **37:** 512–518.

81. EMSLIE, G., J.A. RUSH, W.A. WEINBERG, *et al.* 1997. A double-blind, randomized placebo-controlled trial of fluoxetine in depressed children and adolescents. Arch. Gen. Psychiatry **54:** 1031–1037.

82. WOOD, A., R. HARRINGTON & A. MOORE. 1996. Controlled trial of a brief cognitive-behavioural intervention in adolescent patients with depressive disorders. J. Child Psychol. Psychiatry **37:** 737–746.

83. BRENT, D.A., D. KOLKO, B. BIRMAHER, *et al.* 1999. A clinical trial for adolescent depression: predictors of additional treatment in the acute and follow-up phases of the trial. J. Am. Acad. Child Adolesc. Psychiatry **38:** 263–270.

84. KELLER, M.B., J.P. McCULLOUGH, D.N. KLEIN, *et al.* 2000. The acute treatment of chronic major depression: a comparison of nefazodone, cognitive behavioral analysis system of psychotherapy, and their combination. N. Engl. J. Med. Submitted.

85. CLARKE, G., H. HOPS, P.M. LEWINSOHN, *et al.* 1992. Cognitive-behavioral group treatment of adolescent depression: prediction of outcome. Behav. Ther. **23:** 341–354.

86. EMSLIE, G.J., A.J. RUSH, W.A. WEINBERG, *et al.* 1998. Fluoxetine in child and adolescent depression: acute and maintenance treatment. Depression & Anxiety **7:** 32–39.

87. HAMILTON, J.A. & J. BRIDGE. 1999. Outcome at 6 months for 50 adolescents with major depression treated in a health maintenance organization. J. Am. Acad. Child Adolesc. Psychiatry **38:** 1340–1346.

88. BIRMAHER, B., D.A. BRENT, D. KOLKO, *et al.* 2000. Clinical outcome after short-term psychotherapy for adolescents with major depressive disorder. Arch. Gen. Psychiatry **57:** 29–36.

89. KROLL, L., R. HARRINGTON, D. JAYSON, *et al.* 1996. Pilot study of continuation cognitive-behavioral therapy for major depression in adolescent psychiatric patients. J. Am. Acad. Child Adolesc. Psychiatry **35:** 1156–1161.

90. LEWINSOHN, P.M., D.N. KLEIN & J.R. SEELEY. 1995. Bipolar disorders in a community sample of older adolescents: prevalence, phenomenology, comorbidity and course. J. Am. Acad. Child Adolesc. Psychiatry **34:** 454–463.

91. AXELSON, D.A., B. BIRMAHER, R.E. ULLOA, *et al.* 1998. The clinical presentation of pediatric bipolar disorder. Presented at the Annual Meeting of the American Academy of Child and Adolescent Psychiatry. Los Angeles, CA.

92. STROBER, M., W. MORRELL, J. BURROUGHS, *et al.* 1988. A family study of bipolar I disorder in adolescence. Early onset of symptoms linked to

increased familial loading and lithium resistance. J. Affect. Disorders **15:** 255–268.

93. GELLER, B., COOPER, T.B., SUN, K., *et al.* 1998. Double-blind and placebo-controlled study of lithium for adolescent bipolar disorders with secondary substance dependency. J. Am. Acad. Child Adolesc. Psychiatry **37:** 171–178.

94. MIKLOWITZ, D.J. & M.J. GOLDSTEIN. 1997. Bipolar Disorder: A Family-Focused Treatment Approach. The Guilford Press. New York.

95. TONDO, L., R.J. BALDESSARINI, J. HENNEN, *et al.* 1998. Lithium treatment and risk of suicidal behavior in bipolar disorder patients. J. Clin. Psychiatry **59:** 405–414.

96. BECK, A.T., A.J. RUSH, B.F. SHAW & G. EMERY. 1979. Cognitive Therapy of Depression. The Guilford Press. New York.

97. SIMONS, A.D., S.L. GARFIELD & G.E. MURPHY. 1984. The process of change in cognitive therapy and pharmacotherapy for depression: changes in mood and cognition. Arch. Gen. Psychiatry **41:** 45–51.

98. SHURE, M.B. & G. SPIVACK. 1988. Interpersonal cognitive problem solving. *In* 14 Ounces of Prevention: A Casebook for Practitioners. R.H. Price, E.L. Cowen, R.P. Lorion & J. Ramos-McKay, eds. :69–82. American Psychological Association. Washington, DC.

99. MILLER, A.L., J.H. RATHUS, M.M. LINEHAN, *et al.* 1997. Dialectical behavior therapy adapted for suicidal adolescents. J. Pract. Psychiatry Behav. Health **3:** 86.

100. BRENT, D.A., K. POLING, B. MCKAIN & M. BAUGHER. 1993. A psychoeducational program for families of affectively ill children and adolescents. J. Am. Acad. Child Adolesc. Psychiatry **32:** 770–774.

101. POLING, K. 1997. Living with depression: a survival manual for families. 3rd Ed. University of Pittsburgh, Services for Teens at Risk. Pittsburgh, PA.

102. HENGGELER, S.W. & C.M. BORDUIN. 1990. Treatment of delinquent behavior. *In* Family Therapy and Beyond: A Multisystemic Approach to Treating the Behavior Problems of Children and Adolescents. S.W. Henggeler & C.M. Borduin, eds. :219-245. Brooks/Cole Publishing Co. Pacific Grove, CA.

103. BIFULCO, A., G.W. BROWN & Z. ADLER. 1991. Early sexual abuse and clinical depression in adult life. Brit. J. Psychiatry **159:** 115–122.

104. ROMANS, S.E., J.L. MARTIN, J.C. ANDERSON, *et al.* 1995. Sexual abuse in childhood and deliberate self-harm. Am. J. Psychiatry **152:** 1336–1342.

105. WARNER, V., M.M. WEISSMAN, M. FENDRICH, *et al.* 1992. The course of major depression in the offspring of depressed parents: incidence, recurrence and recovery. Arch. Gen. Psychiatry **49:** 795–801.

106. WEISSMAN, M.M., M. FENDRICH, V. WARNER & P. WICKRAMARATNE. 1992. Incidence of psychiatric disorder in offspring at high and low risk for depression. J. Am. Acad. Child Adolesc. Psychiatry **31:** 640–648.

DISCUSSION

DAVID SHAFFER (*Chairman*): Often adolescents recant their suicidality in the emergency room. Do you discount the recantation and hospitalize anyway?

DAVID A. BRENT: Yes. I like that word "recantation." It does have a prosecutorial ring to it. Often there is a problem, and that's why a child will engage in serious suicidal behavior and then say, "But that was a mistake and I'm not doing that now." That's why you have to look at what they have actually done. If someone is engaged in serious suicidal behavior of at least moderate intent, with some degree of planning and so on, I don't really care what they are saying now. It may very well be true that at that moment the patient really is not suicidal. But you have to look at what's going to be happening over the next couple of weeks. Basically you have to estimate what level of care to recommend on the basis of where they are going to be at their worst point. If someone is engaged in very suicidal behavior, you must assume that the suicidal crisis is not over and recommend a more restrictive level of care.

SHAFFER: What caveats do you have in treating complex borderline traits, cluster B personality, substance abuse, mood disorders, and the parasuicidal patient who isn't amenable to participate in his treatment?

BRENT: That is the problem. Let's start with those kids who are willing to participate in treatment because they are hard enough. The first issue is that of a mismatch in general between the duration of treatment in research and what these people really need. The exception is Marsha Linehan's work; she has a very intensive treatment program that lasts a year. I think it's two or three sessions a week. When you are dealing with a chronic condition in which the person needs to some degree to be reparented and needs many skills that, by their age, they should have had, treatment should be much more intense than traditionally done and it has to be multimodal. In our experience we're dealing with group treatment, aftercare, as well as individual treatment and pharmacotherapy. When you are talking about kids who are unwilling to engage in treatment, this is a parent's nightmare. Our society – I wouldn't necessarily say it errs on the side – tends to go on the side of protection of individual liberty, something that has made this country great. At the same time, a parent of a schizophrenic or a severe borderline personality knows that what that means is that you can't force them to get the treatment they need. I don't really have any wisdom about that except that often there is another person in that person's life who may have more influence on them than the parent. It could be a religious figure, a friend, or a relative. You have to mobilize the whole social network to try and get that person help. Having said that, I've taken care of many kids who we have not been successful in getting them to treatment. You can also use more assertive treatment, where you go into the home and work with the family. Having said that, I think this group is extremely difficult to reach if they don't want to be engaged in treatment.

SHAFFER: How far do you go to try to have patients comply with follow-up? How many letters, phone calls, and how many no-shows do you allow?

BRENT: Good question. I think that when you feel you are harassing some-one, it is probably time to stop. You have to balance the risk to the individual and their previous pattern of behavior with the fact that you don't want to poison their attitude towards mental health treatment in the future. I would say that if a kid doesn't show up, we'll probably call two or three times and leave messages. If we have been involved with the primary care physician or the school, we will contact them to let them know that the kid is not coming in. If that doesn't work, we will send a letter and ask them to call us. If we don't hear from them then, we will send a letter and indicate we're closing the case.

SHAFFER: You don't do a home visit?

BRENT: We would do a home visit if we had done that before, but it feels a bit weird to go to somebody's house if we haven't done so before.

SHAFFER: A very important consideration is what you know about the mental state of the parent, their competence, and everything else. It's a very live question for me, because recently in our clinic we had a death of a teenage girl who had been referred because of suicidal ideation and a suicide attempt. She did very well with treatment, and she stopped coming to the clinic, but her mother had schizophrenia and the girl didn't come for 3 or 4 months. There were the usual things in the letter asking for numerous appointments, telephone calls, and so on, but she didn't comply. In retrospect, we should have taken more account of the mother's mental state and probably should have pursued the child with a home visit, given the circumstances.

Dr. Brent, please comment on the teenager who has learned to use suicidal threats to avoid a situation. How do we differentiate these from a suicidal threat that could be lethal; for example, if I threaten suicide, I'll be hospitalized and I won't have to stay home in the midst of all this conflict.

BRENT: When you first encounter an individual, you may not be able to determine their intent. They may convey that their intent is higher and more towards wanting to die than it really is, because that is more socially acceptable and also people learn quickly that it gets your attention. But you don't lose much at the beginning in erring on the side of being more cautious and assuming that the suicidal behavior is more life threatening than it may be. Then as you get to know the kid and the family, you have a different situation on your hands. Clearly what you need to do is to target the things that they are avoiding. In other words, find out why they are afraid to go to school or what the conflict is. They may have an anxiety disorder and they don't want to go to school, or they may have a conduct disorder and they are truant. You need to address those issues rather than focusing on suicidality. For kids who are chronically suicidal and make a lot of suicidal threats, you sometimes do need to sift out how to deal with this rather than a single or fairly isolated suicidal threat. Often that involves the emergency room, the inpatient unit, all the systems of care that may be involved, and a different sort of treatment plan. For these kids, I make myself one of the first points of call because otherwise they're going to meet someone else, perhaps a resident in the ER, who doesn't know this kid and obviously by behaving responsibly will perceive the threat to be different than it is. So for those kids I will leave instructions at the ER that they can contact me.

SHAFFER: One final question. Is there a place for insight-oriented therapy in adolescents with less serious suicide attempts and with sufficient ego strength?

BRENT: Yes.

Suicide in Elders

YEATES CONWELL AND PAUL R. DUBERSTEIN

University of Rochester Medical Center, Center for the Study and Prevention of Suicide, Rochester, New York 14642-8409, USA

ABSTRACT: Older persons in the United States are at higher risk for suicide than any other segment of the population. The epidemiology and risk factors for suicide in later life and the most promising approaches to its prevention are reviewed. Available data suggest that psychiatric and physical illnesses, functional impairment, personality traits of neuroticism and low openness to experience, and social isolation are important correlates of late-life suicide. Affective illness is the risk factor with the strongest association. As treatable conditions in most cases, mood disorders are critical targets for preventive interventions. Because 70% of older adults who committed suicide saw their primary care provider within 30 days of death, the primary care setting is an important venue for intervention. Mood disorders are common in primary care practice, but often go undiagnosed and inadequately treated. One important approach to late-life suicide prevention, therefore, is to optimize the ability of primary care providers to diagnose and treat late-life mood disorders and suicidality effectively. Other elders at high risk have no active relationship to primary care. Strategies designed to identify this group and provide them with preventive services through outreach to the community have shown promise as late-life suicide prevention measures as well.

KEYWORDS: Elders, suicide in; Epidemiology; Mood disorders; Risk factors for suicide; Suicide prevention

INTRODUCTION

Older adults are at a higher risk for suicide than are any other segments of the population. This fact may reflect the special challenges that the characteristics of suicidal behavior among older people pose for prevention efforts. Treatment of elders in a suicidal crisis, while necessary to save lives, is an insufficient answer to the significant public health problem of suicide among older adults. Instead, treatment and prevention must take a broader approach, addressing recognition and effective intervention at the earliest possible points in the causal sequence that leads to suicide in an older person.

Address for correspondence: Yeates Conwell, M.D., University of Rochester Medical Center, 300 Crittenden Blvd., Rochester, NY 14642-8409. Voice: 716-275-6739; fax: 716-273-1082.
yeates_conwell@urjc.rochester.edu

TABLE 1. Guidelines for disease prevention

#1	The goals of prevention must be based on an analysis of what beneficial outcome is most meaningful to the individual and to society.
#2	The potential benefit of a preventive measure is proportional to: (a) the *prevalence of the disease* ; (b) the *severity of the morbidity* associated with it.
#3	To be effective in older persons, preventive care must take into account the multiple dimensions that impact on their health: (a) biological, (b) psychological, and (c) social.
#4	The effectiveness of a prevention measure depends on: (a) identification of the risk factors characteristic of the individual or group, (b) the strength of the causal relationship between the risk factor and the disease, and (c) the alterability of the causal (risk) factor.

This review considers the epidemiology and risk factors for suicide in later life and their implications for the design of preventive intervention strategies. The discussion focuses on completed rather than attempted suicide, as it is the former that can best lead to our understanding of individuals at greatest risk. Attempted suicide is a far less frequent behavior and a less common cause of morbidity among older than younger adults. Conclusions drawn from studies of attempted suicide may not pertain to completed suicide in later life. Finally, the discussion will be structured by a consideration of four fundamental guidelines for disease prevention (TABLE 1).[1]

GUIDELINES

Guideline 1. The goals of prevention must be based on analysis of what beneficial outcome is most meaningful to the individual and to society.

Suicide among the elderly has received relatively less attention in the scientific literature than has suicide in adolescents and younger adults. A recent search of Medline (1966–1999) revealed almost 10,000 articles that listed suicide as a focus; 31.4% concerned adolescents, 21.4% concerned subjects aged 65 years and over, and 3.1% concerned subjects aged 80 and over. This phenomenon may reflect appropriate concern over substantial increases in suicide rates among adolescents and young adults in the latter half of this century[2] or the added tragedy of potential years of life lost, which is so much greater with the suicide of a younger person. It may also reflect negative perceptions and attitudes towards aging and the aged in our culture. Attitudinal research has demonstrated that suicide is regarded as more acceptable for an

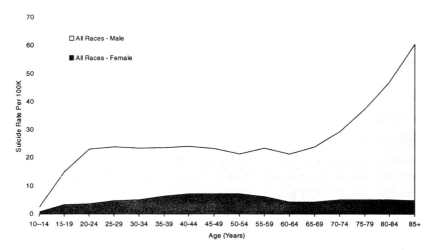

FIGURE 1. U.S. suicide rates by age and gender, 1997 (from Hoyert *et al.*[4]).

older than a younger person.[3] An increasingly larger proportion of the population has approved of physician-assisted suicide in recent serial polls, an issue that is more pertinent to elders than to young adults because of their far greater prevalence of debilitating and terminal medical conditions. The debate goes on concerning the ethics of self-determined death, under what circumstances and for whom it may be acceptable. It remains to be determined, therefore, what importance our society will place on the recognition and treatment of suicidal elders and hence the resources devoted to preventing suicide in this age group.

Guideline 2. *The potential benefit of a preventive measure is proportional to both the prevalence of the disease and the severity of the morbidity associated with it.*

How large a problem is suicide among older people in the United States? In 1997, the last year for which figures are available, there were 5,728 deaths among persons aged 65 years and over.[4] Whereas the elderly constituted 12.7% of the population, they committed 18.8% of all suicides. FIGURE 1 indicates that the substantial increased risk for suicide among older people in this country is specific to men. The suicide rate of 60/100,000 among men aged 85 and over is over five times the nation's age-adjusted rate. This distinctive interaction of age and gender is relatively unique to the United States, however. Pearson and Conwell,[5] for example, noted the age groups of men and women that were at highest risk for suicide in 36 countries reporting such statistics to the World Health Organization between 1988 and 1991. Among men, those aged 75 and over had the highest rates in 35 of the 36 reporting countries. Among women, 25 of 36 countries reported highest rates in the oldest age group (age >75 years) as well. Only the United States and 10 other countries reported peak rates for women at any other stage of life, all between the ages of 45 and 74.

Not only are older people at greater risk for suicide than are younger adults, they are the fastest growing segment of the U.S. population. This trend will continue as the large postwar "baby boom" generation enters later adulthood. Furthermore, cohort studies demonstrated that baby boomers have carried higher suicide rates through each life stage than have earlier or subsequent birth cohorts.[6,7] These demographic shifts suggest the likelihood of substantial increases in coming decades of suicide among older people. Early indication of that trend may be reflected in recent data from the Centers for Disease Control and Prevention, which reported that suicide rates rose 9% between 1980 and 1992 for Americans aged 65 years and over.[8] The change was most marked for men and women in the 80–84-year age range, for whom suicide rates rose 35 and 36%, respectively.

In addition to the prevalence of a disease, Guideline 2 links the potential benefit of prevention efforts to the severity of the morbidity associated with it. Data indicate that suicidal behavior among older people is more highly lethal than that in other age groups. Studies estimate that there may be as many as 200 suicide attempts for each completed suicide among adolescents and young adults.[9] The ratio in the general population has been estimated to be between 10 and 20:1, whereas among older people there may be only four attempts per completed suicide.[10] These differences are accounted for by several factors. In general, older adults have more physical illness burden and less resilience than do younger people; therefore, any self-injurious act is more likely to result in death. Second, older adults are more likely to live alone than are adolescents and younger adults, and therefore their self-destructive acts are less likely to be discovered in time for them to be saved. Finally, the high ratio of completed to attempted suicides in late life results from a greater intent to die among suicidal older people. Merrill and Owens[11] found greater suicidal intent among older than younger people admitted to the hospital after an overdose, and Frierson[12] noted greater planning of the act among older than younger persons who attempted suicide. Among people who committed suicide, studies demonstrated that older victims used more potentially lethal methods,[13] gave fewer warnings to others of their suicidal intentions,[14,15] and were more planning and determined in their self-destruction than were younger victims.[15]

These findings have important implications for intervention and treatment strategies. From a clinical perspective, they indicate the need for immediate, aggressive interventions when suicide risk is identified in an older person—

detailed evaluation, mobilization of resources to guarantee safety, and the institution of diagnosis-specific therapy. From a public health perspective, however, these findings suggest that preventive interventions targeting older individuals already in a suicidal crisis will have limited impact. Because the suicidal behavior of older adults is more planned and deliberate, the likelihood of successful intervention after the initiation of the suicidal behavior is relatively small. Additional efforts, therefore, must be targeted at identification and treatment of conditions predisposing to the development of the suicidal state.

Guideline 3. *To be effective in older persons, preventive care must take into account the multiple dimensions—biological, psychological, and social— that impact on their health.*

Suicide among older people as portrayed in the media is often oversimplified. An older person, for example, may be determined to have taken his life because of grief or physical decline; yet only a small proportion of bereaved or physically ill elders commit suicide. This complexity was captured well by Havens,[16] who described suicide as "the final common pathway of diverse circumstances, of an interdependent network rather than an isolated cause, a knot of circumstances tightening around a single time and place." FIGURE 2 depicts the interactive nature of suicide risk factors as overlapping domains, the weighting and interaction of which determine the individual's vulnerability.[17] From the clinical perspective, accurate assessment of the risk for suicide carried by any individual hinges on an appreciation of promoting and protective influences in each domain. From the public health perspective, the model suggests numerous potential nodes for preventive intervention. As no single factor is universally causal, no single intervention will prevent all suicide deaths. As each death can be understood to result from an interdependent network of factors, numerous opportunities may exist at which to intervene to change the outcome. The multi-determination of suicide presents great challenges, but it also offers hope for its prevention.[18]

Guideline 4. *The effectiveness of a preventive measure depends on the (a) identification of the risk factors characteristic of the individual or group, (b) strength of the causal relationship between the risk factor and the disease, and (c) alterability of the causal (risk) factor.*

In this next section we consider the available evidence base for risk factors for suicide among older adults in each of the domains depicted in FIGURE 2 and whether they are alterable. We then consider the approaches to suicide prevention that appear to hold most promise for decreasing suicide rates in later life.

Social Factors. Social isolation has been associated with suicide among older adults, although the lack of carefully controlled studies prevents its des-

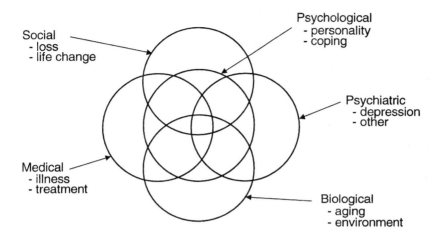

FIGURE 2. Domains of suicide risk in later life (adapted from Blumenthal & Kupfer[17]).

ignation as a risk factor. Barraclough[19] reported in 1971 that 50% of elderly suicide victims lived alone compared with only 20% of all older people in the communities from which they were drawn. He concluded that suicide in this age group was more highly correlated with living alone than with any other social variable. Other investigators have reported in uncontrolled studies that from 19–60% of older suicides were living alone at the time of death.[14,20–23] Studies have also shown no difference between younger and older suicide victims in the amount of social contacts prior to death.[14,24] Luscomb and colleagues[25] found that elderly psychiatric patients who had attempted suicide experienced more stressful life events prior to their self-destructive acts than did nonsuicidal patient controls. No such difference was evident between younger persons who attempted suicide and controls, however. Our group demonstrated that elders who committed suicide had a different profile of stressful life circumstances preceding the act from that of younger victims,[20] a pattern confirmed by analyses of data from the San Diego Suicide Study.[26] Both reports found that in addition to physical illness, interpersonal loss through death was significantly more common in elderly victims than in younger ones, whereas legal and financial problems were more common in young adult and middle-age suicide victims.

McMahon and Pugh[27] demonstrated that suicide risk is elevated during the first 4 years of widowhood. Using psychological autopsy data, Duberstein and colleagues[28] found significant associations between suicide within 4 years of spousal loss and a history of psychiatric treatment, early life loss/ separation, and substance abuse. Spousal bereavement increases the likelihood of physician visits.[29,30] As well, elderly suicide victims are likely to have visited a primary care provider in the last days and weeks of life.[31] Primary care clinicians, therefore, should vigilantly monitor for suicide risk in their recently widowed patients, especially those with histories of mental illness, substance abuse, and early life loss.

Biological Risk Factors. A mounting body of compelling evidence supports the relationship between suicide and altered central neurochemical functions. Serotonergic systems have been most extensively investigated.[32] Moreover, there is intriguing evidence for a heritable component to suicide risk from twin and adoption studies.[33] The extent to which these factors pertain to suicide in older people is unclear, as the number of elderly subjects included has been small. Just as a family history of affective illness is less likely with older age of onset of depressive disorder,[34] it is less likely that genetic predisposition plays a role as a risk factor in suicide at later ages. Aging-related changes, however, could contribute. Relatively little information is available as yet about either normal aging of neurochemical systems or differences in the neurobiological profile of younger and older victims.[35] Additional research is necessary before biological markers can be identified and applied in a clinically useful manner.

Psychological Factors. A number of uncontrolled studies have related suicide in later life to specific personality traits. They include timidity and shy seclusiveness,[36] a tendency to hypochondriasis, hostility, and a rigid, fiercely independent style.[36,37] One study used a standardized measure of personality traits that has been validated for use both in older adults and by informants[38] in the study of elderly completed suicides. Duberstein and colleagues[39] showed that suicide victims over 50 years of age were distinguished from age-matched controls by higher levels of neuroticism and lower levels of "openness to experience" (OTE). Individuals high in neuroticism will be anxious, angry, sad, fearful, and self-conscious. Individuals with low OTE characteristics prefer to follow a familiar routine, have a constricted range of intellectual interests, and have relatively blunted affective and hedonic responses to their environment. The combination of these qualities is indeed reminiscent of many older adults whose suicides we have investigated by the psychological autopsy method. Duberstein and colleagues[40] have examined these same qualities among elderly depressed inpatients, in which low OTE was associated with the *absence of suicidal ideation*. These findings can be reconciled by the proposal that older adults with depression and low OTE are at increased risk for completed suicide, because they are less likely to feel, or report feeling, suicidal. Their affective muting may make suicide risk more difficult to detect.

If personality traits were unmodifiable, they would have less utility as identifiable risk factors for suicide. However, personality traits have been associated with responsiveness to a wide range of psychopharmacologic[41] and psychotherapeutic[42] treatments. As well, personality traits are likely to moderate the effects of interventions on suicidal outcomes in older people, reinforcing the need to consider them in the design of preventive interventions.

Psychiatric Illness. Psychological autopsy studies of older suicides conducted in Great Britain, the United States, and Finland document that from 71–90% of victims had diagnosable major psychiatric disorders.[14,19,43–46] Affective illness, principally unipolar major depression, was present in 54–87% of cases, whereas alcohol and other drug use disorders were present in 3–42%. The diagnosis of dementia is not often made in retrospective studies of suicide, despite its prevalence in community and institutionalized populations of elders. Schizophrenia, other nonaffective psychoses, and anxiety disorders appear to play a relatively small role in later life suicide, although few studies are available that include samples to control for the base rate of these disorders in nonsuicidal elders. Four case control psychological autopsy studies of suicide in older adults are currently in progress (Great Britain, New Zealand, Sweden, and western New York State); a far richer evidence base with which to quantify the risk associated with different psychiatric illnesses in older people will be available soon.

Physical Illness and Functional Impairment. Harris and Barraclough[47] noted four reasons that one might expect an association between physical illness and suicide: (1) Psychiatric illnesses that predispose to suicide may be independently associated with high levels of medical illness, for example, through self-neglect by depressive persons or the toxic effects of chronic substance abuse. (2) Psychiatric illness leading to suicide may be due to the medical illness, for example, brain metastases of cancer or the affective and cognitive sequelae of thyroid disease. (3) Disability or disfigurement resulting from a medical illness may lead to social withdrawal and isolation, predisposing to depression and other psychiatric illnesses. (4) Individuals facing terminal illnesses may choose to preempt the frightening course and inevitable outcome. In a review of 235 published reports, they found sufficient evidence to conclude that there is increased mortality from suicide associated with HIV disease and AIDS, Huntington's disease, malignant neoplasms, multiple sclerosis, peptic ulcer disease, renal disease, spinal cord injuries, and systemic lupus erythematosus. Evidence supporting the risk associated with epilepsy, particularly with temporal lobe foci, is also strong.[48]

In addition to specific illnesses, data suggest a complex association between suicide, physical illness burden, and functional impairment. We compared the physical health and functional status of 42 suicides aged 60 years and over, who saw a primary care provider within 30 days of death with 196 age-matched patients from primary care practices.[49] Suicides had significantly more affective illness, physical illness burden, and functional limitations

TABLE 2. Last appointment with a primary care provider by older adult suicides

Study	Age (yr)	n	Percent seen within: 1 wk	1 mo
Miller (1976)[52]	≥ 60	30	33	77
Barraclough (1971)[53]	≥ 65	30	47	70
Clark (1991)[43]	≥ 65	54	41	70
Cattell & Jolley (1995)[21]	≥ 65	100	19	43
Conwell et al (1994)[54]	55–74	24	25	42
	75+	20	35	75

than did controls. However, when only depressive subjects and controls were considered, physical health measures no longer distinguished the group. The findings indicated that the risk for suicide in older persons with physical illness is mediated by associated affective psychopathology. This interpretation is consistent with the findings of Chochinov and colleagues[50] and Brown and colleagues[51] that suicidal ideation among seriously ill people is rare in the absence of clinically significant mood disturbance.

IMPLICATIONS FOR PREVENTION AND TREATMENT

Suicide Prevention in Primary Care. TABLE 2 lists studies of older adults who committed suicide for whom information was available concerning their most recent visit to a primary care provider (PCP).[21,43,52–54] Up to 76% saw a PCP within 30 days of death, as many as 49% within 1 week of their suicide. This observation is critical for prevention, as it suggests a means for access for elders in, or immediately preceding, the development of the suicidal state. Depression is the most common psychopathology associated with suicide in older people. It may mediate the relationship between physical illness and suicide. Like bereavement, depression is associated with increased utilization of primary care services. Affective illness in older adults is a treatable condition, with 60–80% expected to respond to standard pharmacologic and psychosocial therapies, or their combination. Therefore, preventive interventions designed to increase the recognition and effective treatment of depression in primary care settings appear most consistent with Prevention Guideline 4.

Many studies have demonstrated that PCPs have difficulty recognizing treatable depression in their patients. PCPs typically spend less time with older than younger patients,[55] have insufficient knowledge regarding the symptoms and management of depression, often fail to elicit mood or cognitive symptoms,[56] and all too frequently assume that depression is a "natural" consequence of aging and related stressors.[57] The publication of depression practice guidelines has had relatively little impact on PCP practice. Furthermore, depressive symptoms may be more obscure and difficult to elicit than among younger patients. To address these problems, the routine use of a well-validated screening instrument for depression in primary care elders (e.g., the Geriatric Depression Scale and the Center for Epidemiologic Studies—Depression Scale) has been advocated.[58] In addition, greater emphasis should be placed in undergraduate, graduate, and continuing medical education, as well as in the training of nurses, physicians' assistants, and office staff on the recognition of depressive disorders and suicidal states in older people.

Increased recognition of at-risk individuals through improved screening and diagnostic assessment must be coupled with innovative, effective treatment strategies. Because older people rarely utilize mental health services, active collaborations between psychiatry and primary care in medical settings may yield optimal outcomes. Schulberg and colleagues[59] tested a collaborative care model in which mental health professionals joined the primary care provider to treat depressed patients in the primary care office. Young adult and middle-aged depressive subjects treated with either nortriptyline or interpersonal psychotherapy had significantly better outcomes than did patients who received care as usual. Katon and colleagues[60] provided a multimodal treatment to primary care depressives that included patient and physician education, cognitive behavioral therapy delivered by psychologists, antidepressant therapy prescribed by physicians, and regular ongoing consultation between the two disciplines. Patients with major depression showed significant improvement in adherence to medications, satisfaction with care, and reduction of depressive symptoms, whereas patients with minor depression showed less improvement. Neither study focused specifically on older persons, and outcomes of suicidal subjects could not be examined. Indeed, it is rare, because of liability concerns, that people with active suicidal states are included in clinical trials.

One influential study has tested the hypothesis that improved recognition and treatment of depression reduces suicide rates. Rutz and colleagues[61] have reported the results of an educational intervention conducted on the Swedish island of Götland in which every primary care provider attended an educational program designed to improve his or her knowledge of detection and treatment of depression. In the 2 years following the intervention, suicide rates on the island dropped significantly in comparison to contemporary rates in other parts of Sweden as well as to historical rates on the island of Götland before the educational program took place. In addition, the intervention was temporally associated with reduced sick leave for depressive disorders, decreased inpatient care days for depression, and increased antidepressant prescriptions. However, the effect of the intervention was short lived; its principal influence was on women with depression rather than on men; and the study's relatively small sample size and limited time frame have raised concerns that its results were an artifact of temporal fluctuations in suicide rates.[62,63] Stimulated by the results of the Götland study and the early success of collaborative care models, investigators are currently attempting to replicate and extend these findings.

Community Outreach. The 30% or more of elderly suicides who did not see a PCP in the last days or weeks of life may represent a high risk group that is distinct from those actively in primary care treatment. An important complementary approach to reducing suicide morbidity and mortality in later life hinges on community outreach. Attempts to evaluate four such programs have been described in the literature thus far.

The Tele-Help/Tele-Check system serves elderly residents of Padua, Italy who are referred by Social Service and other providers. It equips users with a portable alarm system and offers active contacts by trained staff who provide information, support, and rapid intervention in medical and psychological emergencies. DeLeo and colleagues[64] report significantly fewer suicides among the over 12,000 elderly subjects enrolled in the program from 1988 through 1991 compared with the number that would have been expected for the general population of that region.

Link-Plus is another telephone-based service designed to provide multidimensional assessment, service arrangement, and supportive therapy for at-risk elders. Its clients are referred from a crisis hotline and by family members, friends, and professionals in the St. Louis area. Morrow-Howell and colleagues[65] reported on a randomized comparison of 30 enrolled participants with 31 wait list controls. After 4 months of Link-Plus involvement, intervention subjects showed significantly greater social contact and a strong trend towards lower depressive symptoms.

A third program has been described by the Center for Elderly Suicide Prevention of San Francisco, California. It includes a 24-hour telephone line for emotional support, crisis intervention, information and referral services for older adults, and an outreach program to provide counseling via scheduled telephone calls and home visits to elders at risk. Fiske and Arbore[66] compared changes in depression, hopelessness, and life satisfaction over 1 year between 116 program participants and 70 elderly controls recruited from local senior centers. Relative to controls, program clients had significantly reduced hopelessness scores; there were no significant changes in depressive symptoms or life satisfaction.

Finally, the Spokane Mental Health Center Elder Services Division has described a comprehensive system of outreach known as the Gatekeeper model, coupled with a comprehensive clinical case management system.[67] The Gate-keeper model relies on nontraditional community referral sources to identify, during the course of their routine business, older individuals at risk for self-harm. Meter readers, utility workers, bank personnel, apartment and mobile home managers, postal carriers, and others likely to observe older people in their homes and the community effectively perform this task with a small amount of education and training. Approximately one-third of the service's referrals were from the gatekeeper mechanism, which tended to identify a more socially isolated, although less physically impaired, population. Gate-keepers were also more likely to refer individuals diagnosed with substance use disorder, bipolar disorder, or schizophrenia than were traditional lines of referral. Elders potentially at risk are then referred to the Clinical Case Man-agement Program, which is equipped to respond with clinical referrals; in-home medical, psychiatric, family, and nutritional assessments; medication management and respite services; and crisis intervention. Program evalua-tions have thus far lacked a control sample with which to measure the benefits to older patients of the Gatekeeper and case management models. Their im-pacts on suicide and other outcomes therefore remain speculative. Prelimi-nary evidence, however, indicates that although the suicide rate of persons aged 60 years and over rose significantly in the state of Washington during the years in which the Gatekeeper program has operated, rates for that age group in Spokane County decreased (R. Raschko, personal communication).

CONCLUSIONS

While considerable information concerning the clinical correlates of sui-cide among older people has accrued, additional preintervention research is needed to help define more precisely the risk factors most strongly associated and alterable. Even as preintervention research continues, however, the ongo-ing loss of senior citizens to suicide demands that preventive interventions be designed and implemented. The recognition and optimal treatment of clinical depressive illness in older people, particularly in primary care settings, must be emphasized. Clinical services should implement routine screening for de-pression among older adults and assure ready access to mental health consul-tation. Mental health providers should develop collaborative relationships with the primary care sector that enable provision of services to older adults in style and settings that the clients find acceptable. Diagnosis and treatment of the associated psychiatric symptoms and disorders of older adults should be aggressively pursued.

At the community level, efforts should be made to educate not only health providers but consumers as well about the risk factors for suicide among old-er adults, its associations with treatable mental illness, and the typical presentations of and treatments available for those illnesses, depression in particular. Such education programs should be coupled with universal interventions designed to reduce the stigma associated with aging and mental health treatment. Outreach to those elders at risk in the community who avoid, or lack access to, medical care is another important element in any comprehensive plan to late-life suicide prevention. The cost effectiveness and reproducibility of these and other strategies informed by preintervention research must be tested in rigorously designed randomized controlled trials. It is especially important that resources be provided to test the effectiveness of existing and newly implemented interventions, so that valid lessons can be learned to guide subsequent efforts.

REFERENCES

1. FRIED, L.P. 1990. Health promotion and disease prevention. *In* Principles of Geriatric Medicine and Gerontology. W.R. Hazzard, R. Andres, E.L. Bierman & J.P. Blass, eds. :192–200. McGraw-Hill, Inc. New York.
2. BRENT, D.A., J.A. PERPER & C.J. ALLMAN. 1987. Alcohol, firearms, and suicide among youth. JAMA **257:** 3369–3372.
3. DELUTY, R.H. 1988. Factors affecting the acceptability of suicide. Omega **19:** 315–326.
4. HOYERT, D.L., K.D. KOCHANEK & S.L. MURPHY. 1999. Deaths: final data from 1997. National Vital Statistics Reports **47**[19]: 1–104.
5. PEARSON, J.L. & Y. CONWELL. 1995. Suicide in late life: challenges and opportunities for research. Introduction. Int. Psychogeriatr. **7:** 131–136.
6. BLAZER, D.G., A.K. BAHN & K.G. MANTON. 1986. Suicide in late life: review and commentary. J. Am. Geriatr. Soc. **34:** 519–525.
7. MANTON, K.G., D.G. BLAZER & M.A. WOODBURY. 1987. Suicide in middle age and later life: sex- and race-specific life table and cohort analyses. J. Gerontol. **42:** 219–227.
8. MMWR. 1996. Suicide among older persons--United States, 1980-1992. Morbid. Mortal. Weekly Rep. **45:** 3–6.
9. FREMOUW, W.J., M. DEPERCZEL & T.E. ELLIS. 1990. Suicide Risk: Assessment and Response Guidelines. Pergamon Press. New York.
10. PARKIN, D. & E. STENGEL. 1965. Incidence of suicidal attempts in an urban community. Br. Med. J. **2:** 133–138.
11. MERRILL, J. & J. OWENS. 1990. Age and attempted suicide. Acta Psychiatr. Scand. **82:** 385–388.
12. FRIERSON, R.L. 1991. Suicide attempts by the old and the very old. Arch. Intern. Med. **151:** 141–144.
13. MCINTOSH, J.L. & J.F. SANTOS. 1985. Methods of suicide by age: sex and race differences among the young and old. Int. J. Aging Human Dev. **22:** 123–139.
14. CARNEY, S.S., C.L. RICH, P.A. BURKE & R.C. FOWLER. 1994. Suicide over 60: the San Diego study. J. Am. Geriatr. Soc. **42:** 174–180.

15. CONWELL, Y., P.R. DUBERSTEIN, C. COX, *et al.* 1998. Age differences in behaviors leading to completed suicide. Am. J. Geriatr. Psychiatry **6:** 122–126.
16. HAVENS, L. 1965. The anatomy of a suicide. N. Engl. J. Med. **272:** 401–406.
17. BLUMENTHAL, S.J. & D.J. KUPFER. 1986. Generalizable treatment strategies for suicidal behavior. Ann. N.Y. Acad. Sci. **487:** 327–340.
18. O'CARROLL, P.W. 1993. Suicide causation: pies, paths, and pointless polemics. Suicide Life Threatening Behav. **23:** 27–36.
19. BARRACLOUGH, B.M. 1971. Suicide in the elderly: recent developments in psychogeriatrics. Br. J. Psychiatry **6** (Spec. Suppl.): 87–97.
20. CONWELL, Y., M. ROTENBERG & E.D. CAINE. 1990. Completed suicide at age 50 and over. J. Am. Geriatr. Soc. **38:** 640–644.
21. CATTELL, G. & D.J. JOLLEY. 1995. One hundred cases of suicide in elderly people. Br. J. Psychiatry **166:** 451–457.
22. YOUNGER, S.C., D.C. CLARK, R. OEHMIG-LINDROTH & R.J. STEIN. 1990. Availability of knowledgeable informants for a psychological autopsy study of suicides committed by elderly people. J. Am. Geriatr. Soc. **38:** 1169–1175.
23. WALSH, D. & P.D. McCARTHY. 1965. Suicide in Dublin's elderly. Acta Psychiatr. Scand. **41:** 227–235.
24. HEIKKINEN, M.E. & J.K. LONNQVIST. 1995. Recent life events in elderly suicide: a nationwide study in Finland. Int. Psychogeriatr. **7:** 287–300.
25. LUSCOMB, R.L., G.A. CLUM & A.T. PATSIOKAS. 1980. Mediating factors in the relationship between life stress and suicide attempting. J. Nerv. Ment. Dis. **168:** 644–650.
26. RICH, C.L., G.M. WARSTADT, R.A. NEMIROFF, *et al.* 1991. Suicide, stressors, and the life cycle [published erratum appears in Am. J. Psychiatry. 1991. **148:** 960]. Am. J. Psychiatry **148:** 524–527.
27. MACMAHON, B. & T.F. PUGH. 1965. Suicide in the widowed. Am. J. Epidemiol. **81:** 23–31.
28. DUBERSTEIN, P.R., Y. CONWELL & C. COX. 1998. Suicide in widowed persons. A psychological autopsy comparison of recently and remotely bereaved older subjects. Am. J. Geriatr. Psychiatry **6:** 328–334.
29. MOR, V., C. McHORNEY & S. SHERWOOD. 1986. Secondary morbidity among the recently bereaved. Am. J. Psychiatry **143:** 158–163.
30. STROEBE, W. & M.S. STROEBE. 1987. Bereavement and Health: The Psychological and Physical Consequences of Partner Loss. Oxford University Press. New York.
31. CONWELL, Y. 1997. Management of suicidal behavior in the elderly. Psychiatr. Clin. North Am. **20:** 667–683.
32. MANN, J.J., C. WATERNAUX, G.L. HAAS & K.M. MALONE. 1999. Toward a clinical model of suicidal behavior in psychiatric patients. Am. J. Psychiatry **156:** 181–189.
33. ROY, A., G. RYLANDER & M. SARCHIAPONE. 1997. Genetic studies of suicidal behavior. Psychiat. Clin. North Am. **20:** 595–611.
34. MENDLEWICZ, J. 1976. The age factor in depressive illness: some genetic considerations. J. Gerontol. **31:** 300–303.
35. CONWELL, Y., W.N. RABY & E.D. CAINE. 1995. Suicide and aging. II: The psychobiological interface. Int. Psychogeriatr. **7:** 165–181.
36. BATCHELOR, I.R.C. & M.B. NAPIER. 1953. Attempted suicide in old age. Br. Med. J. **2:** 1186–1190.

37. CLARK, D.C. 1993. Narcissistic crises of aging and suicidal despair. Suicide Life Threatening Behav. **23:** 21–26.
38. COSTA, P.T. & R.R. MCCRAE. 1992. Revised NEO Personality Inventory and NEO Five Factor Inventory: Professional Manual. PAR. Odessa, FL.
39. DUBERSTEIN, P.R., Y. CONWELL & E.D. CAINE. 1994. Age differences in the personality characteristics of suicide completers: preliminary findings from a psychological autopsy study. Psychiatry **57:** 213–224.
40. DUBERSTEIN, P.R., Y. CONWELL, L. SEIDLITZ, et al. 2000. Personality traits and suicidal behavior and ideation in depressed inpatients 50 years of age and older. J. Gerontol. Psych. Sci. **55:** 18–26.
41. PESELOW, E.D., C.J. ROBINS, M.P. SANFILIPO, et al. 1992. Sociotropy and autonomy: relationship to antidepressant drug treatment response and endogenous-nonendogenous dichotomy. J. Abnormal Psychol. **101:** 479–486.
42. BLATT, S.J., D.M. QUINLAN, P. PILKONIS & M.T. SHEA. 1995. Impact of perfectionism and need for approval on the brief treatment of depression. J. Consult. Clin. Psychol. **63:** 125–132.
43. CLARK, D.C. 1991. Suicide among the elderly. Final report to the AARP Andrus Foundation.
44. CONWELL, Y., K. OLSEN, E.D. CAINE & C. FLANNERY. 1991. Suicide in later life: psychological autopsy findings. Int. Psychogeriatr. **3:** 59–66.
45. CONWELL, Y., P.R. DUBERSTEIN, C. COX, et al. 1996. Relationships of age and axis I diagnoses in victims of completed suicide: a psychological autopsy study. Am. J. Psychiatry **153:** 1001–1008.
46. HENRIKSSON, M.M., M.J. MARTTUNEN, E.T. ISOMETSA, et al. 1995. Mental disorders in elderly suicide. Int. Psychogeriatr. **7:** 275–286.
47. HARRIS, E.C. & B.M. BARRACLOUGH. 1994. Suicide as an outcome for medical disorders. Medicine **73:** 281–296.
48. CONWELL, Y., R. HENDERSON & E.D. CAINE. 1995. Suicide and neurological illness. Neurologist **1:** 284–294.
49. CONWELL, Y., J.M. LYNESS, P.R. DUBERSTEIN, et al. 2000. Completed suicide among older patients in primary care practices: a controlled study. J. Am. Geriatr. Soc. **48:** 23–29.
50. CHOCHINOV, H.M., K.G. WILSON, M. ENNS, et al. 1995. Desire for death in the terminally ill. Am. J. Psychiatry **152:** 1185–1191.
51. BROWN, J.H., P. HENTELEFF, S. BARAKAT & C.J. ROWE. 1986. Is it normal for terminally ill patients to desire death? Am. J. Psychiatry **143:** 208–211.
52. MILLER, M. 1976. Geriatric suicide: the Arizona study. Gerontologist **18:** 488–495.
53. BARRACLOUGH, B. 1971. Suicide in the elderly. Recent developments in psychogeriatrics. Br. J. Psychiatry **6** (special suppl.): 87–97.
54. CONWELL, Y. 1994. Suicide in elderly patients. In Diagnosis and Treatment of Depression in Late Life: Results of the NIH Consensus Development Conference. L.S. Schneider, C.F.I. Reynolds, B.D. Lebowitz & A.J. Friedhoff, eds.: 397–418. American Psychiatric Press, Inc. Washington, DC.
55. KEELER, E.M., D.H. SOLOMON, J.C. BECK, et al. 1982. Effect of patient age on duration of medical encounters with physicians. Med. Care **20:** 1101–1108.
56. SCHULBERG, H.C. & R. MCCLELLAND. 1987. A conceptual model for educating primary care providers in the diagnosis and treatment of depression. Gen. Hosp. Psychiatry **9:** 1–10.

57. CALLAHAN, C.M., N.A. NIENABER, H.C. HENDRIE & W.M. TIERNEY. 1992. Depression of elderly outpatients: primary care physicians' attitudes and practice patterns. J. Gen. Intern. Med. **7:** 26–31.
58. LYNESS, J.M., T.K. NOEL, C. COX, *et al.* 1997. Screening for depression in elderly primary care patients. A comparison of the Center for Epidemiologic Studies-Depression Scale and the Geriatric Depression Scale. Arch. Intern. Med. **157:** 449–454.
59. SCHULBERG, H.C., M.R. BLOCK, M.J. MODONIA, *et al.* 1996. Treating major depression in primary care practice: eight month clinical outcomes. Arch. Gen. Psychiatry **53:** 913–919.
60. KATON, W., P. ROBINSON, M. VON KORFF, *et al.* 1996. A multifaceted intervention to improve treatment of depression in primary care. Arch. Gen. Psychiatry **53:** 924–932.
61. RUTZ, W., L. VON KNORRING & J. WALINDER. 1989. Frequency of suicide on Götland after systematic postgraduate education of general practitioners. Acta Psychiatr. Scand. **80:** 151–154.
62. RUTZ, W., L. VON KNORRRING & J. WALINDER. 1992. Long-term effects of an educational program for general practitioners given by the Swedish Committee for the Prevention and Treatment of Depression. Acta Psychiatr. Scand. **85:** 414–418.
63. RUTZ, W., L. VON KNORRING, H. PIHLGREN, *et al.* 1995. Prevention of male suicides: lessons from Götland study [letter]. Lancet **345:** 524.
64. DE LEO, D., G. CAROLLO & B.M. DELLO. 1995. Lower suicide rates associated with a Tele-Help/Tele-Check service for the elderly at home. Am. J. Psychiatry **152:** 632–634.
65. MORROW-HOWELL, N., S. BECKER-KEMPPAINEN & L. JUDY. 1998. Evaluating an intervention for the elderly at increased risk of suicide. Res. Soc. Work Pract. **8:** 28–46.
66. FISKE, A. & P. ARBORE. 2001. Late life suicide prevention. Omega. In press.
67. FLORIO, E.R., M.S. HENDRYX, J.E. JENSON, *et al.* 1997. A comparison of suicidal and nonsuicidal elders referred to a community mental health center program. Suicide Life Threatening Behav. **27:** 182–193.

DISCUSSION

DAVID SHAFFER (*Chairman*): Do we have information about the frequency of general practitioner contacts in persons who have not been suicidal? What is the base rate?

YEATES CONWELL: In other words?

SHAFFER: Primary practitioner contact, how significant is that? 60% or 70%?

CONWELL: There are as yet no controlled studies. Clearly, behind your question is the observation that older people, just as they are more likely to be sick than younger people, are clearly much heavier users and abusers of primary care services. Therefore, does the fact that they're there—75% of them within 30 days of death—make them different from the general population? It probably does, but we don't have controlled data to establish that finding. The issue, however, is not that going to a primary care provider is a risk factor for suicide; it is that 75% of the people are there. Therefore, if we can find some way to increase recognition, to use that as an opportunity to identify the people at risk, then we have a leg up on the situation.

SHAFFER: Your talk focused primarily on demographics, assessment, and prevention, but very little on treatment. Can you summarize the key issues involved in therapeutic work with the elderly and how it differs from work with a younger population of suicidal individuals?

CONWELL: The bottom line may be that it doesn't differ substantially in approach from that we would take or the outcomes we would expect in middle-aged adults. That is, when we recognize and treat depression in an older person, we ought to expect the same success in terms of remission as in treatment of a younger person. The approaches are the same. For depression we would use either psychotherapy, pharmacotherapy, or a combination of the two. There are good data to show the effectiveness of a variety of psychotherapeutic approaches, interpersonal therapy and cognitive behavioral therapy for depression in older adults have been demonstrated effective. In the use of standard antidepressants the same caveats apply. Tricyclics are somewhat more dangerous and difficult to use in older people than are SSRIs and other antidepressant agents; ECT is an effective intervention. Psychotic features also need to be treated very aggressively with antipsychotic medications or ECT. The special issues really involve the context of that treatment, that is, older people don't go to mental health care settings in any great measure. It's much more important that we find ways within the context of primary care, for example, to diagnose and treat. That is the notion of collaborative care. Instead of expecting that depressed older person to come to the mental health care sector, we need to find ways to reach out to them in the community and in primary care settings where they are going to be much more likely to accept what treatment we have to offer.

SHAFFER: Dr. Conwell, can you elaborate on the TeleHelp/TeleCheck service for the elderly that was used in Italy?

CONWELL: This model has been replicated in many different cases in the United States as well. I offer the TeleHelp/TeleCheck example because it has somewhat better evaluation built into it, that is, more numbers by which we can judge whether or not it is having an effect on suicide rates. But specifically in that example, what they do is take referrals from social services, primary care providers, and families as well; screen older adults for vulnerability and need based on both physical and psychological assessment; equip them in their homes with a series of remote speaker devices and a panic button; and institute regular calls through a bank of trained providers, most of whom are social workers, who will contact this individual on a regular basis indefinitely. Another model of that kind is the LinkPlus system in St. Louis. It uses comprehensive assessment to identify individuals and provide services in the home linking the person with other social and physical health services and providing support; there is also a telephone program for peer support as well as professional evaluation. This is done in San Francisco by the Center for Elderly Suicide Prevention. Both of those organizations have preliminary evaluations suggesting, for example, that in controlled trials, hopelessness may decrease over time for elders enrolled in that program, and depressive symptoms may diminish. There is also a very important gatekeeper program in Spokane, Washington where there is a comprehensive effort in the community to train gatekeepers, people who in the routine course of their business day run across older adults and might be able to recognize people at particular risk. These are people such as meter readers, bank tellers, and pharmacists who make referrals to a central agency. In-home evaluations can be conducted and various kinds of support services provided. That, too, has some preliminary indication of effectiveness.

SHAFFER: Do you think that medically ill elderly patients should be permitted a choice about their plans to end life, like Mr. Eastman? That would apply to both psychiatric and medical illness. What do you do when you are asked to evaluate a patient who is requesting physician-assisted suicide? In your opinion, in terminal illness and in considering quality of life, is there any justification for physician-assisted suicide or speeding up the end of life?

CONWELL: Those are complicated and important questions, and clearly there are no answers that we can all agree on. Everyone has their opinion. Without trying to duck the issue, I would take a clinical perspective. My approach is as a geriatrician who sees his job as serving the individual patient and his or her family in trying to identify and ameliorate the source of the pain that is causing them to feel as if they can't go on. That involves a complex diagnostic process. I'm not looking solely for a major depressive disorder, although in most of those circumstances that's what I will find. I want to understand how that person got to that point in life, what their strengths and weaknesses are, and what their support network has to offer. Is there some other way we can help muster resources that. if only for a day or a week, will help that individual decide that they have a tolerable and acceptable option to ending life or having somebody end it. Also to be taken into account are the family's understanding and preferences and a systems-oriented approach to the situation. I wish that there was an easy answer, but it is a very individual set of circumstances for both the provider and the individual patient.

SHAFFER: I'd like to ask Dr. Hendin, who has really thought about this matter an enormous amount, probably more than anyone else, if he will share his views on this important question.

HERBERT HENDIN (*AFSP, New York, NY*): The first question was whether medically ill elderly persons should have some say in decisions regarding their end-of-life care. Clearly, they should and in most instances they do. That involves a variety of decisions such as the right to refuse or withdraw from invasive or painful treatments. The second question was what should you do when a patient requests assisted suicide. Patients who become suicidal in response to serious illness are not as different from other suicidal patients as most people assume. Whether physically ill or not, the wish to die usually reflects a patient's desperation. The physician needs to determine what is making the patient so desperate. That engagement with the patient usually leads to psychological and physical interventions that relieve suffering, so that patients no longer wish to hasten death. That leaves the question of what to do in the small number of cases where this is not possible. Under current medical practice, proper palliative care requires sedating patients so that they feel no pain. Patients often refuse tube feeding or infusions and die painlessly within a few days. Is that an ideal solution? Obviously not, but it is probably better than the problems that arise when assisted suicide is legalized.

Suicide: What is in the Clinician's Mind?

STEVEN P. ROOSE

Department of Clinical Psychiatry, College of Physicians & Surgeons, Columbia University, New York, New York 10032, USA

ABSTRACT: The assessment and treatment of the suicidal patient challenge all clinicians, regardless of training or theoretical orientation, to draw upon their knowledge and judgment to formulate the best treatment plan possible. As great as the influence of demographics, genetics, and psychobiology are, what is in the mind of the clinician, whether it is anxiety, confidence, knowledge, or uncertainty, will determine the fate of the suicidal patient.

KEYWORDS: Countertransference; Psychotherapy; Suicide

INTRODUCTION

When considering treatment of the suicidal patient, it is necessary to go beyond what is in the patient's mind or brain and to consider what is in the mind of the clinician when in the presence of a suicidal patient, more specifically, the conscious and unconscious conflicts that can significantly interfere with diagnosis and treatment. Treatment of a patient with suicidal potential compels the kind of active intervention that is a component of the medical model. However, this can be problematic for and, indeed, stand in juxtaposition to the orientation, technique, and belief system of the clinician who primarily uses a psychodynamic model of the mind.

Ironically, some of the difficulty for the psychodynamic therapist in ongoing treatment of the suicidal patient arises because the therapist often tacitly adopts a part of the medical model, that is, he feels responsible for what happens to the patient, but may not accept other important components, specifically, authority and a recognition that we do not save all severely ill patients whatever the disease process. Psychodynamic therapists may often consider the suicide of a patient as a personal failure and experience shame in front of their colleagues. However, given their training, dynamic clinicians are especially aware of countertransference obstacles and can successfully negotiate them.

Address for correspondence: Steven P. Roose, M.D., Department of Clinical Psychiatry, New York State Psychiatric Institute, Unit 98, 1051 Riverside Dr., New York, NY 10032.

The assessment and treatment of the suicidal patient challenge clinicians to draw upon their knowledge and judgment to formulate the best treatment plan possible. As great as the influence of demographics, genetics, and psychobiology are, what is in the mind of the clinician, whether it is anxiety, confidence, knowledge, or uncertainty, will also determine the fate of the suicidal patient.

CLINICAL PRESENTATIONS: THE NEW EVALUATIONS

Two clinical situations and the different approaches they require are presented. A problem arises when clinicians do not have flexibility with respect to theory and technique to adapt to the clinical situation. The clinician's flexibility is restricted if there is an allegiance to a specific model of the mind, which is invariably connected to the perpetuation of a mind/body dichotomy.

The first situation occurs when the clinician is faced with a new evaluation of a patient, whether it is in the emergency room or a private office, or even perhaps with the presentation of new symptoms in a patient already in treatment. Considering a patient with delusional depression, a depressive subtype that is associated with an increased risk of suicide, will best illuminate the issues.[1] Given that an appropriate history and mental status report are completed, the clinician will most often make the diagnosis of delusional depression. The problem is that this diagnosis compels intervention, and the scope of the intervention is great. Frequently hospitalization is required, but even hospitalization is not sufficient protection, as is demonstrated by studies on suicide in hospitalized patients.[1] A search is necessary to make sure that there are no potentially dangerous instruments, and restriction of movement and constant observation must also be set in place. This series of interventions, which constitute a significant invasion of privacy, although necessary to prevent suicide, must often be done without the patient's consent or even against the express wishes of the patient.

In this situation, diagnosis and appropriate intervention will be facilitated mostly by the adoption of the medical model; this model organizes the information and attenuates internal conflicts, thereby helping the clinician make the decisions that will most effectively help the patient. Medically trained clinicians have experience with this model. For example, a patient with an acute myocardial infarction arriving in the emergency room will be stripped of his clothes, may be intubated, may receive a central line, and, if necessary, be given electroshock to normalize ventricular fibrillation. These procedures are often done without the express consent of the patient; indeed, the patient's medical condition may leave him or her unable to give consent. Granted, the situation is more complex if the patient explicitly denies consent for these interventions. However, the clinician would not necessarily think of these interventions as an invasion of privacy even if the patient does not agree. If the patient is believed to have an illness that compromises his capacity to consent, for example, uremia or head trauma, the clinician will proceed to do what he determines is medically necessary with or without the patient's express consent or even against the patient's wishes.

The medical model postulates that there is a direct relation between diagnosis and treatment and assumes the necessity of an authoritarian figure; the physician assumes the authority to make decisions for the patient based on the convictions that their decisions are (1) benevolent, that is, in the best interests of the patient and (2) not arbitrary, that is, based on knowledge. The medical model compels the physician to adopt a benevolent, paternalistic role. The model assuages the natural discomfort associated with assuming such control over a person, acting "God-like," because in the medical model the physician's actions are based on the belief that his knowledge of the illness indicates the appropriate treatment.

This coupling of diagnosis and intervention, however, can be problematic for, and indeed stand in juxtaposition to, the orientation, technique, and belief system of a clinician who primarily uses a psychodynamic model of the mind. In this model, a disorder of mental function, such as depression, is considered a "psychological" illness resulting from unconscious psychic conflict. In Freud's theory of depression, as outlined in *Mourning and Melancholia*,[2] depression was associated with the loss of a narcissistic object. Suicide in particular was explained in a highly mechanistic schema in which the lost narcissistic object is taken back within the ego ("the shadow of the object falls upon the ego"), and rage towards the narcissistic object because of its unavailability leads to the desire to obliterate the object. However, the object now resides within the ego, and so any attempt to kill the object requires sacrifice of the self, because the object now resides within the self. Actually, the depressed patient never wants to kill himself; he wants to kill the object. This theory is generally misunderstood, and it is often misstated as depression and suicide are "anger turned against the self." Freud believed that suicide was the unavoidable sacrifice of the self in order to destroy the lost object.

Regardless of whether the psychodynamic clinician believes in Freud's formulation of depression and suicide (many, if not most, modern clinicians do not) with respect to assessing the patient, the psychodynamic clinician may not think in terms of the diagnostic categories that are accepted in clinical psychiatry. As Charles Benner said,

> since depression and anxiety are part of every compromise formation, whether or not they are present in the form of manifest symptomatology…it is a mistake to base a nosology on the premise that the presence of depression distinguishes a class of mental illness in some fundamentally important way. Depression is

an affect, not an illness. The current concept of depressive illness, whatever the words used to designate it, is more misleading than helpful.[3]

Thus, psychodynamic metapsychology does not easily allow for the incorporation of phenomenological diagnostic and psychobiological dimensions when considering suicide, but rather it compels the clinician to conceptualize affective state and suicidal ideation as consequences of psychic conflict and potentially amenable to interpretation. However, there may be another motivation behind the psychodynamic clinician's aversion to diagnostic categories, that is, to avoid a level of activity, authority, and the assumption of power, all of which are inherent in the medical model. The medical model implies a type of doctor/patient relationship that is incompatible with traditional psychodynamic therapy. The dynamically oriented clinician is committed to a technique in which he does not make the decisions for the patient; there is no physical contact, much less physical restraint:, and there is a reliance on interpretation rather than prescription. It is understandably foreign for a dynamically oriented clinician to adopt a medical model. Allegiance to a theory creates inflexibility that interferes with the diagnosis and treatment of depressed patients with significant suicide potential. A paradigm shift from a psychodynamic model to a medical model can be very difficult, particularly in a climate when adoption of the medical model can be seen as the abandonment of psychology in favor of biological psychiatry.

In summary, the accurate diagnosis of a depressed or psychotic patient with suicide potential compels intervention. A clinician will be inhibited from making the proper diagnosis if he or she is reluctant to initiate the interventions that the proper diagnosis mandates. To insure that a theoretical model of the mind does not become an obstacle to diagnosis and treatment, the dynamically oriented clinician must use the dynamic model of the mind when appropriate and recognize that in certain situations it is not as germane as the medical model. Just because it may not always be helpful is not to say that the dynamic model of the mind is incorrect.

CLINICAL PRESENTATIONS: THE PATIENT IN THERAPY

A second clinical situation is one in which suicidal ideation or behavior occurs in the context of ongoing psychotherapy. Although it is possible that in the course of ongoing therapy a patient may develop a new episode of depression with suicidal ideation, the more frequent situation is that certain conditions, such as borderline personality disorder, other severe personality disorders, and chronic depression, are associated with both suicidal ideation and, in some cases, suicide attempts. In addition to diagnosis, many clinicians distinguish the impulsive patient, who may engage in self-destructive acts, from the suicidal patient, who is not necessarily impulsive or, ironically, self-destructive. Clinicians have come to accept that they may not be able to prevent the death of the impulsive patient who takes a drug overdose or drives while under the influence of alcohol, but nonetheless feel that as the therapist they should be able to prevent suicide. Although chronic suicidal ideation may preexist the beginning of therapy, chronic suicide risk in the course of therapy takes on another dimension, as an interaction within the treatment dyad. It not only stems from the patient, but now also exists between patient and therapist.

Therapists have adopted many different strategies for the suicidal patient with the express intent of keeping the focus of therapy on the patient and not on suicide. However, the multitude of strategies seems to have two goals in common: to reduce the constant pressure experienced by the therapist when treating the suicidal patient and to prevent suicide, express statements of the therapist to the contrary notwithstanding. Some therapists adopt the position that in certain severely ill patients suicide is inevitable, and therefore the effectiveness of the treatment is measured not by preventing the suicide, which is a foregone conclusion, but by the quality of the patient's life before that event occurs. The therapist's tacit belief is that if the therapy improves the quality of life sufficiently, the suicide may be averted. Some clinicians will state directly to the patient that preventing suicide is the patient's responsibility, not that of the clinician; they will treat the patient as long as he or she is alive, but it is the patient who must keep himself/herself alive. The question arises as to what the therapist would do if the patient calls with a suicide threat. Some therapists will tell the patient, "I will save you once, but if you use that save, the treatment will be terminated."

What would create in a therapist such a strong desire to both distance himself from the suicidal patient and yet be determined to save him? Unlike a patient with terminal cancer, for whom it is acknowledged by the doctor that there is nothing that the doctor can do to prevent death, there is a strong belief among clinicians that when treating a suicidal patient, if you do the right thing, the patient will stay alive. Therefore, the suicide of a patient is experienced as a failure and seen by colleagues as a failure, and whatever the therapist's public position, the internal experience is shame. Emphasizing suicide as an interaction within the dyad further reinforces this feeling of failure, because it fosters the belief that if the patient commits suicide, then the clinician did not properly use the power of the relationship. Therapists seem to tacitly accept both the premise that they can prevent suicide and the responsibility that this implies. However, our actual knowledge about the veracity of this assumption is limited and there has been little systematic research.

Ironically, much of the difficulty for the psychodynamic therapist arises because he/she often tacitly adopts part of the medical model, that is, he feels responsible for what happens to the patient, but he may not accept other important components, that is, the authority and the recognition that we do not save all severely ill patients whatever the disease process. Of all the clinical specialties, psychiatrists and specifically psychodynamic clinicians have perhaps the least experience with death in the clinical setting. They have little opportunity to develop the perspective that comes from taking responsibility for a patient's life and exercising authority to make difficult decisions, that is, doing one's best and accepting a patient's death with disappointment and sadness, but without a sense of shame or failure. Many therapists, perhaps realizing that they do not have this perspective, avoid treating suicidal patients.

SUMMARY

In summary, two conflicts in the therapist's mind, (1) an aversion to the medical model and (2) the fear of shame and failure, are obstacles to the optional assessment and treatment of the suicidal patient. What is one to do? Though the psychodynamic clinician may be in a predicament, another part of their training, in fact, uniquely equips him/her to deal with the problem. Dynamically trained therapists presumably have had treatment of their own, in many cases a classical (or not too classical) psychoanalysis. Thus, they are trained to be aware of their feeling states, particularly when they are in response to the patient and potentially influence treatment. They can draw on this self-awareness to assess if countertransference, whether it takes the form of refuge in theory, intellectualization, avoidance, or anxiety, is significantly influencing their cognition and behavior in the clinical situation. Dynamic clinicians can be especially aware of countertransference obstacles and successfully negotiate them. Indeed, if they can also incorporate nondynamic models of illness into their working mind, they may be uniquely capable of formulating a therapeutic plan for the suicidal patient. After all, countertransference does not exist only in the dynamically trained therapist. Exclusive adherence to a phenomenologic diagnostic or biological model of depression and suicide can also produce less than optimal, or even egregiously flawed, clinical treatment. Indeed, anxiety over what will be the collective wisdom voiced in morning rounds has influenced more than one ER physician's decision about whether to hospitalize a patient with suicidal ideation or send him/her home.

REFERENCES

1. ROOSE, S.P., A.H. GLASSMAN, T.B. WALSH, *et al.* 1983. Depression, delusions and suicide. Am. J. Psychiatry **140:** 1159–1162.

2. FREUD, S. 1915. "Mourning and Melancholia." Standard Edition, 1964, Vol. 14: 237–239. Hogarth Press. London.
3. BRENNER, C. 1991. A psychoanalytic perspective on depression. J. Am. Psychoanal. Assoc. **39:** 25–43.

Treating the Suicidal Patient

Basic Principles

JOHN T. MALTSBERGER

Departments of Psychiatry, Harvard Medical School and Massachusetts General Hospital; Department of Psychiatry, McLean Hospital, Brookline, Massachusetts 02146, USA

ABSTRACT: Successful psychotherapy with suicidal patients requires an emotionally full, active engagement from the therapist with his patient. Emphasis is on the real relationship, not the transference, and the therapist must be available to the patient as a sturdy, reliable object with whom to identify. The therapist's attitude must be loving, not neutral; the alliance is built upon the therapist's devotion to the patient's growth and the development of the attributes necessary for successful autonomous adult functioning. Patients require emotional containment and support, assistance in modulating painful affect, validation, education, help with reality testing, and kindly limit setting. Countertransference reactions must be expected and kept in check, so that the therapist does not get in the patient's way as he tries to build up the faulty mental structures that got him into trouble in the first place.

KEYWORDS: Countertransference; Psychotherapy; Suicide; Transference

INTRODUCTION

What is the best psychotherapeutic method for treating patients at risk to die of suicide? In truth, we do not know, in an acceptable scientific way, how best to reduce the incidence of death by suicide among patients who come to us for treatment.[1] No psychotherapeutic method has yet been shown to reduce the likelihood of a suicide outcome.

It is true that some therapies have been effective in reducing self-injurious behavior, at least for a while, included under which rubric are some attempted suicides. Cognitive behavioral approaches, typically time limited and organized towards immediate problem solving, very notably dialectical behavioral therapy, have been proven valuable by controlled clinical trials.[2] Other

Address for correspondence: Dr. John T. Maltsberger, 38 Fuller Street, Brookline, MA 02446. Voice: 517-731-2488; fax: 617-277-2619.

maltsb@3b.com

problem-solving methods have been demonstrated and described by Hawton and Kirk.[3] Cognitive therapy approaches developed by Beck and his students have empirically demonstrated value in the self-injurious group.[4,5] The value of interpersonal psychotherapy for depression, a time-limited treatment that has a bearing on suicidal cases, has been empirically shown. A recent book is advertised as a manual for treating suicidal patients according to a time-limited, empirically supported method, specifically designed with the managed care environment in mind.

Scientific rigor comes at a certain price. It is difficult to devise empirical trials for some of the more complex approaches to the treatment of patients inclined towards suicide.[7]

Furthermore, most treatment methods described in the last 15 years presume that the patient is reasonably well disposed to enter into an alliance with the therapist and to work in the direction of overcoming suicidal forces. Some are pointedly time limited. But many suicidal patients will not be suitable for such treatments. Virtually all suicidal patients suffer from significant mental illnesses, most from significant depression, alcoholism, or schizophrenia. Many patients are too distressed to cooperate in cognitive retraining or problem solving. Many are unable to cooperate in a psychodynamic interpretive method. Many of the most desperate patients refuse to play by our rules and will fly in the face of treatment manuals. Their illnesses are often treated only in the most superficial ways by inflexible time limits as imposed by "managed care."

Before the modern psychopharmacological era, there was considerable interest in psychotherapeutic approaches for deeply disturbed patients, many of whom were labeled "schizophrenic" according to the diagnostic mode of the time. (Now we would find most of the suicidal ones in the categories of bipolar illness, chronic depression, personality disorder diagnoses, and substance abuse.) Fromm-Reichmann[8] and Semrad[9] were among the pioneers who developed and taught several generations of psychiatrists a psychotherapeutic approach that appeared to have some success with profoundly disturbed patients. The basic principles of that approach, which with slight modification still have value, aim at promoting the gradual development of narcissistic autonomy by inviting the patient's identification with an empathic, realistic, and loving therapist.

Psychoanalytic treatment in the sense of five-times-a-week sessions conducted on a couch with the therapist out of the patient's view is hardly an appropriate method for suicidal patients, although psychoanalytic theory casts a helpful light for our understanding of such patients. Most suicidal patients who become significantly involved in psychotherapy that lasts more than a few weeks suffer from narcissistic character disturbances of a borderline nature. Their egos are defective, and defective in specific ways that make classical on-the-couch treatment unsuitable. Specifically, their capacity to distinguish between the therapist's real qualities and their transference to him is very faulty. For these patients, to *feel* that the therapist is filled with hate is to know that he is so. They have very limited capacity to distinguish between what they think and feel about others and the reality of others. In this respect, the patients are very close to psychotic cases; they are vulnerable to transference psychoses, and, indeed to other psychotic phenomena, although usually brief in nature. In short, their capacity for reality testing is deficient.

Other characteristics that make the couch unsuitable for these patients is their difficulty in containing affects without going into action, their incapacity to form and work through a reasonably coherent transference, their lack of a stable sense of self, and, in general, their incapacity to adapt to the restrictions and limitations imposed by the classical method.

I have said their egos are defective. In particular, they have constricted capacities to modulate and contain affect without going into action. They are prone to develop psychotic fantasies about the therapist and the nature of death. They may have little sense of self-continuity from one day to the next or even hour to hour. They may hate themselves with great passion and feel they have no worth to others. To treat patients with such formidable difficulties as these, the therapist must come out from behind the couch and join the patient in a face-to-face encounter. In this encounter, the therapist offers himself as an auxiliary ego, providing special narcissistic assistance to the patient which the patient is unable to provide for himself. We hope that if the therapy can be sustained for a sufficiently long time, the patient will identify with the narcissistic assistance he is offered, strengthening his own ego by building it up through identification with what he is given.

WHAT DO I MEAN BY NARCISSISTIC ASSISTANCE?

First of all, the treatment must be carried out with an emphasis on the real relationship, not the transference relationship. The therapist must give the patient the full benefit of his own ego as a model for identification. He must become for the patient that which the patient needs to become in order to carry forward as a reasonably autonomous adult. One of the principal characteristics of the real relationship must be that the therapist will love the patient and not conceal this fact.

> A chronically self-lacerating, suicidal patient suffering from a schizoaffective disorder reduced her first-year resident psychotherapist to a state of helpless self-doubt and anxiety by escalating her behavior in the face of his somewhat detached, rather impersonal interpretive approach. He consulted Elvin Semrad. During their discussion he burst into tears, so great was his distress at his patient's plight. Semrad said, "I think if you will show your patient what you have

just shown me, she will stop cutting herself." The resident confessed his distress and helplessness to his patient, and told her he desperately wanted to help her, but did not know how. She stopped cutting herself.

Obviously the therapist need not love the patient erotically. Of course therapists do react erotically to patients sometimes, but such responses belong to the countertransference and must be inhibited. The essential love is the disinterested kind – the warm, concerned, and caring respect a good teacher feels for a student. It is unselfish, disinterested, loyal, and benevolent. The theologians call it *agape*. You can find it between the lines in Socrates's dialogues with his students or on morning hospital rounds conducted by a truly good attending physician or surgeon. You can find it in the manner of a good first-grade teacher.

Every intervention that the therapist makes with these patients needs to be informed with this feeling. The greatest deficiency of all in suicidal patients is their incapacity to feel any loving concern for themselves. They need to take the respect and care of the therapist into themselves and learn it from the therapist. It was said that Fromm-Reichman, that tiny little old German lady, would return time and again for sessions with a withdrawn and uncooperative patient until at last the patient could bear it no longer and opened up to her, concluding that if she so obviously felt him worth so much time and effort, maybe he was wrong about himself and could learn from her.[10]

In the context of this attitude the therapist learns to experience his own countertransference responses to the patient consciously, yet not to act on them. Indeed, sometimes the responses may be erotic, but more often, the patient's relentless hostile barrage will generate intense feelings of countertransference hate.

The therapist who has the capacity to know himself deeply will be aware at times that he would like to make the patient suffer: he will feel anger and, beyond anger, sadistic impulses to retaliate on the patient and torment him in return. If the therapist is not able to contain his sadistic excitement in reasonable comfort, he will begin to experience impulses to get rid of the patient. The two components of countertransference hate are malice (sadism) and aversion. Neither should be acted out, but aversive, or rejecting, actions by the therapist are particularly likely to generate suicide attempts.[11]

A suicidal borderline patient made her therapist very anxious by repeated self-cutting. One day he told his patient she had to stop this behavior, and that if she did not, he would terminate the treatment. (Such rules are made only to be broken, of course.) She cut herself again, and he discharged her from his care, whereupon the patient killed herself. In retrospect the therapist was able to acknowledge that his effort to control the patient by fiat arose from a sense of intense dislike. His termination of the treatment was driven by countertransference aversion.

A therapist must be prepared to help the patient contain anxiety, rage, and rage against the self and to assist in quieting him down and modulating him without going into destructive action. This is the soothing function of psychotherapy, sometimes called too generally simply "supportive"; the patient requires emotional "holding," not in the physical sense, but in the relational.[12,13]

The patient requires validation, also. In the course of development these patients have received little by way of encouraging positive reactions from important others. How is a child to know that he has any valuable qualities if the parents or their surrogates do not acknowledge them, name them, and praise them? By naming and acknowledging good qualities, the therapist validates the patient's worth and slowly helps him build up self-respect. If a patient is generous, intelligent, musically talented, or possesses any other admirable qualities or traits, the therapist should point them out and express admiration directly.

The patient requires education from his therapist. This therapeutic intervention can be a very broad one, but few of these patients are skilled in social relationships.

> A young patient in analysis, bitterly teased and humiliated as a boy by his father, had improved sufficiently to fall in love with a pretty young woman for the first time in his life. Pausing at a traffic light, he leaned toward her and gave her a kiss. He had not noticed the car just behind which was filled with young sailors. When the sailors broke out in cheers and blew their horn, the patient felt humiliated and enraged. He had not thought that the sailors might have been cheering in congratulation and camaraderie, not jeering at him, until his analyst suggested this several hours later when he was still in a rage about the event.

When the therapist can notice more adaptive ways in which the patient might respond in common situations of stress, the therapist should teach the patient the new adaptation. These patients commonly need to learn, as Benjamin Franklin said, that "a teaspoon of honey will catch more flies than a cup of vinegar." This is not an easy lesson for persons who have been raised on vinegar and much deprived of honey.

Another important educative function of the therapist is to teach patients that there are better ways to obtain emotional help from others than by making suicidal threats or by self-injury. They must learn to put their feelings into words and to speak to others in such a way that others grasp what they suffer and will be disposed to respond constructively.

Reality testing is an important therapeutic intervention. The patient's hateful projections, which distort the good will and intentions of the therapist into something cruel and ugly, need careful, respectful examination as the therapist helps the patient compare what he feels with what he knows has been the constructive history of the therapeutic relationship. When the therapist is told, for example, that the patient is sure the doctor wants to get rid of him, the patient must be asked what he has observed in their interaction, recent or past, that would support such a view. When a distortion is presented in support of the hateful projection, the distortion should be discussed and the patient shown the real perspective. I would call this clarification in the service of defense analysis, viz., the defense of distortion.

If the patient discerns that the therapist has made a mistake or has slipped into some small angry acting out, the therapist must be prepared to acknowledge the mistake and to apologize for it.

Limit setting is difficult but essential in the treatment of these patients. When the therapist discerns that the patient is on the edge of some self-destructive activity, he needs to help the patient see where his behavior will lead. If the patient is in such passionate excitement that discussion and anticipatory investigation are not enough, the therapist must be prepared to intervene, firmly but kindly, in such a way that the patient is prevented from harming himself or others, but prevented in a loving way. This kind of activity may sometimes involve involuntary hospitalization of a patient bent on suicide or a gentle but firm insistence that the patient surrender a cache of pills that are being saved up in preparation for an overdose. Interfering with a patient in this way almost always invites a rage reaction from the patient, who will respond with the accusation that the therapist is being punitive. Loving education and persuasion are called into play here, as the patient is shown that not every frustration is motivated by hate and that frustrations can be imposed out of caring concern.

> A suicidal patient, rejected by her boyfriend, arrived at her treatment session in a rage and declared that she was going to leave the session and jump in front of the subway. Her therapist acknowledged that she felt terribly hurt and angry, and then told her this story, kindly and lovingly: "Once upon a time," he said, "There was a little girl named Suzy who had set her heart on going on a picnic with a friend. The picnic plans were spoiled by rain, and Suzy, after staring out the window for a while, began to cry, and then she had a terrible tantrum, smashing her toys and tearing her books. Her mother came into the room and said, very gently, 'Suzy I know you are disappointed by the rain. But you love those toys and books, and tomorrow you will be sorry they are ruined. Wouldn't you rather come on out into the kitchen with me and make some fudge?' Suzy stopped the destruction, cried for a while, and decided she would make fudge with her mother." On hearing this the patient fell silent for several minutes, and then she began to cry. She stopped the suicidal threatening and rejoined her analyst, beginning to work through yet another disappointment.

In conclusion, you may have noticed that I have said little about interpretation as a therapeutic measure. The process of growth can be helped if patients learn how their current reaction patterns repeat those of the past and that they arise from painful interactive patterns with the adults of childhood. But I would contend that no amount of interpretation without loving concern, soothing, validation, education, reality testing, and limit setting will be enough to help the patient grow.

Whatever "method" one may employ in the treatment of suicidal patients, little lasting success can be expected unless the basic attitude towards the patient I have described informs the therapist's attitude. The late Ernst Kris once remarked that patients never learn anything of lasting emotional value except in an atmosphere of love, and the experience of many therapists, struggling with the problems of suicidal persons, has often shown this is correct.[14] Excessive adherence to a set of treatment rules, concentrating on "problem solving" in the immediate present, rushing through predetermined steps in the limited amount of time dictated by managed care requirements, is not so likely to result in genuine emotional growth that may be expected to last.

REFERENCES

1. LINEHAN, M.M. 1997. Behavioral treatments of suicidal behaviors. Definitional obfuscation and treatment outcomes. *In* The Neurobiology of Suicide. D.M. Stoff & J.J. Mann, eds. Ann. N.Y. Acad. Sci. **836:** 302–328.
2. LINEHAN, M.M. 1993. Cognitive-Behavioral Treatment of Borderline Personality Disorder. The Guilford Press. New York.
3. HAWTON, K. & J. KIRK. 1989. Cognitive behaviour therapy for psychiatric problems. *In* Cognitive Behaviour Therapy for Psychiatric Problems: A Practical Guide. K. Hawton, P.M. Salvkovskis, J. Kirk & D.B. Clark, eds. :406–427. Oxford University Press. Oxford.
4. BECK, A.T., A.J. RUSH, B.F. SHAW & F.G. EMERY. 1979. Cognitive Therapy of Depression. Guilford Press. New York.
5. FREEMAN, A. & M.A. REINECKE. 1993. Cognitive Therapy of Suicidal Behavior. Springer. New York.
6. KLERMAN, G., M.M. WEISSMAN, B. ROUNSAVILLE & E.S. CHEVRON. 1995. Intrpersonal psychotherapy for depression. J. Psychother. Practice Res. **4:** 342–351.
7. RUDD, M.D., T.E. JOINER & M.H. RAJAB. 2000. Treating Suicidal Behavior: An Effective, Time Limited Approach. Guilford Press. New York.
8. FROMM-REICHMAN, F. 1950. The Principles of Intensive Psychotherapy. University of Chicago. Chicago.
9. SEMRAD, E.V. & D. VAN BUSKIRK. 1969. Teaching Psychotherapy of Psychotic Patients: Supervision of Beginning Residents in the "Clinical Approach." Grune & Stratton. New York.
10. SEMRAD, E.V. 1961. Personal communication.
11. MALTSBERGER, J.T. & D.H. BUIE. 1974. Countertransference hate in the treatment of suicidal patients. Arch. Gen. Psychiatry **30:** 625–633.

12. ADLER, G. & D.H. BUIE. 1979. Aloneness and borderline psychopathology: the possible relevance of child development issues. Int. J. Psycho-Analysis **60:** 83–96.
13. BUIE, D.H. & G. ADLER. 1982–1983. Definitive treatment of the borderline personality. Int. J. Psychoanal. Psychother. **2:** 51–87.
14. KRIS, A. 1961. Personal communication.

DISCUSSION OF PAPERS BY DR. MALTSBERGER AND DR. ROOSE

DAVID SHAFFER (*Chairman*): Dr. Maltsberger, would you care to respond to Dr. Roose?

JOHN T. MALTSBERGER: Dr. Roose, your points about the conflict between the medical model and the dynamic model take me back to the early days of my training. My teachers made a tremendous effort to stop me from being prepared to go into action at the drop of a hat, which medical students and interns are taught, and to sit down and listen with not much actual interference with a patient's life. The fact of the matter is that I wanted to be a doctor since I was 6 years old, and my most important role model was a family doctor. He took care of me when I was a scared kid. It is very important in my identification as a physician, and I am a physician first and a psychoanalyst second, although in my view, it's possible to put the two together, because psychoanalysis can supply valuable information for our medical interventions with these patients. For instance, you asked whose responsibility it is to keep the patient alive? Many patients want to entrap us, not on purpose but it's in their dynamics, into saving them, and they will get out on the George Washington Bridge or call from a motel to demand rescue. Dr. Hendin wrote a very interesting paper that discusses this problem. After all these years I think it is not possible, particularly early in treatment, to decide exactly who is responsible for the patient's staying alive. Certainly, we wish over time to get the patient to accept more responsibility, but particularly early on we may expect the test. We have to respond in a caring way; otherwise we're going to have a dead patient. Ultimatums, such as "I will rescue you once, but never again" or "if you cut yourself, you're out of here because cutting is forbidden in my treatment," conceal a considerable amount of countertransference hate in the form of aversion. They say, "I can't stand the whole of you, that is you in your entirety and I'm not going to have anything to do with this destructive part of you and you damn well better control yourself if you want to be my patient." Ultimatums, like rules, are made to be broken. You can't do it. You have to respond to emergencies judiciously, and you must keep the anger out of it.

STEVEN P. ROOSE: I can understand the difference in our attitude from our early life. At 6 years old I wanted to be the center fielder for the New York Yankees. I still do, and I believe I could do it. In a sense there has been a long tradition within psychoanalysis of this conflict. We saw it first when medications were introduced. Originally, medications were greeted with skepticism and concern because it was felt that medications would be deceptively helpful. They might reduce symptoms, but they would actually undercut the patient's motivation for the in-depth, painful, long-term treatment that many analysts felt was going to cure the illness. For example, even though medications and psychodynamic treatments and psychoanalysis are frequently used together, the fact that they are given concurrently doesn't make them theoretically compatible. As things go forward, there is a point at which there is a division in the model of the mind that interferes with treatment. For example, we run a workshop at the American Psychoanalytic Association on the use of antidepressant medications in the psychoanalytic process. One of the senior clinicians presented a case in which the patient was put on medication for severe depression. Analysis was very successful. Termination was coming up and the analyst wanted to take the patient off medication. He later realized that he wanted to do so because he believed that if his treatment had really been helpful, he would have changed the internal structure so that the depressive illness would no longer exist. The patient, under the influence of the analyst, went off medication, became depressed, went back on medication, and said to the analyst, "Listen. You have been very helpful to me, and so was the medication. I don't want to have to choose between the two of you." For psychodynamic clinicians, it's very important to be vigilant and to be aware of this conflict, because it leads to treatment decisions. Let me just make two other brief comments. As you said, you are a doctor first and a psychoanalyst second. Many of our colleagues, however, reveal the analytic attitude, the analytic posture, and believe that is to be used at all times, that it comes first, and abandonment of it is considered to be abandonment of our field. The problem is that we do not perceive certain things that are going on.

MALTSBERGER: To come back to a point I made, every intervention that you make with a patient must be for the patient's good. The story of the analyst who influenced the patient to go off an antidepressant raises a question. The patient is not there for our narcissistic gratification; the patient is not there to better enable us to cover ourselves with garlands and flowers because our wonderful psychoanalytic ideas are being confirmed or not. That analyst has a narcissistic problem and needs more analysis.

SHAFFER: Dr. Roose, there are several questions. What are your thoughts on the use of a psychodynamic diagnostic evaluation, as proposed by Canberg and more recently elaborated by Nancy McWilliams, in bridging medical and psychodynamic models? Do you think this system would allow the clinician to act appropriately and effectively with respect to suicidal patients, and perhaps in answering that you could tell us more about the Canberg/ McWilliams model.

ROOSE: We can bring some data to bear on this. For example, in the treatment of depressed patients, we refer to them as depressed patients or depression. The person has depression and that illness exists in the context of the particular person. If we take a look at depression, which is probably the illness most closely associated with suicide, we know that depression is a recurrent illness and many patients, especially after their second episode, are judged to be best treated if they are on maintenance medication for the prevention of recurrence. We also know that only about 30 or 40% of patients after 3 months are still adhering to the recommendation of maintenance medication. That's not just specific to depression; it's true for hypertension and other chronic illnesses as well. One of the issues is not simply to approach what the person is taking, but who is it that is taking the medication. We recently completed a study in combination with our depression evaluation service at Columbia, looking at defense mechanisms in patients who are undergoing treatment of depression in standard medication clinical trials. This group of depressed patients, average age 35, average Hamilton score 22, were outpatients with essentially nonmelancholic major depression in a drug-versus-placebo medication trial. We assessed them using Bond's defense mechanism questionnaire, which really highlights four dimensions: maladaptive defenses and defenses that go along with things like splitting image-distorting defenses, infantile defenses, and adaptive defenses. Lo and behold, the dynamic formulation or the defense mechanism profile at the beginning predicted who dropped out of treatment and that the more image-distorting defenses, the more likely the patient was to have problems with his doctor and how he saw the doctor and experienced the treatment. That predicted dropout. If you look at the multiple studies on combination psychotherapy and medication trials, they don't necessarily study in which patients they would be most effective. If we use a dynamic formulation in assessment, we may understand more about our patients whom we are treating for certain illnesses. That may be helpful in addressing particular issues to keep the patient on the treatment that will, in the long run, be most helpful in preventing recurrence of depression and therefore in reducing suicidal risk. The incorporation of a dynamic formulation, which is not difficult (people have the incorrect fantasy that it requires 10 hours of sitting with the patient), is an investment that can markedly enhance our treatment plans.

SHAFFER: Dr. Maltsberger, which would you consider of greater importance in the treatment of suicidality, serotonin reuptake or love?

MALTSBERGER: Before any SSRIs were available, we had only one thing to offer the patients, ourselves. I have seen patient-informed, loving psychotherapy save patients lives long before we had good antidepressants to get them out of their suicidal state. It takes longer and it's more dicey, because there's more room for mistakes. I'm very grateful for the SSRIs, and I think that you need a combination of the two.

SHAFFER: Another question for Dr. Roose. If you think that depression is not an illness or disease, but an affect, how do you ascribe all the signs and symptoms to affect and not to a diagnosis of depression and all that comes with the diagnosis? Is depression not a disease of the brain?

ROOSE: I would certainly agree. Unfortunately, Freud has been misread, because Freud, in *Mourning and Melancholia,* recognized that he was focusing on one aspect of the illness, the depressed mood. He was the first to say that there are many other features of depressive illness for which we cannot develop a psychodynamic formulation, such as diurnal variation. One problem is that unfortunately this syndrome of depression was named for one symptom and it is a symptom that we also use to connote many other things, mood states that we all experience. In psychodynamic theory, we think that the inability to experience sadness and so forth is pathologic. But sadness and feeling down are not the equivalent of depression. Certainly many older patients who have a clear syndrome of depression do not experience depressed mood; they will not use those phrases at all. Part of the problem in bridging our clinical psychiatric practices with our psychodynamic theory is that the word "depression," which is just one symptom of the illness, is used to designate the illness. That unfortunately leads to much of our confusion.

MALTSBERGER: If we had more time, I'd be glad to discuss what is the matter with the DSM-IV definition of depression, at least as far as suicide studies are concerned. Suicidal people do not kill themselves simply because they have a loss of appetite or don't sleep well, although those items are both in the DSM-IV list. The deadly, in fact one very deadly, phenomenon of depression that is not in the DSM-IV list is the subjective experience of anguish. Anguish is much more specific than is a depressed or blue mood. The definitions in that book, therefore, are not as helpful as they might be.

Recognizing and Responding to a Suicide Crisis

HERBERT HENDIN, JOHN T. MALTSBERGER,[a] ALAN LIPSCHITZ,
ANN POLLINGER HAAS, AND JENNIFER KYLE

American Foundation for Suicide Prevention, New York, New York 10005, USA

*Department of Psychiatry, New York Medical College, Valhalla,
New York 10595, USA*

[a]*Department of Psychiatry, Harvard Medical School, Cambridge,
Massachusetts, USA*

ABSTRACT: Data from therapists who were treating 26 patients when they
committed suicide were utilized to identify signs that warned of a suicide
crisis. Three factors were identified as markers of the suicide crisis: a precipitating event; one or more intense affective states other than depression;
and at least one of three behavioral patterns: speech or actions suggesting
suicide, deterioration in social or occupational functioning, and increased
substance abuse. Problems in communication between patient and therapist, often originating in therapeutic anxiety over the patient's possible suicide, were identified as factors interfering with crisis recognition.
Evaluation of the identified affects and behaviors may help therapists recognize a suicide crisis.

KEYWORDS: Behavioral patterns; Intense affective states; Precipitating
events; Suicide crisis; Suicide crisis recognition

INTRODUCTION

Family and friends of individuals who commit suicide have proven to be a
valuable source of information, but in most cases they are not able to provide
a detailed picture of the inner life and motivations of those they have lost to
suicide.[1–3] Therapists who treat these patients are a relatively untapped
source of such information. Over the course of a professional lifetime, any
one psychotherapist may see one or a small number of patients who kill themselves while in treatment. About 20% of psychologists and over 50% of psy-

Address for correspondence: Herbert Hendin, M.D., Medical Director, American Foundation
for Suicide Prevention, 120 Wall Street, 22nd Floor, New York, NY 10005. Voice: 212-348 4035;
fax: 212-363-6237.

hhendin@afsp.org

chiatrists are estimated to have had this experience.[4-6] What is learned by these therapists remains uncollected and anecdotal.

The Suicide Data Bank of the American Foundation for Suicide Prevention was designed to accumulate and analyze such information in order to better understand patients' thoughts, feelings, and behavior prior to suicide. This report on the first 26 patients in this ongoing project looks at the clinical features that mark a suicide crisis and examines how therapists recognize and respond to the crisis.

METHODS

Therapists who contributed cases learned of the Suicide Data Bank project from a variety of sources, including colleagues, notices in psychiatric publications, mailings from the American Foundation for Suicide Prevention, and relatives of patients who died by suicide. Six of the therapists were known to the investigators, three as colleagues and three as acquaintances. To qualify for inclusion, cases had to be actual suicides and the person had to have been seen by the therapist for at least six visits. Twenty-four of the 26 patients had been seen on a regular basis, 13 two or more times a week and 11 once a week; the remaining 2 were seen less regularly. These patients received treatment for periods from 3 weeks to 48 months, with a median duration of 12 months.

Participant therapists prepared a comprehensive, 15-page, narrative description of the case and completed semistructured questionnaires on the demographic, clinical, and psychodynamic features of the patient and the therapist's reactions to the suicide. Following submission of these materials, three therapists at a time were scheduled to participate in an all-day case presentation workshop with the project clinicians and the project coordinator. Three patients were usually discussed in each workshop; their identities were disguised in the narratives, questionnaires, and other case materials that participants reviewed in advance. As will be seen in the cases to be discussed, the therapist's perception of the case was not always shared by the group.

Eleven of the 26 cases were presented within 2 years of the suicide, 12 within 3 to 5 years, and 3 many years later by therapists who had kept detailed treatment records. Twenty-one of the 26 participating therapists were male; 5 were female; and 21 were psychiatrists, 4 were psychologists, and 1 was a psychiatric social worker. At the time of the suicide, six therapists had been in practice over 15 years, seven between 10 and 15 years, eight between 5 and 10 years; and five were trainees.

Sample

The 26 patients ranged in age from 17–63 years, with a median age of 33.5; half were male and half were female. The demographic distribution of the cases differs considerably from the predominantly male, predominantly older profile of suicide cases in general, likely because women and younger adults more often seek psychiatric treatment.

Nineteen of the 26 cases were outpatients at the time of suicide; six were inpatients; and one had recently transferred from a hospital to a group home. Two of the inpatients killed themselves on pass from the hospital, two eloped to do so, and two did so in the hospital. Almost all the outpatient cases (16 of 19) had had at least one psychiatric hospitalization.

Diagnoses

For each case, DSM-IV criteria were used to make a diagnosis of the patient at the time of suicide. (The first 12 cases, which used DSM-III-R criteria, were reviewed to ensure conformity with DSM-IV criteria.) In addition to the treating therapist, each project psychiatrist made an independent diagnosis to make sure the criteria had been followed. In three cases in which the therapist's diagnosis did not conform to the recognized criteria, the diagnosis recorded for the patient was the one agreed upon by the project psychiatrists.

The diagnosis for 16 of the 26 patients was major depressive disorder, and 4 were diagnosed with bipolar disorder, 2 in mixed states and 2 in major depressive episodes. Four patients were diagnosed with schizoaffective disorder; one had a general anxiety disorder and one an adjustment disorder. Nine patients had an additional Axis I diagnosis of substance abuse; two had the additional diagnosis of panic disorder, and one the added diagnosis of posttraumatic stress disorder.

Fifteen of the 26 patients also had Axis II personality disorder diagnoses. Five were diagnosed with borderline personality disorder, four with narcissistic personality disorder, three with an unspecified (mixed) personality disorder, two with avoidant personality disorder, and one with dependent personality disorder.

All 26 patients had received an antidepressant or other psychotropic medication; it was prescribed by a psychiatric consultant for the five patients who were not being treated by a psychiatrist. Not all of the patients, however, were receiving medications at the time of their death. About half of the patients were correctly and adequately prescribed medications, while in the others medication doses were low or ineffective or not directed to the therapist's primary diagnosis. Detailed evaluation of the psychopharmacologic treatment of these patients will be the subject of a separate review.

RESULTS

Crisis Markers

Three factors were identified as markers of the suicide crisis, usually occurring in combinations of two or three in a single patient: a precipitating event; one or more intense affective states; and one or more behavior patterns including speech or actions suggesting increasing suicidal interest, deterioration in social or occupational functioning, or increasing substance abuse (TABLE 1, Part A).

Precipitating Event. In 21 of the 26 cases a major life event appeared to contribute to the suicide crisis such as the loss of a relationship on which the patient was dependent, the collapse of a career, or the potentially fatal illness of a child. In almost all cases, the precipitating event appeared to be closely linked to the patient's preexisting affective state. In many patients, the event clearly resulted from the emotional difficulties the patient was experiencing, as in the case of an attorney whose uncontrolled bipolar illness led to the collapse of her career. In other cases, the occurrence of the event intensified the patient's preexisting affective state or the affective state magnified the event's importance to the patient.

In only 2 of the 20 cases was there no evidence of an affective disorder prior to the precipitating event: in one case, the suicide of his older brother led to behavior that culminated in the suicide of a 17-year-old young man (Case 3); in another, learning that his 3-year-old son had acute leukemia was the stimulus for guilt and agitation that culminated in the suicide of a 34-year-old noncommissioned military officer (Case 14). More important than the occurrence of a precipitating event per se was the meaning of the event for the patients and the fact that they and/or their therapists attributed their affective states and behavior to such events.

Patients' Affective States. A depressed mood was present in all 26 patients. The therapist rated the depression as "severe" in 18 cases, "moderate" in six cases, and "mild" in two cases (TABLE 2). Chronic affective states typically were interwoven with the patients' depression and included a longstanding sense of abandonment or rejection, chronic hopelessness, loneliness, and self-hatred. These were not clear signs of the suicide crisis. The sense of abandonment, seen in 15 patients, was sometimes acute in response to a specific rejection, but more often reflected longstanding feelings of being alone and unsupported.

Consistently linked to the suicide crises were acute, intense affective states associated with real or perceived occurrences in the patient's life. These feelings—desperation, an acute sense of abandonment, anxiety, rage, guilt, or hu-

TABLE 1. Crisis markers and other factors indicating risk of suicide

Case #	ID	Diagnosis	Status[a]	A. Crisis markers					B. Other factors indicating risk		
							Behavioral manifestations of a crisis				
				Precipitating event	Intense affective state	Speech/ action	Deteriorating functioning	Increasing substance abuse	Number of previous attempts	Impulsivity	Current substance abuse
1	34M	PTSD, MajDep, SubsAbuse (cannabis & alcohol)	op	•	•	•	•	•	3	Severe	•
2	33F	GenAnxDis, SubsAbuse(alc), BPD	op	•	•	•	•	•	3	Moderate	•
3	17M	AdjDisorder, SubsAbuse, Dysthymia, BPD	ip	•	•	•	•	•	1[b]	Severe	•
4	53M	Bipolar Mixed, PersDisNOS	op	•	•	•	•			Severe	•
5	21M	MajDep, recur, PanicDis, AvoidantPersDis	ip	•	•	•			1[b]		
6	37F	MajDep	op	•	•	•				Moderate	
7	32F	Schizoaffective, BPD	op	•	•		•		4		
8	22M	MajDep, Bulimia	op	•	•					Severe	
9	56F	MajDep, recur w psychotic features	ip	•	•		•				
10	26M	Schizoaffective, PanicDis	ip	•	•						
11	39M	Bipolar w psychot fs, NarcPersDis	gh	•	•	•			1		
12	27F	MajDep, recur w psych, Bulimia	ip	•	•	•			5[b]	Moderate	
13	23F	MajDep, Dysth, SubsAbuse (alcohol), PersDisNOS	op	•	•	•	•		4[b]	Severe	•
14	34M	MajDep, mixed mood disorder due to meds	op	•	•	•	•			Severe	
15	23F	MajDep, Dysthymia, BPD, NarcPersDis	op	•	•		•		3[b]		
16	44F	MajDep, recur, SomatizDis,Dysth, BPD, SubsAbuse (sed & analg)	op	•	•	•	•	•	6	Moderate	
17	22F	Schizoaff, SubsAbuse (cannb&alc)	op	•	•	•	•	•	>5		
18	49M	MajDep, Dependent PersDis	op		•		•				
19	63F	MajDep, NarcPersDis	op	•	•	•			1		
20	49F	Bipolar	op		•					Moderate	
21	58F	MajDep, recur, Body dysmorphDis, NarcPersDis	op	•	•	•	•		1[b]	Moderate	
22	17M	MajDep w psychotic fs in partial remission	op	•	•				1		
23	44M	Bipolar Mixed, SubsAbuse (alc)	op		•					Moderate	•
24	27F	Schizoaffective disorder	ip	•	•	•			2[b]	Moderate	•
25	41M	MajDep, recur, SubsAbuse (alc), Avoidant PersDis	op	•	•	•	•		1	Moderate	•
26	21M	MajDep,recur, Eating Dis NOS, SubsAbuse (alc), PersDis NOS	op	•	•		•		1	Moderate	•
				21	26	17	14	5	17	15	9

[a]op, outpatient; ip, inpatient; gh, group home. [b]Made suicide attempt within 3 months of death.

miliation—appeared to have compounded the patient's depression. The acute affective state most associated with a suicide crisis was desperation. Defined as a state of anguish accompanied by an urgent need for relief, desperation was intense in 22 of the 26 patients.

In three depressed patients with borderline, narcissistic, or mixed personality disorders (Cases 7, 16, and 19), abandonment and rage appeared to be as important as desperation in influencing the suicide. In two other patients, guilt and rage, precipitated in one case by the suicide of a brother (Case 3) and in another by the diagnosis of leukemia in an infant son (Case 14), were the affects that appeared to trigger the suicides. In four patients (Cases 4, 18, 23, and 25), acute humiliation resulting from social or occupational failures played a major role along with desperation in precipitating an already depressed patient into suicide.

Behavioral Manifestations of the Suicide Crisis. In addition to an intense affective state, 21 of the 26 patients showed at least one of three behavioral signs that warned of the suicide crisis. Seventeen patients showed by speech or action that they were contemplating suicide; the form this took varied from a patient (Case 15) who reported suicidal ideation she would not detail, to another (Case 12) who bluntly reported feeling acutely suicidal. Several did not confide their suicidal intent directly to the therapist, but to someone else whom they knew would relay the information to the therapist.

Other patients communicated their impending suicide through their actions. Seven patients (Cases 3, 5, 12, 13, 15, 21, and 24) made actual suicide attempts within 3 months of their suicide and while in their current therapy. Others engaged in escalating self-mutilating or self-destructive behaviors. One patient (Case 26) dealt with his anxiety every night by drinking and burning a pattern across his chest with a heated paper clip. Still another, a Vietnam veteran with posttraumatic stress disorder (Case 1), began shooting at trees while intoxicated. When the police were called, he challenged them to shoot him.

Fourteen of the patients showed marked deterioration in functioning immediately before their suicide. Two (Cases 9 and 20) gave up longstanding professional careers; one (Case 25) quit a long-held job. Several others were in danger of losing their jobs because of growing absenteeism or were experiencing difficulties with employers or supervisors. Other patients' deterioration was signaled by increasing loss of control and by rage explosions. A nurse's aide, for example, who worked with retarded children (Case 7) hit one shortly before killing herself. She was terrified by her loss of control.

Socially, the patients' deterioration was expressed in frequent arguments, breakups in relationships, or social withdrawal. Two patients (Cases 20 and 25) used the last session before their suicide to announce that they were stopping therapy.

TABLE 2. Therapists' ratings of patient's affective sate prior to suicide

Case #	Status[a]	ID	Depression	Desperation	Rage	Anxiety	Abandonment	Hopelessness	Self-hatred	Guilt	Loneliness	Humiliation
1	op	34M	Severe	Intense	Intense	Intense	Intense		Intense	Intense		
2	op	33F	Moderate	Intense	Intense	Intense	Intense	Intense		Intense		
3	ip	17M	Severe		Intense		Intense			Intense		
4	op	53M	Severe	Intense	Intense		Intense	Intense			Intense	Intense
5	ip	21M	Severe	Intense	Intense	Intense		Intense			Intense	Intense
6	op	37F	Severe	Intense	Intense		Intense					
7	op	32F	Severe	Intense	Intense		Intense	Intense	Intense		Intense	
8	ip	22M	Severe	Intense	Intense		Intense	Intense			Intense	
9	op	56F	Severe	Intense		Intense	Intense	Intense	Intense	Intense	Intense	Intense
10	ip	26M	Mild			Intense						
11	gp	39M	Severe	Intense	Intense	Intense		Intense	Intense			Intense
12	ip	27F	Severe	Intense	Intense	Intense	Intense	Intense	Intense	Intense		Intense
13	op	23F	Severe	Intense		Intense	Intense	Intense		Intense		
14	op	34M	Severe	Intense[b]	Intense				Intense	Intense		
15	op	23F	Severe	*Intense*	Intense		*Intense*	*Intense*	Intense			
16	op	44F	Severe	Intense	Intense	Intense	Intense		Intense	Intense	Intense	
17	op	22F	Moderate						Intense			
18	op	49M	Moderate	Intense		Intense	Intense	Intense				Intense
19	op	63F	Severe	Intense	Intense	Intense	Intense	Intense		Intense	Intense	Intense
20	op	49F	Mild	Intense				Intense		Intense	Intense	
21	op	58F	Moderate	Intense	Intense	Intense			Intense		Intense	Intense
22	op	17M	Moderate	Intense	Intense					Intense		
23	op	44M	Moderate	*Intense*	*Intense*							Intense
24	ip	27F	Severe	Intense	Intense	Intense	Intense	Intense	Intense	Intense	Intense	
25	op	41M	Severe	Intense	Intense	Intense		Intense	Intense		Intense	Intense
26	op	21M	Severe	Intense	Intense	Intense		Intense	Intense			Intense
				22	18	16	15	15	11	10	10	9

[a] op, outpatient; ip, inpatient; gh, group home. [b] Italics indicate affects not originally listed by therapist.

Fourteen of the 26 patients had a history of substance abuse; 9 were currently abusing, and in 5 of these 9 an increase in alcohol abuse, used to deal with increasing anxiety, marked the suicide crisis.

As summarized in TABLE 1, each of the 26 patients showed at least one of these three crisis markers: a precipitating event, an intense affective state other than depression, and a pattern of behavior indicative of the suicide crisis. In 16 of the cases, all three markers were present.

Other Indicators of Suicide Risk

Three other factors contributing to the suicide risk were frequently identified in our 26 patients (TABLE 1, Part B). The first of these was a history of previous suicide attempts, which was more frequent in our sample than in the general population of suicides. Seventeen of our patients had made at least one prior suicide attempt; 9 had made two or more attempts.

Impulsivity was the second factor that played a role in determining suicide risk, although it was not a sign of crisis. Therapists rated the patients' impulsivity as severe or moderate in 15 of the 26 cases. Finally, an ongoing pattern of substance abuse, even if not worsening, was seen frequently (9 cases), warranting its inclusion as a suicide risk factor.

Factors Impeding Recognition of the Suicide Crisis

In 14 of our 26 cases, the therapist did not recognize the suicide crisis. In 1 patient (Case 19), a precipitating event led to an impulsive suicide before the therapist could intervene. Eight of the 14 patients (Cases 2, 4, 6, 9, 14, 17, 20, and 26), however, provided warning signs by their intense affective states, combined with one or more behaviors associated with a suicide crisis. Awareness of the importance of these factors as crisis markers likely would have alerted the therapist to the patient's risk.

Among the other 5 patients in whom the suicide crisis was not recognized (Cases 5, 10, 15, 18, and 22), problems in communication appeared to contribute to the lack of recognition. In a number of cases, including the two that follow, disrupted or flawed communication between patient and therapist led the patient to deliberately conceal suicidal feelings and intention. In one case, what had been good communication between patient and therapist was disrupted by the threat of hospitalization, misleading the therapist to assume a suicide crisis had been resolved when it had actually intensified. In the second, restrictions by the hospital treatment team prevented the patient from communicating the intensity of his suicide crisis.

The therapist had treated this 23-year-old woman (Case 15) with major depressive disorder and borderline personality disorder for 2 years subsequent to her hospitalization for a suicide attempt. Early in treatment, the patient sought assurance that her thoughts of suicide would not alarm the therapist into putting her into a hospital. She was reassured by the therapis's affirming that while she was committed to the patient's living, she could not force her to remain alive. The young woman again became suicidal after 2 years of therapy, but said she would no longer discuss her desire for suicide because the therapist would try to dissuade her. This time the therapist replied that if the patient could not share such feelings, she would have to be hospitalized.

The patient related feeling alarmed and threatened by the therapist's response but said that she would not kill herself. She seemed more cheerful in the following weeks and denied any suicidal intentions but then proceeded to tape a long suicide message to her parents just before killing herself:

> ...Dr. (X) sort of threatened me. She said that if I didn't open up to her, she was going to have me put in the hospital...I stopped trusting her and started acting. I'm not that good an actress, but I just tuned out the part that I didn't want to tell her, but I did let myself get all emotional about how bad I was feeling and seemed like I was really opening up to her, but I started planning then about suicide...I lost faith in Dr. (X) and I couldn't come up with any reason to change those plans...It's going to be harder to work out the problems in my life after having lost the connection with Dr. (X) in which I had really felt sort of committed to tell the truth, so I just stuck with those plans...

The therapist did not observe any strong affective state in the patient prior to the suicide. The taped message, however, revealed the patient's feelings of desperation, hopelessness, rage, and abandonment. The therapist's anxiety over the patient's disclosure that she was withholding her thoughts of suicide led to the threat of hospitalization, blocking the patient's communication with the therapist and forcing the patient to dissemble, like "an actress." Had this threat not impeded their communication, this patient may not have needed hospitalization. A simple statement that if the patient did not talk about her feelings, the therapist could not help her, might have been sufficient.

A young man of 21 (Case 5) was treated for 9 months in an inpatient unit for major depressive disorder with severe anxiety and avoidant personality disorder. A few months before his death he exhibited aggressive behavior and made several suicide attempts. His treatment team was frustrated by his persistent reference to himself as "brain dead" and his demand for electroshock therapy. He was told that he would be transferred if he continued his suicidal behavior, and he was required to sign a contract that he would no longer refer to himself as "brain dead." His behavior seemed to improve, and he was allowed supervised excursions with other patients. He disclosed to his therapist, a resident who was leaving the ward, that his improvement was a masquerade to conceal and control his rage and agitation. Her note in the patient's chart was seemingly not read or understood, because soon afterwards he eloped from a group excursion and killed himself in a motel with stockpiled medications.

In his multiple suicide attempts, his statements that he felt "brain dead," and his insistence on electroshock therapy, this patient was telling his caregivers that his medication and therapy were not helping him. This obviously needed to be heard, and not suppressed by a contract or the threat of expulsion from the hospital. Like the previous patient, he felt obliged to put on a "masquerade" to hide his feelings. In both these cases, coercion on the part of treatment providers resulted not only in concealment of the suicide crisis, but also in a power struggle in which the patient distorted suicide into a victory.

A different kind of communication problem was seen in a hospital inpatient whose symptomatic improvement in the period preceding his death served as an impediment to recognizing his suicide crisis.

A 26-year-old man (Case 10) was intensively treated in a private hospital for 4 years for schizoaffective disorder and panic disorder. Although when delusional he feared being murdered and talked of himself as already dead, he never attempted suicide, never talked of suicide or of suicidal ideation, and, apart from severe anxiety, showed no other warning signs or affects associated with suicide. He became one of the first patients to be treated with clozapine. He showed marked improvement in both the positive (delusions and hallucinations) and negative (emotional withdrawal) symptoms of his disorder, although he was still intermittently delusional and continued to have panic attacks that were only partly relieved by clozapine and klonopin. He seemed to accept the plans being made for his discharge, but while on pass he threw himself in front of a train.

The improvement of this patient's psychotic and depressive symptoms on clozapine therapy seemed dramatic, and the absence of any previous history of suicide made anticipation of danger more difficult. Nevertheless, his chronic intense anxiety appears to have been exacerbated by his impending discharge, and the therapist subsequently realized this should have been addressed. In retrospect, the therapist thought that the patient was overly compliant about his discharge to please the therapist and his overburdened family and that more active elicitation of the patient's fears of trying to make a life outside of the hospital might have led to recognition of the suicidal danger.

Therapeutic Responses to the Suicide Crisis

In twelve of the 26 patients, the therapists identified crises that were propelling their patients towards suicide. The following cases illustrate two of the most common problems therapists experienced in attempting to respond to the crisis.

Suggestion of Hospitalization. In five cases in which therapists suggested hospitalization because of a patient's suicidal intentions, the suggestion was rejected by the patient and the suicide soon followed. The following case is illustrative.

A 44-year-old single male with bipolar disorder (Case 23) was in considerable debt because of his grandiose and unrealistic plans to open an art gallery. He and his friends also faced eviction from lofts they occupied illegally. One year earlier he was hospitalized for a psychotic episode when he became agitated and threw furniture while drinking. It took a month until he could be discharged, but he made a good recovery, Subsequently, however, he discontinued his prescribed medications and became verbally abusive to his parents.

He began therapy by reporting his intent to kill himself if he could not make a success of his gallery. He also indicated that he owned a handgun but that he had pawned it. After a brief improvement, he relapsed, and told his mother that he was going to get the gun back and she informed the therapist. When the therapist confronted him, he said he would not kill himself without talking about it first in therapy. The therapist proposed hospitalization; when the patient declined, the therapist offered to drive him to visit a prestigious hospital, and the patient agreed to consider this. Early in the morning after this conversation the patient hung himself in his studio.

This patient's refusing hospitalization, while agreeing to the therapist's request to consider it, suggests that his demurral and apparent cooperation masked a determination to kill himself and a fear that the therapist might prevent his suicide by involuntary hospitalization. In other cases, therapists arranged family meetings to elicit support for hospitalizing the patient. These efforts were largely controlled by the patient, however, and were unsuccessful.

Failure to Address Factors Underlying the Suicidal Intent. In several cases in which the suicidal intent was apparent, the therapist's response did not adequately address the patient's desire to die. In the following case, the therapist appeared to be more attentive to the needs and feelings of the patient's mother than to those of the patient himself.

A 39-year-old man (Case 11) with a history of bipolar disorder since the age of 17 never managed to establish a life independent of his mother. He had been hospitalized 20 times for his illness, and at the age of 21 he had attempted suicide. He was treated by his current therapist for 10 months, first while in the hospital and then while living in a group home and attending a day hospital. His mother was actively involved in his therapy and insisted that he should leave the group home, get his own apartment and a full-time job, and become financially independent.

When the patient told other residents in the group home that he was feeling suicidal, they called the therapist, who went to see him there. The patient showed him the rope and cinder blocks he was planning to use to drown himself. The therapist saw this suicide threat as a test of the commitment to free the patient of his dependency on the hospital, while recognizing it as a response to the pressure he and the patient's mother had been exerting. Although the therapist confiscated the blocks and the rope, he indicated to the patient that his reactions to discharge should be worked through in treatment with no change in plans. When the therapist reported what occurred to the mother, she replied, "He'd be better off dead if this is the way it's going to be for the rest of his life."

In his last session the patient discussed his continuing anxiety about moving out on his own. The therapist praised him for continuing to work at a part-time job despite his anxiety. The patient related a dream: "My father is sweeping me into the mouth of a big fish, and I get stuck in the fish's throat… or maybe I do get swallowed, I'm not so sure." The therapist's notes reported that in an earlier dream, the patient represented himself as trying to swim under water with weights attached to his body, an image that suggested how impossibly burdened he felt by his condition. The current dream suggested the patient's awareness that the therapist was actively participating in permitting his mother to control what was happening. He may have felt that the therapist was as helpless to deal with her as were he and his father, who had long been invalided by multiple sclerosis. Perhaps he hoped that his death would at least stick in her throat. The patient left the session and drowned himself in the manner he had indicated to the therapist.

The therapist recognized that in pursuing a strategy dictated by the patient's mother, he did not heed the dramatic warning that the patient conveyed in showing how he intended to kill himself, nor did he pay sufficient attention to the anxiety and anger reflected in the patient's dream.

CONCLUSIONS

The 26 suicide cases we studied suggest that therapists working with suicidal patients frequently do not recognize the severity of the emotional crises they experience. Our data indicate that only a small percentage of persons who are intent on killing themselves while in treatment give the therapist no indication of their crisis. We anticipate that consideration of the specific markers we have identified may aid therapists in recognizing the immediate danger of a suicide crisis.

A suicide crisis is a time-limited occurrence signaling immediate danger of suicide. Suicide risk, by contrast, is a broader term that includes factors such as age and sex, psychiatric diagnosis, past suicide attempts, and such traits and behaviors as impulsivity and substance abuse, known to be correlated with suicide.[7–10]

While therapists look at past events and ongoing behaviors in evaluating suicidal patients, our schema is designed to encourage evaluation of a range of current behaviors and intense affects to help identify a suicide crisis. Rage, hopelessness, and guilt, for example, have been shown to distinguish depressed patients who are suicidal from those who are not.[11–13] Anxiety has been shown to be a better short-term predictor of suicide than is hopelessness.[14] Our study suggests, however, that a wider range of acute intense affects including desperation, abandonment, humiliation, guilt, rage, and anxiety, often in combination, contribute to generating a suicide crisis with immediate danger to the patient.

In our analysis, problems in patient-therapist communication were central in preventing therapists from recognizing a suicide crisis and in impeding their effective response when they did. When patients appeared to be considering suicide but did not confide this to the therapist, asking if they were suicidal usually elicited the automatic "no" response that patients believed the therapist wanted to hear, or believed would deter the therapist from interfering with their plan for suicide. It would probably be more useful in this situation for therapists to indicate their awareness of the patient's mood or to convey their impression that the patient is considering suicide. Whatever the patient's response, it is likely to be more informative. Asking the patient at such a time to agree to a suicide contract or to reaffirm a prior contract may relieve the therapist's anxiety, but it is likely to be seen by the patient as primarily serving the therapist's need for reassurance and may unwittingly substitute for more careful clinical evaluation.[15]

In a number of the cases, the therapist's anxiety on hearing patients discuss their suicidal intent blocked communication and derailed the therapy. The communication of suicidal intent, however, is usually the patients' dramatic way of informing the therapist how desperate they feel. The first response should be to try to understand the nature and source of the desperation.

Hospitalization was often presented to patients as necessary to prevent their suicide—a motivation patients may not share with their therapists—rather than as a way for the patient to gain relief from desperation, anguish, and anxiety. If a therapist is unable to persuade a patient to be hospitalized and is convinced that there is an immediate threat of suicide, it seems warranted to initiate an involuntary hospitalization at once and not permit the patient to go home to think about it. Involuntary hospitalization might damage the relationship between therapist and patient, so that a change in therapists would be necessary, but it is worse to continue outpatient treatment when inpatient admission seems required. Obviously, hospitalization is not a guarantee of safety, but it may be the best possible way to address and resolve an acute suicide crisis.

Recognizing the suicide crisis is clearly as important in treating inpatients as well as outpatients. Although some patients, like one young woman who made four suicide attempts over the last 10 years, may appear chronically suicidal, they were not suicidal all the time. There were often several years between their attempts, and knowledge of when they were in crisis was important. Such patients appear to be particularly vulnerable when being pressed to make a transition to outpatient status.[16,17]

Several different explanations have been given for the observation that the mood of some depressed patients appears to be better in the days before their suicide, an observation made about several of these patients. The vegetative symptoms of depression have been said to improve in response to medication before affective symptoms such as desperation can resolve, providing the patient with the energy to commit suicide.[18] The improvement has also been seen as reflecting the calm of patients who know that their suicidal death will soon end their anguish.[19] Patients in this study suggest two other explanations. In some cases the improvement was a deception, ensuring that the therapist took no action to prevent the suicide. In other cases recovery from depression led to expectations of work and independent living that generated intolerable anxiety. Suicide in these cases seemed triggered by the expectations that recovery produced, not by recovery from depression per se.

Limitations

We initiated the Suicide Data Bank project with the goal of utilizing a relatively untapped source of information—therapists treating patients at the time of their suicide—to gain greater understanding of the psychology and behavior of patients who commit suicide. Rather than beginning with an *a priori* set of hypotheses, our approach was broadly exploratory, based essentially on our clinical sense that patient suicides occur within a dynamic set of relationships and forces that come together to create what we describe here as a suicide crisis. Our primary aim in looking at these first 26 cases has been to identify common patterns among such patients and their therapists, which might assist the development of more effective strategies for treating those at high risk of suicide. While we believe that this approach has yielded a valuable perspective, it is subject to a number of methodologic limitations that may restrict the ability to generalize the observations offered in this report.

The therapists who have participated in the project to date were, of necessity, volunteers, and therefore we cannot estimate how representative they are of the population of therapists who have experienced the suicide of a patient.

They cut across a wide range of professional experience, therapeutic orientations, and personal styles of interaction. Although our clinical experience supervising and consulting in patient suicide cases does not lead us to believe that these therapists are different from other therapists with the same experience, it is possible that therapists not volunteering their cases may be more troubled about their treatment of their patients than are those willing to have their cases reviewed. The requirements and procedures of this study may also have served to select a group of more highly involved and motivated therapists. On the other hand, it is also possible that participating therapists may be more than ordinarily disturbed about the death of their patients. Our earlier analysis of the reactions of the therapists to the deaths of their patients suggests that both of these possibilities were represented among our participating therapists.[20]

Our initial concern as to whether therapists could be frank in discussing cases they regard as treatment failures did not turn out to be a problem. The therapists who participated were generally eager to reveal all they could about the case in the hope of learning from the experience, and they welcomed the opportunity to present their cases to others with comparable experiences. Virtually all felt their participation was, to some degree, therapeutic as well as educational.

Persons who kill themselves while in psychotherapy are also not representative of all who commit suicide. Studies show, however, that there are basic clinical similarities between patients and nonpatients with psychiatric problems,[21,22] with attitudes toward utilization of psychiatric services rather than psychopathology often determining whether those in need of help seek treatment.[23] The 26 patients whose cases we analyzed in this project have had more suicide attempts in their past history then have suicides in general. Indeed, suicide attempts were often responsible for initiating their treatment. Comprehensive data do not currently exist on the demographic and clinical characteristics of patients who kill themselves in treatment. It would not be surprising, however, if there were more prior suicide attempts in the histories of such individuals than in the general population of people who commit suicide, many of whom have never had psychiatric treatment and kill themselves on their first attempt.

We are currently undertaking a survey of psychiatrists in the United States to ascertain whether or not their experience confirms this observation. Parenthetically, we have been led by our current project to suspect that a suicide attempt by a patient in treatment is a more serious warning of an impending suicide than is an attempt by a person not in treatment, because the attempt may be an indication that the patient does not feel that he or she is getting enough help. Indeed, in some of the cases presented here, suicide attempts and actual suicides appeared to be partly directed against the therapist.

Even if the findings here described are applicable only to those who seek treatment, the implications are important, because a considerable proportion of suicidal patients do seek treatment, and clinicians are in a position to help these individuals. Our work to date suggests the need for additional studies to be conducted to provide reliable empirical testing of our observations related to such suicides. In this regard, it might seem desirable to compare patients who commit suicide while in treatment with a matched control group of patients who did not kill themselves while being treated by the same therapists. While seemingly sound from a methodologic perspective, such a study design would be difficult to implement. It would also need to incorporate recognition of the fact that even comparable patients of the same therapist do not have the same relationship with the therapist and that such dynamics are essential to understanding why one patient commits suicide and another does not.

Perhaps a sounder and more feasible approach would be a prospective study involving a control group of depressed patients who do not kill themselves, against whom the experiences of those who do could be compared. In such a design, it would also be possible to elicit patients' descriptions of their affective experiences and compare them with therapists' evaluations.

We believe that the therapists participating in this study have provided information that has been missing from retrospective studies of suicide. We hope that a central finding of our work, that certain intense affective states together with other crisis markers can help therapists recognize the presence of a suicide crisis, will stimulate further study.

ACKNOWLEDGMENTS

This work was supported in part by unrestricted grants to the American Foundation for Suicide Prevention from the Mental Illness Foundation and Janssen Pharmaceutica. The material is this chapter is also being published as an article in *Suicide and Life-Threatening Behavior.*

REFERENCES

1. ROBINS, E., G. MURPHY, R. WILKINSON, *et al.* 1959. Some clinical considerations in the prevention of suicide based on a study of 134 successful suicides. Am. J. Public Health **49:** 888–899.
2. BARRACLOUGH, B. & J. HUGHES. 1987. Suicide. Clinical and Epidemiological Studies. Croon Helm. London.
3. RICH, C., R. FOWLER, L. FOGARTY & D. YOUNG. 1988. San Diego suicide study. III. Relationships between diagnoses and stressors. Arch. Gen. Psychiatry **45:** 589–592

4. CHEMTOB, C.M., R.S. HAMADA, G. BAUER, *et al.* 1988. Patients' suicides: frequency and impact on psychiatrists. Am. J. Psychiatry **145:** 224–228.
5. CHEMTOB, C.M., G.B. BAUER, R.S. HAMADA, *et al.* 1989. Patient suicide: occupational hazard for psychologists and psychiatrists. Prof. Psychol. Res. Pract. **20:** 294–300.
6. ALEXANDER, D.A., S. KLEIN, N.M. GRAY, *et al.* 2000. Suicide by patients: questionnaire study of its effects on consultant psychiatrists. Br. Med. J. **320:** 1571–1574.
7. ÅSBERG, M., D. SCHALLING, L. TRASKMAN, *et al.* 1987. Psychology of suicide, impulsivity and related phenomena. *In* Psychopharmacology: The Third Generation of Progress. H.Y. Meltzer, ed. Raven Press. New York.
8. APTER, A., R. PLUTCHIK & H.M. VAN PRAAG. 1993. Anxiety, impulsivity and depressed mood in relation to suicidal and violent behavior. Acta Psychiatr. Scand. **87:**1–5.
9. MURPHY, G.E. 1986. Suicide in alcoholism. *In* Suicide. Alex Roy, ed. Williams & Wilkins. Baltimore, MD.
10. FLAVIN, D.K., J.E. FRANKLIN & R. FRANCES. 1990. Substance abuse and suicidal behavior. *In* Suicide Over the Lifecycle. S. Blumenthal & D. Kupfer, eds. American Psychiatric Press. Washington, DC.
11. PLUTCHIKK, R. & H.M. VAN PRAAG. 1990. Psychosocial correlates of suicide and violence risk. *In* Violence and Suicidality: Perspectives in Clinical and Psychological Research. H.M. Van Praag, R. Plutchik & A. Apter, eds. Brunner/ Mazel. New York.
12. BECK, A.T., R.A. STEER, J.S. BECK & C.F. NEWMAN. 1993. Hopelessness, depression, suicidal ideation, and clinical diagnosis of depression. Suicide Life Threatening Behav. **23:** 139–145.
13. HENDIN, H. & A.P. HAAS. 1991. Suicide and guilt as manifestations of PTSD in Vietnam combat veterans. Am. J. Psychiatry **148:** 586–591.
14. FAWCETT, J., W. SHEFTNER & L. FOGG. 1990. Time-related predictors of suicide in major affective disorders. Am. J. Psychiatry **147:**1189–1194.
15. STANFORD, E.J., R.R. GOETZ & J.D. BLOOM. 1994. The no harm contract in the emergency assessment of suicidal risk. J. Clin. Psychiatry **55:** 344–348.
16. FAWCETT, J., D.C. CLARK & K.A. BUSCH. 1993. Assessing and treating the patient at risk for suicide. Psychiatr. Ann. **23:** 244–255.
17. KLEEPSIES, P.M., S. MARSHALL, T. POKRAJAC & R. AMODIO. 1994. Case consultation. The transition from inpatient to outpatient care: comment. Suicide Life Threatening Behav. **24:** 305–307.
18. HIMMELHOCH, J.M. 1987. Lest treatment abet suicide. J. Clin. Psychiatry **12** (suppl): 44–54.
19. HENDIN, H. & G. KLERMAN. 1993. Physician-assisted suicide: the dangers of legalization. Am. J. Psychiatry **150:** 143–145.
20. HENDIN, H., J. MALTSBERGER, A. LIPSCHITZ, *et al.* 2000. Therapists' reactions to patients' suicides. Am. J. Psychiatry **157.** In press.
21. HENDIN, H., W. GAYLIN & A. CARR. 1965. Psychoanalysis and Social Research: The Psychoanalytic Study of the Non-patient. Doubleday. New York.
22. LEAF, P.J., M. LIVINGSTON, G. TISCHLER, *et al.* 1985. Contact with health professionals for the treatment of psychiatric and emotional problems. Med. Care **23:** 1322–1337.

23. LEAF, P.J., M.L. BRUCE, G.L. TISCHLER & C.E. HOLZER, 3D. 1987. The relationship between demographic factors and attitudes toward mental health services. J. Commun. Psychol. **15:** 275–284.

DISCUSSION

JAN FAWCETT (*Rush Medical College, Chicago, IL*): It's very important to have the kind of data that Dr. Hendin has presented from analyzing cases of suicide. Suicide is such a tragic loss that the one thing we can do in suicides is to try and learn something from the cases. Our natural instinct is to try and forget about them. It's a very painful thing to lose a patient, for instance. There are all the fears of legal reprisals. There's a lot to suppress in our thinking about these suicides, and yet I think that by studying them we stand a chance of learning to be better at preventing them. If you think of a suicide as a useless death, certainly if it contributes to someone's life being saved through our study of it, it can be a very valuable thing. Studying these cases is very important. Every time I look into a suicide case that someone brings to me, I learn something that I didn't know before. Every case has another aspect to it. Secondly, I think the use of the terms "anguish" and "desperation" is very interesting. To me, the language of anxiety is something we don't think about much in clinical psychiatry. The patient has another language. Every patient has a different language. I spend most of the time with my depressed patients talking about their anxiety in whatever language they want to give it to me. I try and learn their language of anxiety. Everyone speaks a different language, uses different words, but it comes down to the same thing, to psychic pain. It's something we should be looking for very actively in every depressed patient. It's a lethal combination and needs to be treated and addressed. We are not doing it enough, perhaps because of the artificial separation of anxiety disorders from depressive disorders. It's because we don't consider anxiety as severe. There are many reasons, but the point is we need to focus on this. Dr. Hendin and his colleagues are starting to do this through their studies.

DAVID SHAFFER (*Columbia University, New York, NY*): Jan, I think that what you found in your follow-up was that agitation and arousal were the best predictors of imminent suicide. In our New York Youth Suicide Study, our findings were consistent in that death frequently followed a stress event by a short period of time. The most characteristic situation was that of a youngster who found that he was in trouble and he committed suicide within the few hours between discovering he was in trouble and learning what the consequences would be. Death might have occurred shortly after a girlfriend said she wasn't going to see a young man anymore. It might have occurred shortly after a youth was arrested and told that his parents were going to be informed.

It might have occurred after a youth was found out at school for doing something wrong and told that her parents would be informed. It was during that
phase of acute unease and "dread," a word I sometimes use which is similar
to anguish and psychic pain, of really acute psychological distress, malaise,
and pain, when the youth didn't know where he/she was and when the parameters or the outcome were not known to them. Of course, the situation in Dr.
Hendin's study was very different, because most of those people were in
treatment and were not responding acutely.

HERBERT HENDIN: Only two of our patients were adolescents. One of them
would fit your description in his response to an acute event. Our work indicated that in addition to anguish there was a quality of urgency in the patient's
need for relief. In our view, "desperation" best conveyed that anguish was accompanied by a sense of urgency.

Circumstances are different in evaluating the danger of suicide in patients
who are in ongoing therapy. Dr. Hirschfeld points out that patients coming to
an ER for help usually reveal readily that they are suicidal. That is seldom
true for patients in ongoing therapy. They usually do not want to admit that
they are imminently suicidal, which they fear might lead to their being hospitalized. In addition, Dr. Fawcett's work suggests that a suicide attempt is
not a particularly good short-term predictor of suicide. Our experience suggests that it is a better short-term predictor in patients engaged in ongoing
psychotherapy. After all, for a patient not in treatment the suicide attempt
may be a way of indicating great distress and the need for help. For patients
in treatment the attempt is likely an expression of the feeling that treatment
is not helping. Such an attempt has more serious prognostic implications.

When to Hospitalize Patients at Risk for Suicide

ROBERT M.A. HIRSCHFELD

Department of Psychiatry and Behavioral Sciences, University of Texas Medical Branch, Galveston, Texas 77555-0188, USA

ABSTRACT: The decision to hospitalize patients at imminent risk for suicide requires careful assessment of risk factors, including sociodemographic, psychiatric, general medical, and mental status considerations. Assessment of these risk factors is essential and can usually be accomplished in a straightforward manner, although clinical obstacles sometimes make assessment more difficult. Key issues regarding imminent suicide risk are intent and means, severity of psychiatric illness, the presence of psychosis or hopelessness, lack of personal resources, and older age among men. Once the decision to hospitalize is made, reasonable care should be taken to assure that the patient is transported to the treating hospital safely and is not left alone. On arrival at the hospital, the patient should be closely monitored, and reasonable precautions must be taken to assure the patient's safety at all times, especially during the first few days. Proper assessment, monitoring, and treatment of patients at imminent risk for suicide save lives. A person who is determined to kill himself/herself will probably prevail despite our best efforts. However, most people who are imminently suicidal at one time will feel very differently at some later time.

KEYWORDS: Hospitalization; Involuntary hospitalization; Risk factors for suicide; Suicide; Suicidal risk assessment

INTRODUCTION

Suicide is not a rational act. Jamison illustrates this point dramatically in her latest book, *Night Falls Fast,* in which she writes, "Suicide is simply the end of what I could bear. No amount of love from or for other people could help.... No advantage of a caring family was enough to overcome the pain and the hopelessness I felt. I knew my life to be in shambles and I believed incontestably that my family, friends, and patients would be better off without me." [1]

Address for correspondence: Robert M.A. Hirschfeld, M.D., Department of Psychiatry and Behavioral Sciences, University of Texas Medical Branch, 1.302 Rebecca Sealy, 301 University Boulevard, Galveston, TX 77555-0188. Fax: 409-747-8300.
Rohirsch@UTMB.udu

Jamison was profoundly depressed when she experienced these thoughts and feelings. Fortunately, she did not commit suicide. After she recovered, she felt very differently. She relished life again and experienced love and warmth from family and friends. A person determined to kill himself or herself may prevail despite our efforts, but like Jamison, most people will feel dramatically differently in time, especially if they are treated for their depression. Jamison's words and story illustrate how important it is for clinicians to protect patients when they are in danger of acting on suicidal thoughts and feelings arising from depression.

Clinicians often have the opportunity to detect suicidal risks and to intervene. As many as two thirds of individuals who commit suicide had seen a physician within the month preceding their suicide.[2–6] A clinician who believes that a patient is at risk for suicide must then assess the patient for imminent risk (i.e., suicide attempt within 48 hours), short-term risk (i.e., suicide attempt within days or weeks), or long-term risk. For the most part, the clinical options depend on this important judgment. Patients presenting with imminent suicidal risk usually should be hospitalized to protect them and to begin aggressive treatment. An overview of the risk factors for suicide is presented here, with a focus on imminent risk. Evaluation of imminent suicidal risk, how to make the decision to hospitalize, and how to deal with a suicide in one's practice are discussed.

EVALUATION OF THE PATIENT FOR SUICIDAL RISK

Several issues must be addressed in the evaluation of suicidal risk. First, can the patient be evaluated? Often by the time a clinician sees a patient, the patient has already made a suicide attempt and has been transported to the emergency room for evaluation and treatment. The patient may have taken an overdose of medication or may be stuporous, somnolent, or unable to communicate for other reasons. In such circumstances, the clinician's judgment may be that the patient cannot be evaluated for suicidal risk at that time and that disposition decisions will have to be postponed.

A second consideration is intoxication. Many suicide attempts occur during periods of alcohol or other types of intoxication. Patients may make suicidal threats when intoxicated. These threats may have been fostered by intoxication-lowered levels of inhibition or anger, aggression, impulsivity, and emotional lability. Patients often feel very differently following resolution of alcohol or cocaine intoxication and do not necessarily require protective psychiatric hospitalization. Disposition decisions may need to be postponed until the patient's intoxication resolves.

A third consideration is the extent to which the patient is being cooperative and honest during the psychiatric evaluation. An example of this situation is a young woman who was brought to the emergency room because of profound depression with command hallucinations to kill herself. When protective hospitalization was recommended, her husband, a long-distance truck driver, informed the emergency room staff that the patient was not suicidal. He then mentioned that he was scheduled to leave on a trip the next day and that his wife was needed to care for their young children. On hearing this, the patient reversed herself and said that she was not suicidal and would not hurt herself. Allowing her to return home at that moment would have been extremely dangerous.

A fourth consideration is whether the patient has a general medical condition that precludes psychiatric hospitalization. For example, unstable angina pectoralis, malignant hypertension, and gastroenterologic bleeds usually cannot be safely managed on a psychiatric unit.

RISK FACTORS FOR SUICIDE

Once the patient can be evaluated, the clinician should seek to assess the risk factors for suicide, of which there are four basic types: (1) demographic and psychosocial; (2) clinical or psychiatric; (3) general medical; and (4) mental status (TABLE 1).

Sociodemographic risk factors can be assessed by simple observation and straightforward questioning. As can be seen in FIGURE 1, suicide rates in white men skyrocket beginning in their late sixties.[7] We can speculate that men have fewer coping skills to deal with economic and interpersonal losses that are common in later life. Why white men have higher rates of suicide than men of other races is a mystery. In addition to considering the patient's age and gender, it is also important to find out if the patient is married or lives alone. Patients who live alone are generally at higher risk than married patients. At any rate, when weighing the risk factors to make a clinical judgment, older white men should be treated with greater caution, especially those living alone.

The most powerful risk factor for suicide is depression.[8] Rates in psychotic depression are especially high, particularly when there are auditory hallucinations commanding the person to kill himself or herself. Mixed manic states can also be very dangerous, particularly when the patient is aggressive. Mania, dysphoria, and lack of judgment can be a very lethal combination. Substance abuse, anxiety, and borderline personality disorder are also important clinical risk factors. Comorbidity of any of the foregoing, especially with anxiety, should be assessed. A history of suicide attempts is a particularly im-

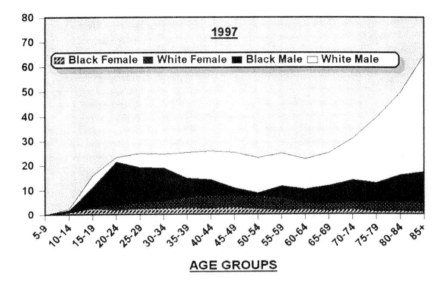

FIGURE 1. US suicide rates by age, gender, and racial group. Reprinted from National Institute of Mental Health.

portant risk factor that should also be assessed. Moreover, a family history of suicide may also be a risk factor, considering the amazing tendency for suicide to run in families.

In some instances, patients with general medical conditions may also be at risk for suicide. Such illness may include cancer (especially breast and genital), epilepsy, multiple sclerosis, head injury, cardiovascular disease, dementia, and AIDS.[9]

The patient's mental status is fundamental in evaluating suicide risk. Level of intoxication and ability to resist impulses should be evaluated. Pessimistic, hopeless cognitions and severe depression (especially with comorbid anxiety symptoms) are of concern. Direct assessment of suicidality is key: intentions, thoughts, plans, and availability of lethal means. Can the patient resist suicidal impulses? Is the patient psychotic?

CLINICAL EVALUATION FOR IMMINENT SUICIDAL RISK

The previous discussion focused on basic risk factors for suicide. If the evaluation leads to a judgment of no suicide risk or long-term suicide risk,

TABLE 1. Risk factors for suicide

Demographic and psychosocial	Clinical / psychiatric	General medical	Mental status

• Male
• Older age
• Living alone
• Lack of significant others
• Lack of dependents
• Acute distress
• Interpersonal conflict
• Humiliation/disgrace
• Financial
	• Depression, especially psychotic
	• Schizophrenia / schizoaffective disorder
	• Mixed mania
	• Substance abuse
	• Personality disorder, especially borderline
	• Comorbidity of above, especially with anxiety
	• History of suicide attempts
	• Family history of suicide
		• Cancer, especially breast and genitals
		• Epilepsy
		• Multiple sclerosis
		• Head injury
		• Cardiovascular disease
		• Dementia
		• AIDS
		• Cushing's syndrome
		• Klinefelter's syndrome
		• Porphyria
		• Hemodialysis
		• Prostatic hypertrophy
			• Intoxication
			• Suicidality
			  −Thoughts
			  −Intention
			  −Availability of lethal means
			• Mood
			  −Depression
			  −Anxiety symptoms, especially panic attacks
			  −Anger
			• Substance abuse
			• Psychosis
			  −Command hallucinations
			• Cognition
			  −Hopelessness
			  −Pessimism
			  −Despair
			• Personality
			  −Impulsivity
			  −Risk taking
			  −Emotional lability

there are many options to consider, such as informing and involving a friend or family member of the patient and limiting access to the means of suicide. A judgment of imminent suicide risk requires definitive action (usually hospitalization). The steps to this judgment are described below (FIG. 2).

The best way to determine if a patient is at imminent risk of suicide is simply to ask him or her. Many physicians are amazed at how frank people can be about suicidal intent if asked directly. One would think that if a person really wanted to do it, he or she would not tell the physician because the physician may stop him or her. However, the desire to commit suicide is often accompanied by a desire to ask for help.

Patients with borderline personality disorder, antisocial personality disorder, or features of these disorders, such as impulsivity and aggression, are often at high imminent risk. Risk taking and the emotional lability associated with borderline personality disorder can be lethal. Moreover, when such patients are depressed and angry, they will often make attempts or actually kill themselves in order to communicate to someone how angry or upset they are. Thus, when a patient is harboring a great deal of anger or meets criteria for borderline or antisocial personality disorder, these factors must be considered seriously in terms of whether hospitalization is necessary.

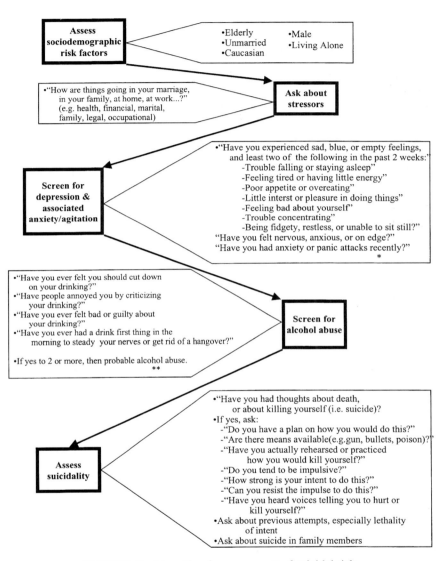

FIGURE 2. Algorithm for assessment of suicidal risk.

Cognition deserves close attention during the clinical evaluation. Patients are at greater risk when they feel hopeless and pessimistic. This can be determined by the patient's general attitude and by asking about stress and distress at home. Legal or financial problems should also be queried. If patients relate a sense of no hope or no future relief, they are likely at imminent risk. Auditory hallucinations commanding the patient to kill himself are indicators of imminent risk. Delusions about suicide with special religious themes or other meanings should also be carefully evaluated.

Another key assessment issue for imminent suicidal risk is availability of lethal means. Firearms are the number one means for suicide; 58% of suicides are committed with firearms, according to the Centers for Disease Control and Prevention.[7] Firearms should be removed from accessibility of patients.

MAKING THE DECISION TO HOSPITALIZE

The key issues in the evaluation of *imminent* suicidal risk are: (1) suicidal intent; (2) severity of psychiatric illness, especially depression; (3) presence of psychosis; (4) hopelessness and pessimism; (5) lethal means; (6) lack of personal resources; and (7) being an older white man.

VOLUNTARY OR INVOLUNTARY

Once a physician has determined that hospitalization is necessary, the next question is whether admission should be voluntary or involuntary. In most states the legal standard for involuntary commitment is that: (1) the person must be mentally ill; (2) the person evidences a substantial risk of serious harm to himself or others; (3) the described risk of harm is imminent unless the person is immediately restrained; and (4) emergency detention is the least restrictive means by which the necessary restraint may be accomplished.[10]

AFTER THE DECISION TO HOSPITALIZE IS MADE

A patient who is to be hospitalized because of imminent suicide risk should not be left alone. The patient should be maintained in a safe place and accompanied by a competent person. There are all too many tragic instances of patients committing suicide while the physician is making arrangements for transfer.

In general, do not allow the person to be taken to the hospital by a family member. The patient may manipulate the family member out of taking them to the hospital. Furthermore, the patient may commit suicide on the way to the hospital. This situation can be unfortunate from both a clinical as well as a legal liability perspective. In some communities (e.g., Texas) there are mental health deputies who can be very helpful in transporting patients to the hospital. Whenever available, resources such as these should be used. If a mental health deputy is unavailable, consider an ambulance service or the police to ensure the patient's safety during transportation to the hospital.

SUICIDE IN THE HOSPITAL

Patients at imminent suicidal risk require close supervision in the hospital as well. Patients with comorbid depression and anxiety or panic are at particular risk for attempting suicide in the hospital. Suicides in the hospital generally occur within the first few days of hospitalization. Suicide attempts are more likely during times of staff rotation or disorganization. Many patients may also make attempts when they are off the ward or on pass.

WHEN SUICIDE OCCURS

Despite our best efforts, a suicide may occur. When it does, how should the clinician handle this? The clinician should be humane, concerned, and express condolences, but should not break his/her professional demeanor. The clinician should completely avoid the issue of blame, neither accepting nor assigning it. Defensive statements are unwise. When death first occurs, people are often in shock. After things begin to settle, relatives may look for someone to blame. The clinician can be a target.

Whenever there is a suicide, a thorough records review is in order. A post-dated addendum is perfectly appropriate to record events, such as phone calls, which had not been previously documented. Records should not be altered or destroyed. If there are particular concerns or questions, it might be advisable to consult an attorney.

CONCLUSION

Safety of the patient is our primary concern. If suicidal intentions are suspected, the risk of suicide and the necessity of hospitalization should be assessed. Evaluation of suicidal risk often involves difficult and stressful clinical judgments. It is important to proceed cautiously. The patient should be in a proper mental state to be evaluated, and we should always be on guard for the patient who is not forthright about his/her feelings. Careful note should be made of demographic, psychosocial, psychiatric, general medical, or mental status risk factors. If the patient appears to represent a suicidal risk based on these factors, we should determine whether the patient is at imminent as opposed to long-term risk of suicide. If the patient is not at imminent risk, he/she may be treated on an outpatient basis, provided sufficient psycho-social support by family and/or friends is available and secure arrangements are in place. If the patient is at imminent suicide risk, hospitalization is usu-ally necessary. Regardless of whether hospitalization is voluntary or involun-tary, the patient should not be left alone, and proper arrangements (e.g., ambulance) should be made to safely transport the patient to the hospital. Evaluation of the suicidal patient is a serious matter and should be taken very seriously. With proper detection and intervention lives can be saved.

REFERENCES

 1. JAMISON, R.K. 1999. Night Falls Fast: Understanding Suicide. Knopf. New York.
 2. BARRACLOUGH, B.M., J. BUNCH, B. NELSON & P. SAINSBURY. 1974. A hundred cases of suicide: clinical aspects. Br. J. Psychiatry 125: 355–373.
 3. HAGNELL, O., J. LANKE & B. RORSMAN. 1981. Suicide rates in the Lunby study: mental illness as a risk factor for suicide. Neuropsychobiology 7: 248–253.
 4. MURPHY, G.E. 1975. The physician's responsibility for suicide I. An error of commission. Ann. Intern. Med. 82: 301–304.
 5. MATTHEWS, K., S. MILNE & G.W. ASHCROFT. 1994. Role of doctors in the pre-vention of suicide: the final consultation. Br. J. Gen. Pract. 44: 345–348.
 6. ROBINS, E., G.E. MURPHY, R.H. WILKINSON, JR., et al. 1959. Some clinical considerations in the prevention of suicide based on a study of 134 successful suicides. Am. J. Public Health 49: 888–899.
 7. CENTERS FOR DISEASE CONTROL AND PREVENTION. National Center for Health Statistics. Atlanta, GA. (http://www.cdc.gov)
 8. RICH, C.L. & B.S. RUNESON. 1992. Similarities in diagnostic comorbidity between suicide among young people in Sweden and the United States. Acta. Psychiatr. Scand. 86: 335–339.
 9. ROY, A. 1999. Psychiatric emergencies. In Kaplan & Sadock's Comprehensive Textbook of Psychiatry. B. J. Sadock & V. A. Sadock, eds. Brandon/Hill. New York, NY.
10. TEX. HEALTH & SAFETY CODE. 2000. §573.022.
11. HIRSCHFELD, R.M.A. & J.M. RUSSELL. 1997. Assessment and treatment of sui-cidal patients. N. Engl. J. Med. 337: 910–915.
12. National Institute of Mental Health. In harm's way: suicide in America. (http://www.nimh.gov). NIH Publication No. 01-4509.

DISCUSSION

J. JOHN MANN (*Chairman*): Based on your clinical assessment or gut reac-tion or otherwise, when do you decide that the patient doesn't need to be hos-pitalized?

ROBERT M.A. HIRSCHFELD: In many ways that's a more difficult decision than deciding to hospitalize. First of all, the patient has to say, "I will not kill myself. I may be having some thoughts of suicide but I can resist them," and you have to believe him. They must have a very supportive environment with other people, and their psychiatric illness must not be overwhelmingly severe.

MANN: You place a fair bit of reliance on patients saying that they definitely don't feel suicidal.

HIRSCHFELD: That's where I'd start, but you can't use that as your only criterion. Also, there have been many cases where in the emergency room the person says that he is not suicidal and yet their significant other says exactly the opposite, that the person has been making threats and has been stockpiling medicines, etc., for several days. But that is actually not answering your question about hospitalization.

MANN: But that's very helpful, that is, to seek corroborative information.

HIRSCHFELD: I'm always astonished when people come to my office and say, "I've seen a whole bunch of psychiatrists and they have never wanted my wife to come." I often get more information from the significant other than I do from the patient.

MANN: What about the patient who keeps coming back to the emergency room, that is, three times in the last couple of weeks; does that affect your assessment? The second question, which is related, is what if you are a nonphysician and you refer the patient to the emergency room because you think he is a serious suicide risk, and the hospital or emergency room staff don't agree with your assessment?

HIRSCHFELD: It is not hard to play the system, and again we have a cadre of patients who do that. Our census goes up and down depending on the weather and it's very frustrating. If someone says they are going to kill themselves, you are at substantial risk if you don't hospitalize them. You really need to be very careful about not hospitalizing someone even if you know for sure that he has been in three times this week. In those circumstances, if they just spend some time, a day and so on, they often feel better, but it's a very difficult problem. You end up having to do something when you know it's really not necessary. The second question, if the hospital doesn't agree with your assessment, they are really at risk if something does happen. Ultimately, again I know only the laws in Texas, it has to be a physician or a judge who decides. If the emergency room does not agree and discharges that person, medicolegally you're in reasonable shape. Hopefully they have not made a mistake, but it's their responsibility.

JACK R. CORNELIUS (*University of Pittsburgh, Pittsburgh, PA*): In my experience, when the emergency room decides not to admit somebody even though the outpatient doctor or clinician thinks they should, it's often because the outpatient clinician has some information that wasn't necessarily fully appreciated by the emergency room staff. A call by that outpatient clinician to the emergency room, making them aware of that fact and emphasizing it duly, can sometimes help. Often you can prevent that from ever happening if the outpatient clinician calls before and speaks with the emergency room staff before the final decision is made. Even after a decision has been made, if the outpatient doctor immediately calls to say that he disagrees, you still can get the ER people to change their mind if you can provide a convincing rationale. However, I don't want to necessarily encourage this on a regular basis. All those things can lead to disagreements with various people, so I'm not trying to advocate that as a standard course of action, but to make you aware of it.

MANN: It all adds up to being a more activist caregiver, although I can see you may want to have a relationship with more than one hospital. About the complexities of assessing the veracity of what people are saying, what about the particular problems of assessing an adolescent's true level of suicidal intent, particularly when adolescents often change their story when they arrive at a hospital?

HIRSCHFELD: I'd like to suggest that we defer to someone who actually has knowledge in that area. Dr. Brent covers this in his presentation. It certainly is true that adolescents exaggerate. They often have much difficulty in seeing that the current situation is not going to continue for the rest of their lives, so it makes evaluation much more difficult.

MANN: Somebody writes here that hanging used to be a very common method for committing suicide and is a lot less frequent now. Could you comment on that. I would like to add that I believe that it's still a common method in prisons. I know there are some people here who work in forensic services. It's always a vexing question when to admit somebody to hospital from the prison system. Would you tackle those two concerns.

HIRSCHFELD: Actually it's a good question for which I don't know the answer. The first thing is to see if the reduction in the number of people hanging themselves is made up by an increase in the use of firearms. Firearms are much more available and certainly easier to use and at least as lethal, if not more so. The issue of hanging in prisons is an example of means available; people obviously don't have firearms and other things available to them. It is a serious problem. Actually, UTMB does take care of most prisoners in the state of Texas, so that's a huge issue for us. In general, you don't have the same problem of involuntary hospitalization because they are already there involuntarily. The real issue is just observing them very closely and putting them on suicide precautions.

MANN: Dr. Hirschfeld, apparently some states require the diagnosis of mental illness in conjunction with the decision to hospitalize involuntarily. If I understand the question correctly, does that mean that they have to have an axis I diagnosis, or can an axis 2 or adjustment disorder or some such other situational dysthymia type diagnosis suffice?

HIRSCHFELD: That's an interesting question. I assume, and certainly it is true in Texas, in order to hospitalize someone to a psychiatric hospital involuntarily on an EAD, they need to have a mental illness. Their suicidality must presumably be related to that. That would include axis 2, and that's certainly an issue. I don't know that anyone has ever raised that issue of borderline personality disorder in court, but now that you have brought it up here, it may wend it's way down there.

MANN: Let's say you have a very bright, insightful patient that you are hospitalizing against his or her will. What consideration in your decision is given to the thought that the next time the patient feels the same way, he is likely to withhold key information; are you less likely to detect the risk?

HIRSCHFELD: My experience is that even though patients may be bright and insightful, they are remarkably frank. When they get pessimistic and seriously depressed, it affects their whole judgment. They will talk just the way Kay Jamison spoke. That's how they see life.

Suicide and the Media

MADELYN S. GOULD

Division of Child and Adolescent Psychiatry and Division of Epidemiology, Columbia University and New York State Psychiatric Institute, New York, New York 11024, USA

ABSTRACT: Evidence continues to amass on the significant impact of media coverage on suicide. The research literature on the impact of news reports of nonfictional suicides as well as fictional suicide stories is reviewed in order to determine the nature and scope of the influence of the mass media on suicide. The current review, building upon earlier reviews, is limited to English language publications or English translations of articles and/or abstracts. The interactive factors that may moderate the impact of media stories are also reviewed. Such interactive factors include characteristics of the stories (agent), individuals' attributes (host), and social context of the stories (environment). Recommendations are presented for the reporting of suicide stories, which may minimize the risk of imitative suicides. The media's positive role in educating the public about risks for suicide and shaping attitudes about suicide is emphasized. In summary, the existence of suicide contagion no longer needs to be questioned. We should refocus our research efforts on identifying which particular story components promote contagion under which circumstances and which components are useful for preventive programming.

KEYWORDS: Behavioral contagion; Imitative suicide; Media coverage of suicide; Prevention of suicide

INTRODUCTION

The media affords the opportunity for indirect transmission of suicide contagion, the process by which one suicide becomes a compelling model for successive suicides.[1,2] This means of influence is potentially more far reaching than direct person-to-person propagation. Suicide contagion can be viewed within the larger context of behavioral contagion, which has been described as the situation in which the same behavior spreads quickly and spontaneously through a group.[3] Behavioral contagion has also been conjectured to influence the transmission of conduct disorder, drug abuse, and teenage

Address for correspondence: Madelyn S. Gould, Ph.D., M.P.H., Division of Child and Adolescent Psychiatry, Columbia University/New York State Psychiatric Institute, 1051 Riverside Drive, Unit 72, New York, NY 11024. Voice: 212-543-5329; fax: 212-543-5966.
gouldm@child.cpmc.columbia.edu

pregnancy.[4,5] According to behavioral contagion theory, an individual has a preexisting motivation to perform a particular behavior, which is offset by an avoidance gradient, such that an approach-avoidance conflict exists.[6] The occurrence of suicides in the media may serve to reduce the avoidance gradient—the observer's internal restraints against performing the behavior. Social learning theory also provides a foundation on which aspects of suicide contagion may build. According to this theory, most human behavior is learned observationally through modeling.[7] Imitative learning is influenced by a number of factors, including the characteristics of the model and the consequences or rewards associated with the observed behavior.[8] Consequences or rewards, such as public attention, may lower behavior restraints and lead to the disinhibition of otherwise "frowned upon" behavior.[9] Last, a public health or infectious disease model of contagion is also useful for a conceptualization of suicide contagion. This model acknowledges the role that the agent, host, and environment play in the overall transmission process. Applying these three classic theoretical models, the current chapter presents available information on the agent (i.e., model), host (i.e, vulnerable individual), and environmental characteristics that may moderate the impact of the media. The presentation of these interactive factors follows the review of the studies on the impact of nonfictional suicide stories and fictional stories.

NONFICTIONAL SUICIDE STORIES

The occurrence of imitative suicides following media stories is largely known as the "Werther effect," derived from the general impression that Goethe's novel *The Sorrows of Young Werther* in 1774 triggered an increase in suicides, leading to its ban in many European states. Research on the Werther effect was advanced by the systematic work of Phillips,[10–15] whose research consistently found a strong relationship between reports of suicide in newspapers or on television and a subsequent increase in the suicide rate. Several studies within the past decade[16–30] have reported findings that are consistent with the substantial number of earlier studies (see TABLE 1). This body of research has clearly demonstrated that extensive newspaper coverage of suicide is associated with a significant increase in the rate of suicide. The magnitude of the increase is proportional to the amount, duration, and prominence of media coverage. While most of the studies examined an excess of deaths following the appearance of suicide stories, other early studies examined the *decrease* in deaths during the cessation of stories, which occurred during newspaper strikes.[31,32]

Prior to 1990, most of the studies focused on U.S. populations, raising the question of whether the findings could be generalized to other countries. Since 1990, the effect of media coverage on suicide rates has been document-

TABLE 1. Studies examining media influences on imitative suicides: nonfictional suicide stories

Citation	Country studied	Source of study	Support of imitation
Prior to 1990			
Baron & Reiss (1985)[33]	USA	TV network news (partial replication of Bollen & Phillips (1982),[11] using multiprogram suicide stories)	Mixed
Barraclough, Shepherd & Jennings (1977)[90]	England	Newspaper (reports of suicide inquests in daily newspaper)	Yes (age-sex specific)
Blumenthal & Bergner (1973)[31]	USA	Newspaper *cessation* (no specific articles per se; compared suicide mortality during newspaper strike to periods without strike)	Yes (age-sex specific)
Bollen & Phillips (1981)[10]	USA	Newspaper (front page suicide stories)	Yes
Bollen & Phillips (1982)[11]	USA	TV network news (multiprogram suicide stories, i.e., aired on 2 or more networks)	Yes
Ganzeboom & de Haan (1982)[70]	Netherlands	Newspaper (front page suicide stories)	Trend (nearly significant)
Horton & Stack (1984)[34]	USA	TV network news (number of seconds of coverage of suicide on 6 o'clock national news)	No
Kessler, Downy, Milavsky & Stipp (1988)[35]	USA	TV network news (any suicide news report on ABC, CBS, *or* NBC)	Yes/No
Kessler, Downy, Stipp & Milavsky (1989)[36]	USA	TV network news (any suicide news report on ABC, CBS, *or* NBC)	Yes/No
Littman (1985)[96]	Canada	Newspaper (all suicide-related reports: articles, features, editorials)	No
Motto (1967)[97]	USA	Newspaper *cessation* (no specific articles per se; compared suicide mortality during newspaper strike to periods without strike)	No
Motto (1970)[32]	USA	Newspaper *cessation* (no specific articles per se; compared suicide mortality during newspaper strike to periods without strike)	Yes (age-sex specific)

TABLE 1. Studies examining media influences on imitative suicides: nonfictional suicide stories (*contd*)

Citation	Country studied	Source of study	Support of imitation
Phillips (1974)[12]	USA	Newspaper (front page suicide stories in *New York Times, New York Daily News, Chicago Tribune, London Daily Mirror,* and listed in *Facts on File*)	Yes
Phillips (1979)[13]	USA	Newspaper (front page suicide stories in *Los Angeles Times* and *San Francisco Chronicles*)	Yes
Phillips & Carstensen (1986)[14]	USA	TV network news (news or feature stories on ABC, CBS, *or* NBC)	Yes
Phillips & Carstensen (1988)[15]	USA	TV network news (multiprogram suicide stories, i.e., aired on 2 or more networks)	Yes
Stack (1983)[79]	USA	Newspaper/TV network (no articles per se; examined suicide mortality after extensive media coverage of Jonestown mass suicide)	No
Stack (1984)[37]	USA	TV network (number of seconds per month devoted to suicide stories)	No
Stack (1987)[74]	USA	Newspaper (nationally publicized suicide story of a celebrity - separate analyses for front page stories and for number of column inches)	Yes[a]
Stack (1988)[92]	USA	Newspaper (front page suicide stories in *New York Times* <u>and</u> two other papers	Yes[a]
Wasserman (1984)[73]	USA	Newspaper (front page suicide stories in *New York Times*)	Yes
Since 1990			
Cantor, Tucker & Burnett (letter) (1991)[98]	Australia	Newspaper/TV/multimedia (all types of media and word-of-mouth negative publicity about a psychiatry unit experiencing patients' suicides)	Yes
Deisenhammer, Kemmler, Fleischhaker & Hinter-huber (1997)[16]	Austria	TV network (television report on stress suffered by train engineers due to railway suicides)	Yes
Etzersdorfer, Sonneck & Nagel-Kuess (1992)[17]	Austria	Newspaper (no specific articles per se; examined period following implementation of newspaper guidelines)	Yes

TABLE 1. Studies examining media influences on imitative suicides: nonfictional suicide stories (*contd*)

Citation	Country studied	Source of study	Support of imitation
Etzersdorfer & Sonneck (1998)[18]	Austria	Newspaper (no specific articles per se; examined period following implementation of newspaper guidelines)	Yes
Fekete & Macsai (1990)[19]	Hungary	Newspaper/book/TV/film (extensive publicity following suicide of beauty queen in Hungary)	Yes
Gundlach and Stack (1990)[75]	USA	Newspaper (front-page suicide stories in *New York Times*)	Yes
Hassan (1995)[20]	Australia	Newspaper (any suicide story—weighted according to it's position, size, and contents)	Yes
Ishii (1991)[21]	Japan	Newspaper (any suicide story — total amount of suicide news calculated based on number of headlines and circulation of papers)	Yes
Jobes, Berman, O'Carroll, Eastgard & Knickmeyer (1996)[77]	USA	Newspaper/TV/multimedia (extensive publicity in Seattle following suicide of Kurt Cobain)	No[a]
Jonas (1992)[22]	Germany	Newspaper (any story about a suicide of a prominent person)	Yes
Koepping, Ganzeboom & Swanborn (1989)[99]	Netherlands	Newspaper (any story including obituaries)	No
Martin & Koo (1997)[78]	Australia	Multimedia (extensive publicity following suicide of Kurt Cobain)	No[a]
Sonneck, Etzerdorfer & Nagel-Keuss (1994)[23]	Austria	Newspaper (no specific articles per se; examined period following implementation of newspaper guidelines)	Yes
Stack (1990a)[24]	USA	Newspaper (front-page suicide stories in *New York Times* and listed in *Facts on File* also indicating marital problems)	Yes[a]
Stack (1990b)[25]	USA	Newspaper (front-page suicide stories in *New York Times* and listed in *Facts on File*)	Yes[a]
Stack (1990c)[76]	USA	TV network news (multiprogram suicide stories, i.e., aired on 2 or more networks)	Yes[a]

TABLE 1. Studies examining media influences on imitative suicides: nonfictional suicide stories (*contd*)

Citation	Country studied	Source of study	Support of imitation
Stack (1991)[26]	USA	TV network news (multiprogram suicide stories, i.e., aired on 2 or more networks)	Yes[a]
Stack (1992)[27]	USA	Newspaper (front-page suicide stories in at least five of seven newspapers searched)	Yes/No
Stack (1993)[28]	USA	TV network news (multiprogram suicide stories, i.e., aired on 2 or more networks)	Yes[a]
Stack (1996)[29]	Japan	Newspaper (front-page suicide stories)	Yes
Wasserman (1992)[30]	USA	Newspaper (front-page suicide stories—replicated Stack, 1988)	Yes[a]

[a]Examined specific type of story (e.g., celebrity status), individual characteristic (e.g., specific age group), or environmental context (e.g., depression, crisis intervention).

ed in many other countries besides the U.S.—Western countries, including Austria,[17] Germany,[22] and Hungary;[19] Australia;[20] and East Asian countries, such as Japan.[21,29] While most of the recent studies investigating the impact of nonfictional suicide stories have continued to find an increase in rates of suicide following exposure to media reports, one group of researchers found a significant *decrease* in rates of suicide following implementation of media guidelines for news reporting by the Austrian Association for Suicide Prevention in 1987.[17,18,23] These latter studies are consistent with the earlier ones reporting a decrease in the suicide rate during periods of "blackouts" due to newspaper strikes.[31,32]

As can be seen in TABLE 1, the vast majority of studies have examined the impact of *newspaper* coverage of suicide. Fewer studies have examined the association of *television* coverage and subsequent suicides.[11,14,16,26,28,33–37] While earlier findings were equivocal, recent studies support an imitative effect of television news reports on suicide.

FICTIONAL SUICIDE STORIES

Studies of the effects of fictional stories on suicide have produced varying results, with some indicating a significant effect[38–50] and others reporting no association between media reports and subsequent suicides[51–55] or equivocal results[56,57] (TABLE 2).

TABLE 2. Studies examining media influences on imitative suicides: fictional suicide stories

Citation	Country studied	Source of study	Support of imitation
Prior to 1990			
Berman (1988)[56]	USA	Partial replication of Gould & Shaffer (1986)[41] evaluating two of four made-for-TV movies and one additional broadcast not in original study	No
Daniels (1986) (letter)[51]	UK	TV soap opera episode, *East-Enders*, depicting an overdose	No
Ellis & Walsh (1986) (letter)[39]	UK	TV soap opera episode, *East-Enders*, depicting an overdose	Yes
Fowler (1986)[40]	UK	TV soap opera episode, *East-Enders*, depicting an overdose	Yes
Gould & Shaffer (1986)[41]	USA	Four made-for-TV movies	Yes
Gould, Shaffer & Kleinman (1988)[42]	USA	Replication and extension of Gould & Shaffer (1986)	Yes
Häfner & Schmidtke (1989)[43]	Germany	Six-episode TV movie, *Death of a Student* (rebroadcast 18 months after original broadcast)	Yes
Holding (1974, 1975)[45, 46]	Scotland	11-episode weekly series on BBC TV, *The Befrienders* portraying the Samaritans	Yes
Jackson & Potkey (1974)[100]	USA	One-act stage play shown to college undergraduates	No
Kessler & Stipp (1984)[52]	USA	Replication and extension of Phillip (1982)	No
Ostroff *et al.* (1985, 1987) (letters)[47, 48]	USA	Made-for-TV movie	Yes
Phillip (1982)[58]	USA	TV soap opera episodes in which a suicide or suicide attempt occurred	Inconclusive because an inaccurate and nonexhaustive index of TV suicide stories was used (see Kessler & Stipp, 1984)

TABLE 2. Studies examining media influences on imitative suicides: fictional suicide stories (*contd*)

Citation	Country studied	Source of study	Support of imitation
Phillips & Paight (1987)[53]	USA	Partial replication of Gould & Shaffer (1986), evaluating three of four made-for-TV movies	No
Platt (1987, 1989)[59, 101]	UK	TV soap opera episode, *East-Enders*, depicting an over-dose	Equivocal (sex and age spe-cific effects noted)
Range, Goggin & Steede (1988)[67]	USA	Videotaped vignette of an emotionally distressed female high school student shown to college under-graduates	Yes[a]
Sandler, Connel & Welsh (1986) (letter)[49]	UK	TV soap opera episode, *East-Enders*, depicting an over-dose	Yes
Schmidtke & Häfner (1988)[50]	Germany	Six-episode TV movie, *Death of a Student* (rebroadcast 18 months after original broadcast)	Yes
Steede & Range (1989)[68]	USA	Videotaped vignette of an emotionally disturbed female high school student, shown to high school students	No[a]
Since 1990 Biblarz, Biblarz, Pil-grim & Baldree (1991)[62]	USA	Films on suicide or violence or neutral films shown to college undergraduates	Yes[a]
Collins (1993) (let-ter)[38]	UK	One episode on TV series, *Casualty* (Jan. 1993), depicting teenage girl's overdose	Yes
Gibson & Range (1991)[64]	USA	Vignettes read by high school students	Yes[a]
Hawton, Simkin, Deeks, O'Connor, Keen, Altman, Philo & Bulstrade (1999)[44]	UK	One episode on TV series, *Casualty* (Nov. 1996), depicting an RAF's pilot's overdose	Yes

TABLE 2. Studies examining media influences on imitative suicides: fictional suicide stories (*contd*)

Citation	Country studied	Source of study	Support of imitation
Higgins & Range (1996)[65]	USA	Fictitious newspaper article about a high school student who committed suicide, read by college undergraduates	Mixed[a]
McDonald & Range (1990)[66]	USA	Vignettes read by high school students	Mixed[a]
Simkin, Hawton, Whitehead, Fagg & Eage (1995)[60]	UK	Episode on TV series, *Casualty* (Jan. & July 1993), depicting teenage girl's overdose	No
Stack (1990d)[54]	USA	Same made-for-TV movies as Gould & Shaffer (1986)[41]	No
Veysey, Kamanyire & Volans (1999) (letter)[61]	UK	An episode on TV series, *Casualty* (Feb. 1997), depicting attempt with antifreeze	Yes
Waldron, Walton & Helowicz (1993) (letter)[57]	UK	Replication of Collins (1993)[38]	Mixed
Williams, Lawton, Ellis, Walsh & Reed (1987) (letter)[55]	UK	TV soap opera episode, *East-Enders*, depicting an overdose	No

[a]Experimental studies.

While the studies on nonfictional suicide stories have been confined to reports of *completed* suicides, the investigations of fictional suicide stories have often focused on suicide *attempts* as the modeled behavior.[38–40,44,49,51,52,58–61] The impact of the stories does not appear to vary by the nature of the suicidal behavior modeled. Moreover, studies on fictional suicide stories have often examined suicide attempts as the outcome of inquiry, providing the opportunity to measure actual exposure to the stories.[44] This is a notable advance, since earlier studies were limited by not knowing whether the victims had actually seen the broadcasts. Hawton and colleagues[44] reported that of the interviewed patients who presented to emergency rooms and psychiatric services after a television broadcast of a deliberate self-poisoning with paracetamol, 20% stated that the broadcast had influenced their decision to take an overdose, and 17% stated the broadcast had influenced their choice of drug.

Newer paradigms to examine the impact of suicide stories include experimental designs, which examine youths' reactions to media dramatizations or written vignettes about suicide.[62–68] Biblarz and colleagues[62] randomly assigned healthy college students to one of three experimental conditions involving exposure to a film depicting teenage suicide, physical violence, or neither. Subjects exposed to the suicidal movie reported transient increases in arousal, and changes in arousal were associated with some attitudinal change. The research by Range and colleagues[64–68] has focused on the assessments of *attitudes* and *perceptions* of suicide contagion, rather than on actual behavior of high school or college students who have been exposed to vignettes about suicidal individuals. The evidence of suicidal contagion from these experimental studies has been mixed. Another experimental study[63] examined the physiological reactions to a suicide film by suicide attempters, suicide ideators, and nonsuicidal patients. The suicide attempters had significantly lower postscreening heart rates and significantly lesser change in heart and respiration rates than the other two groups. Furthermore, the suicide attempters revealed less anxiety than nonsuicidal psychiatric patients following exposure to a simulated suicide. These results emphasize the need to consider host characteristics when evaluating the impact of a suicide story (to be discussed under INTERACTIVE FACTORS).

Another new research design to examine the impact of televised suicide stories employed a cross-sectional survey of normal high school students to assess television viewing habits, television life events, symptomatology, and suicidal ideation and attempts.[69] Students reporting frequent exposure to television suicide reported more suicide attempts. A strong association was also found between knowledge of a real-life suicide, reporting of frequent television suicide, and a suicide attempt. When knowledge of a suicide in real life was controlled, the relationship between television suicide and suicide attempts was no longer significant. The cross-sectional nature of the study precludes the determination of causality; the associations could have resulted from self-selected viewing of television suicides by suicide attempters or selective memory of viewing such programs. Nevertheless, the reported associations are intriguing and warrant further study.

Despite the contradictory results from the studies on the impact of fictional suicide stories, there is ample evidence of an imitative effect from these broadcasts. As discussed in the next section, interactive factors, such as stimulus variability, may moderate the impact of the media. It is unrealistic to expect a monolithic effect from a heterogeneous set of broadcasts.

INTERACTIVE FACTORS

There is an increasing effort to examine the media's differential impact as a function of the characteristics of the stories (agent), individuals' attributes (host), and social context of the stories (environment). Many theoretical perspectives, as discussed previously, predict that an individual's motivation and attention will moderate the impact of the media stories. Such motivation and attention may reflect the life situation or demographic characteristics of the victim, features of the story, and/or a correspondence between the victim and the story.

Agent/Stimuli Characteristics

There is overwhelming evidence that the magnitude of the increase in suicidal behavior after newspaper coverage is related to the amount of publicity given to the story and the prominence of the placement of the story in the newspaper.[10–14,70,71] Imitation appears more likely when the suicide is covered on the front page, in large headlines, and is heavily publicized, suggesting a "dose-response" relationship.[72] Phillips[72] has argued that repetition is a key factor for news stories' imitative potential.

In contrast to these "structural" elements of the story, there is less information on what characteristics of the models or content of the story have an imitative effect. One characteristic of the model that has been studied is the celebrity status of the suicide victim. Wasserman[73] found that a significant rise in the national suicide rate occurred only after celebrity suicides were covered on the front page of the *New York Times*. Stack[74] replicated this study, but upon correcting substantial measurement error, a later analysis[25] found that noncelebrity stories also had a significant impact, although not as great as publicized celebrity stories. Gundlach and Stack[75] reported that noncelebrity stories yielded imitative suicides if they received enough publicity. Continuing the examination of celebrity suicides, Stack[76] found that only celebrity suicide stories had an imitative effect on suicides among the elderly. Yet, celebrity suicides do not always yield imitative suicides, as evidenced by the lack of a significant increase in suicides following the death of Kurt Cobain.[77,78] As discussed in a later section, the substantial efforts by Kurt Cobain's widow, Courtney Love, to present his suicide in a negative fashion may have counteracted any potential glamorization of his death.

Stories about group or mass suicides[36,79] or about people who first harm others before committing suicide (e.g., murder-suicide)[13,36] do not appear to have an imitative effect. This has been postulated to be due, in part, to the "nonattractiveness" of the victims or the circumstances of the deaths.[80]

Another characteristic of a model to be studied has been the marital background of the suicide victim in the story. Stack[24] found a differential impact of the presence or absence of divorce or marital problems in the suicide stories. Stack[24] conjectured that the victim's marital problems in the story yielded greater identification by suicidal individuals.

Given the vast heterogeneity of the news stories, including villains and heroes, further research is needed to determine which features of the models or stories have an impact on suicide. Only a few studies have formally investigated the specific story elements believed to either facilitate or limit the contagious effects of a news report on suicide. In one study Fekete and Schmidtke[81] conducted a content analysis of suicide-related headlines in German and Hungarian newspapers to examine cross-cultural differences in reporting style. German accounts reflected a tendency to characterize suicidal behavior as criminal or psychiatric in nature, whereas Hungarian newspapers more frequently depicted suicide in a romantic manner. The investigators conjectured that this may partially account for the higher rates in Hungary. Fekete and colleagues[82] expanded the comparison of newspaper headlines to other countries— Austria, West and East Germany, Greece, Hungary, and Lithuania. Consistent with the earlier findings, there were more depictions of attractive, prominent personalities and positive consequences and fewer "negative" prominent people and negative consequences of suicides in the Hungarian and Lithuanian press than in the German and Austrian newspaper headlines.

In another study Castellanos et al.[83] developed and performed a content analysis of the four televised suicide dramatizations that were the focus of the 1986 report by Gould and Shaffer.[41] Thirty adult subjects viewed the four films in a randomized fashion and rated the films' content on a structured scale developed for the study. The ratings included the extent to which specified characteristics applied to each movie, including depictions of the suicide methods, consequences of the suicidal behavior, presentation of mental health problems, stressors, precipitants, personal characteristics of the victims, and help-seeking behavior. Knowledge and attitudes about suicide were assessed. This study found that the movies could be significantly differentiated by their content profiles. In addition, the movies had a small but definite impact on viewer beliefs about suicide (both appropriate and inappropriate).

Weimann and Fishman[84] conducted a systematic content analysis of more than 430 suicide cases published in the two leading daily newspapers in Israel. Each suicide report was analyzed for the *form* of its coverage—including space allocation, placement in the paper, and inclusion of picture—and for the *content* of its coverage—including demographic characteristics of the victim, mode of suicide, attribution of responsibility, and general attitude toward the act or person. They found that the space devoted to suicide stories and the prominence of the stories increased steadily during the 1980s and 1990s. Newspaper reports focused on the more violent modes of suicide. An economic/financial motive was attributed mainly to males, while romantic motives or problems with a partner were attributed mainly to females. Most of the reports were neutral, but among those that did express an attitude, approximately 18% were positive and 8% were negative. Positive coverage was more likely when external causes were presented and when suicides were committed during military service.

A quantitative and qualitative analysis of suicide reports in Swiss print media was conducted by Michel and colleagues.[85–87] Quantitative aspects of the review included the length and positioning of the article, presence or absence of a picture, size of headline, and frequency of reporting. Qualitative aspects included contents of the report, whether articles might serve as a model, and presence of prevention or treatment resources. A coding and scoring scheme was devised, such that an "imitation risk score" was calculated for each report. Approximately 400 newspapers and magazines were examined. During an 8-month period, 74 newspapers and magazines were found to have articles about suicide, yielding 151 articles. The headline in 47% of the stories was considered to be sensational. In 13% of the articles, the headline was judged as romanticizing the event or glorifying the person. This was the case for 26% of the articles' text. Inappropriate pictures were found in 20% of the articles. Overall, 44% of the articles were considered to be in the high imitation risk group. The topic of prevention was covered in detail in only about 11% of the articles, and therapeutic advice was also scarce (9%). Considerable differences were found between newspapers. The results of these analyses were presented at a national press conference as a means to launch guidelines for suicide reporting; they were sent to all newspaper editors. These efforts are discussed in a later section.

Host Characteristics

While there is a paucity of research on the specific host characteristics that may yield a greater susceptibility to suicide imitation, age- and sex-specific effects have been noted. Phillips and Carstensen[14,15] found that the impact of suicide stories on subsequent completed suicides was greatest for teenagers. Similarly, the most marked reduction in suicides during a newspaper strike period was reported for women in the younger age groups, 15–24 and 25–34.[31,32] This is consistent with the findings that the incidence of cluster suicides is highest among teenagers and young adults.[88,89] Thus, younger individuals appear more susceptible to suicide contagion. The effect of gender is equivocal: some studies reported the greatest impact among women,[31,32] others found men to be most susceptible,[20,90] while no difference for males or females was also reported.[15] Generally, the imitative impact of media reports does not appear to be stronger for demographic groups that are already strongly predisposed to suicide—males, whites, unmarried people, or retired persons.[15]

There are some data to suggest that prior suicidal behavior may be a moderating host characteristic. Suicide attempters, suicide ideators, and nonsuicidal patients have been reported to have different physiological reactions to a suicide film.[63] Furthermore, Fekete and Schmidtke[91] found, in an interview study of suicide attempters, psychiatric patients without suicidal history, and nonpsychiatric controls in Germany and Hungary, that suicide attempters reported experiencing more media presentations of fictional suicides than normal controls. The attempters were more apt to report the description of these presentations in more detail and report more imitation fantasies concerning the models. Thus, preliminary evidence suggests that prior suicidal behavior may moderate the imitative effect of the media.

Host/Agent Correspondence

Stack[24,26] has postulated that certain stories promote "differential identification" among individuals who are similar to the suicide victim in the story in certain key respects, such as shared life and demographic circumstances. There is increasing research evidence to support this postulation. Schmidtke and Häfner[50] found that imitation effects were most notable in the groups whose age and sex were closest to those of the victim in a weekly serial in Germany. Following the showing of a railway suicide of a 19-year-old male student, the number of railway suicides increased most sharply among 15- to 19-year-old males. Fekete and Macsai[19] examined the number of suicides attributable to lidocaine overdose following the highly publicized suicide by this method of a nationally recognized teenage beauty contest winner in Hungary. The subsequent increase in suicides attributable to lidocaine overdose was most evident in females ages 15–39 years old, who were most similar to the victim with respect to age and gender. Stack[29] reported that exposure to newspaper coverage in Japan triggered subsequent suicides only if the reported victims were Japanese; non-Japanese victims did not yield these imitative effects. Phillips[13] found, in an examination of motor vehicle fatalities as "disguised" suicides, that the age of drivers in motor vehicle fatalities was correlated to the age of the suicide victims described in the story. Similarly, Stack[76] found evidence for age identification an increase in subsequent suicides among individuals aged 65 and over was greatest following stories about elderly suicides.

Environmental Characteristics

Much of the work examining the effect of the social context of the suicide story has been conducted by Stack.[24–28,92] Stack,[92] studying the period of 1910 to 1920, found that publicized suicide stories during war had no impact on suicide. In contrast, suicide stories during peacetime were associated with a significant increase in subsequent suicides. Another environmental characteristic examined was the Great Depression (1930s). Stack[27] did not find support for his hypothesis that audience receptivity to suicide stories would be high in the Great Depression, given widespread unemployment. Similarly, using a more recent set of data (1968 to 1980), Stack[28,76] found that suicide stories' influence on subsequent suicides was *independent* of economic conditions.

MEDIA EDUCATION

Given the substantial evidence for suicide contagion, a recommended suicide prevention strategy involves educating reporters, editors, and film and television producers about contagion in order to yield media stories that minimize harm. Moreover, the media's positive role in educating the public about risks for suicide and shaping attitudes about suicide should be encouraged.

In the United States, the Centers for Disease Control published a set of recommendations on reporting of suicide that emerged from a national workshop.[93] The American Association of Suicidology[93] has adopted these as their official guidelines for journalists in an attempt to minimize contagious effects from news reports of suicides. Guidelines for media reporting now exist in several countries, including Australia, Austria, Canada, Germany, Japan, New Zealand, and Switzerland. Additional guidelines have recently been developed by the World Health Organization and the American Foundation for Suicide Prevention (AFSP). (The AFSP guidelines are described later in this chapter.) These guidelines generally include descriptions of factors that should be avoided because they increase attention to the media reports and are more likely to induce contagion (e.g., front-page coverage). Also included are suggestions on how to increase the usefulness of the report (e.g., describing treatment resources).

Regrettably, the media guidelines that have been developed thus far have not, for the most part, had the advantage of empirical validation. An evaluation of the implementation of media guidelines has been conducted in Austria.[17,18,23] Following implementation of media guidelines for news reporting by the Austrian Association for Suicide Prevention in 1987, a significant decline in suicide rates occurred within the first year (7% decline). In the 4-year period following implementation, the suicide rate decreased nearly 20%, with an even sharper decline (75%) in subway suicides (a particular focus of the media guidelines). Another evaluation of media guidelines implemented in Switzerland was conducted by Michel and colleagues.[87] As previously discussed, this team of investigators had conducted an 8-month analysis of newspaper and magazine reports prior to the implementation of the media guidelines. Following implementation of the guidelines, a second analysis was conducted in order to evaluate the effect of the guidelines on the style and content of the media reports. Although the number of articles increased, the articles were significantly shorter and less likely to be on the front page; headlines, pictures, and text were rated as less sensational or glorifying; there were relatively fewer articles with pictures; and the overall imitation risk scores were lower. Given the successful strategy of engaging the media in Austria and Switzerland as a means of suicide prevention, efforts to systematically evaluate its efficacy in the United States are warranted. A promising application of media recommendations appeared in Seattle in the aftermath of the suicide of Kurt Cobain.[77] However, the substantial efforts by Kurt Cobain's widow to present his suicide in a negative fashion may have had an impact on influencing attitudes toward preventive ends.

While it is important to begin educating the media on our current state of empirical knowledge, we need to simultaneously improve that knowledge base. In particular, we need to better understand which particular story elements under which circumstances act as the active ingredients for promoting contagion and which components of stories and broadcasts are useful for preventive programming. There are only a few studies that have formally investigated the specific story elements believed to either facilitate or limit the contagious effects of a news report on suicide (see Fekete and Schmidtke[81] and Castellanos et al.,[83] described above). Until this systematic work is completed, interim efforts to disseminate the current state of knowledge are necessary. The findings from the reviewed research literature form the basis for the following interim recommendations, which the author originally compiled for the American Foundation for Suicide Prevention in its efforts to disseminate information on suicide contagion to the media.

Recommendations

The following suggestions may be useful in minimizing the risk for contagion, while still maintaining the integrity of the report:

(1) Question if the suicide is newsworthy. Suicide is a common cause of death. Indeed, it accounts for more teen deaths than all natural causes combined.
(2) Do not misrepresent suicide as a mysterious act by an otherwise "healthy" or "high achieving" person.
(3) Indicate that suicide is most often a fatal complication of different types of mental illness, many of which are treatable.
(4) Do not present suicide as a reasonable way of problem solving.
(5) Do not portray suicide in a heroic or romantic fashion.
(6) Exercise care with pictures of the victim and/or grieving relatives and friends to avoid fostering overidentification with the victim and inadvertently glorifying the death.

(7) Avoid providing a detailed description of method and site.
(8) Limit the prominence, length, and number of stories about a particular suicide. Avoid front page coverage.
(9) Try to oversee headlines. Some responsibly written stories are spoiled by sensational and inappropriate headlines.
(10) Provide local treatment resource information.

These recommendations are forming the basis for national consensus guidelines that are currently under development[94] and can be found on the website for the American Foundation for Suicide Prevention (www.afsp.org). The website also provides examples of appropriate and problematic coverage.

CONCLUSION

Overall, the evidence to date suggests that suicide contagion is a real effect. There is substantial evidence of the significant impact of nonfictional stories on subsequent suicides. While the research on fictional suicide stories is contradictory, there is ample research evidence that highlights the imitative effect of suicide dramatizations. A review of the influence from other modes of media, such as music and the internet, is beyond the scope of this chapter. For a review of this burgeoning research effort see Martin[95] and Schmidtke and Schaller.[80]

Evidence of imitation should not negate the role of individual susceptibility and stresses in suicide. Nevertheless, it is crucial for mental and public health professionals and the media to develop a partnership to enhance the effectiveness of the reporting of suicide, while minimizing the risk of imitative suicides. The media's power to educate the public in an appropriate fashion and change attitudes toward suicide needs to be underscored. The Society of Professional Journalists' Code of Ethics aptly summarizes our joint goals, "Seek Truth and Report It" and "Minimize Harm."

REFERENCES

1. GOULD, M.S. & L. DAVIDSON. 1988. Suicide contagion among adolescents. *In* Advances in Adolescent Mental Health. A.R. Stiffman & R.A. Feldman, eds. :29–59. JAI Press. Greenwich, CT.
2. VELTING, D.M. & M. GOULD. 1997. Suicide contagion. *In* Annual Review of Suicidology, 1997. R. Maris, S. Canetto & M.M. Silverman, Eds.: 96–136. Guilford. New York.
3. GOULD, M.S. 1990. Suicide clusters and media exposure. *In* Suicide Over the Life Cycle. S.J. Blumenthal & D.J. Kupfer, eds. American Psychiatric Press. Washington, D.C.

4. JONES, M.B. & D.R. JONES. 1994. Testing for behavioral contagion in a case-control design. J. Psychiatr. Res. **28:** 35–55.

5. JONES, M.B. & D.R. JONES. 1995. Preferred pathways of behavioral contagion. J. Psychiatr. Res. **29:** 193–209.

6. WHEELER, L. 1966. Toward a theory of behavioral contagion. Psychol. Rev. **73:** 179–192.

7. BANDURA, A. 1977. Self-efficacy: toward a unifying theory of behavioral change. Psychol. Rev. **84:** 191–215.

8. BANDURA, A., N.E. ADAMS & J. BEYER. 1977. Cognitive processes mediating behavioral change. J. Pers. Soc. Psychol. **35:** 125–139.

9. BANDURA, A. 1986. Social Foundations of Thought and Action. Prentice Hall. Englewood Cliffs, NJ.

10. BOLLEN, K.A. & D.P. PHILLIPS. 1981. Suicidal motor vehicle fatalities in Detroit: a replication. Am. J. Sociol. **87:** 404–412.

11. BOLLEN, K.A. & D.P. PHILLIPS. 1982. Imitative suicides: a national study of the effect of television news stories. Am. Sociol. Rev. **47:** 802–809.

12. PHILLIPS, D. 1974. The influence of suggesions on suicide; substantive and theoretical implications of the Werther effect. Am. Sociol. Rev. **39:** 340–354.

13. PHILLIPS, D. 1979. Suicide, motor vehicle fatalities, and the mass media: evidence toward a theory of suggestion. Am. J. Sociol. **84:** 1150–1174.

14. PHILLIPS, D. & L.L. CARSTENSEN. 1986. Clustering of teenage suicides after television news stories about suicide. N. Engl. J. Med. **315:** 685–689.

15. PHILLIPS, D.P. & L.L. CARSTENSEN. 1988. The effect of suicide stories on various demographic groups, 1968–1985. *In* Understanding and Preventing Suicide: Plenary Papers of the First Combined Meeting of the AAS and IASP. R. Maris *et al.*, eds. :100–114. Guilford Press. New York.

16. DEISENHAMMER, E.A., G. KEMMLER, C. DE COL, *et al.* 1997. Eisenbahnsuizide und suizidversuche in Osterreich von 1990–1994. Nervenartz **68:** 67–73.

17. ETZERSDORFER, E., G. SONNECK & S. NAGEL-KUESS. 1992. Newspaper reports and suicide. N. Engl. J. Med. **327:** 502–503.

18. ETZERSDORFER, E. & G. SONNECK. 1998. Preventing suicide by influencing mass-media reporting. The Viennese experience 1980–1996. Arch. Suicide Res. **4:** 67–74.

19. FEKETE, S. & E. MACSAI. 1990. Hungarian suicide models, past and present. *In* Suicidal Behavior and Risk Factors. G. Ferrari, ed. :149–156. Monduzzi Editore. Bologna.

20. HASSAN, R. 1995. Effects of newspaper stories on the incidence of suicide in Australia: a research note. Aust. N.Z. J. Psychiatry **29:** 480–483.

21. ISHII, K. 1991. Measuring mutual causation: effect of suicide news on suicides in Japan. Soc. Sci. Res. **20:** 188–195.

22. JONAS, K. 1992. Modelling and suicide: a test of the Werther effect. Br. J. Soc. Psychol. **31:** 295–306.

23. SONNECK, G., E. ETZERSDORFER & S. NAGEL-KUESS. 1994. Imitative suicide on the Viennese subway. Soc. Sci. Med. **38:** 453–457.

24. STACK, S. 1990. Divorce, suicide, and the mass media: an analysis of differential identification, 1948–1980. J. Marriage Fam. **52:** 553–560.

25. STACK, S.A. 1990. A reanalysis of the impact of non-celebrity suicides: a research note. Soc. Psychiatry Psychiatr. Epidemiol. **25:** 269–273.

26. STACK, S. 1991. Social correlates of suicide by age: media impacts. *In* Life
    Span Perspectives of Suicide: Time-Lines in the Suicide Process. A. Leenaars
    et al., eds. :187–213. Plenum Press. New York.
27. STACK, S. 1992. The effect of the media in suicide: the Great Depression. Sui-
    cide Life Threatening Behav. **22:** 255–267.
28. STACK, S. 1993. The media and suicide: a nonadditive model, 1968–1980. Sui-
    cide Life Threatening Behav. **23:** 63–66.
29. STACK, S. 1996. The effect of the media on suicide: evidence from Japan,
    1955–1985. Suicide Life Threatening Behav. **26:** 132–142.
30. WASSERMAN, I.M. 1992. The impact of epidemic, war, prohibition and media
    on suicide: United States, 1910–1920. Suicide Life Threatening Behav. **22:**
    240–254.
31. BLUMENTHAL, S. & L. BERGNER. 1973. Suicide and newspapers: a replicated
    study. Am. J. Psychiatry **130:** 468–471.
32. MOTTO, J.A. 1970. Newspaper influence on suicide. Arch. Gen. Psychiatry **23:**
    143–148.
33. BARON, J.N. & P.C. REISS. 1985. Same time next year: aggregate analyses of
    the mass media and violent behavior. Am. Sociol. Rev. **50:** 347–363.
34. HORTON, H. & S. STACK. 1984. The effect of television on national suicide
    rates. J. Soc. Psychol. **123:** 141–142.
35. KESSLER, R.C., G. DOWNEY, J.R. MILAVSKY, *et al.* 1988. Clustering of teenage
    suicides after television news stories about suicides: a reconsideration. Am. J.
    Psychiatry **145:** 1379–1383.
36. KESSLER, R.C., G. DOWNEY, H. STIPP, *et al.* 1989. Network television news sto-
    ries about suicide and short-term changes in total U.S. suicides. J. Nerv.
    Ment. Dis. **177:** 551–555.
37. STACK, S. 1984. The effect of suggestion on suicide: a reassessment. Paper
    read at the Annual Meetings of the American Sociological Association, San
    Antonio, TX.
38. COLLINS, S. 1993. Health prevention messages may have paradoxical effect
    [letter to the editor] [see comments]. Br. Med. J. **306:** 926.
39. ELLIS, S.J. & S. WALSH. 1986. Soap may seriously damage your health [letter
    to the editor]. Lancet **1:** 686–686.
40. FOWLER, B P. 1986. Emotional crisis imitating television. Lancet **1:** 1036–
    1037.
41. GOULD, M.S. & D. SHAFFER. 1986. The impact of suicide in television movies:
    evidence of imitation. N. Engl. J. Med. **315:** 690–694.
42. GOULD, M.S., D. SHAFFER & M. KLEINMAN. 1988. The impact of suicide in
    television movies: replication and commentary. Suicide Life Threatening
    Behav. **18:** 90–99.
43. HÄFNER, H. & A. SCHMIDTKE. 1989. Increase of suicide due to imitation of fic-
    tional suicide on television. *In* Epidemiology and the Prevention of Mental
    Disorders. B. Cooper & T. Helgason, eds. :338–347. Routledge. London.
44. HAWTON, K., S. SIMKIN, J.J. DEEKS, *et al.* 1999. Effects of a drug overdose in a
    television drama on presentations to hospital for self poisoning: time series
    and questionnaire study. Br. Med. J. **318:** 972–977.
45. HOLDING, T.A. 1974. The B.B.C. "Befrienders" series and its effects. Br. J.
    Psychiatry **124:** 470–472.
46. HOLDING, T.A. 1975. Suicide and "The Befrienders." Br. Med. J. **3:** 751–753.

47. Ostroff, R.B., R.W. Behrends, K. Lee, *et al.* 1985. Adolescent suicides modeled after television movie [letter to the editor]. Am. J. Psychiatry **142:** 989.
48. Ostroff, R.B. & J.H. Boyd. 1987. Television and suicide [letter to the editor]. N. Engl. J. Med. **316:** 876–877.
49. Sandler, D.A., P.A.R. Connell & K. Welsh. 1986. Emotional crisis imitating television [letter to the editor]. Lancet **1:** 856.
50. Schmidtke, A. & H. Häfner. 1988. The Werther effect after television films: new evidence for an old hypothesis. Psychol. Med. **18:** 665–676.
51. Daniels, R.G. 1986. Emotional crisis imitating television [letter to the editor]. Lancet **1:** 856.
52. Kessler, R.C. & H. Stipp. 1984. The impact of fictional television suicide stories on U.S. fatalities: a replication. Am. J. Sociol. **90:** 151–167.
53. Phillips, D. & D.J. Paight. 1987. The impact of televised movies about suicide: a replicative study. N. Engl. J. Med. **317:** 809–811.
54. Stack, S. 1990. The impact of fictional television films on teenage suicide, 1984–85. Soc. Sci. Q. **71:** 391–399.
55. Williams, J.M., C. Lawton, S.J. Ellis, *et al.* 1987. Copycat suicide attempts [letter to the editor]. Lancet **2:** 102–103.
56. Berman, A.L. 1988. Fictional depiction of suicide in television films and imitation effects. Am. J. Psychiatry **145:** 982–986.
57. Waldron, G., J. Walton & R. Helowicz. 1993. Medical messages on television. Copycat overdoses coincidental [letter to the editor; comment]. Br. Med. J. **306:** 1416.
58. Phillips, D.P. 1982. The impact of fictional television stories on U.S. adult fatalities: new evidence on the effect of the mass media on violence. Am. J. Sociol. **87:** 1340–1359.
59. Platt, S. 1987. The aftermath of Angie's overdose: is soap (opera) damaging to your health? Br. Med. J. **294:** 954.
60. Simkin, S., K. Hawton, L. Whitehead, *et al.* 1995. Media influence on parasuicide: a study of the effects of a television drama portrayal of Paracetamol self-poisoning. Br. J. Psychiatry **167:** 754–759.
61. Veysey, M.J., R. Kamanyire & G.N. Volans. 1999. Effects of drug overdose in television drama on presentations for self poisoning. Antifreeze poisonings give more insight into copycat behaviour [letter to the editor; comment]. Br. Med. J. **319:** 1131.
62. Biblarz, A., R.M. Brown, D.N. Biblarz, *et al.* 1991. Media influence on attitudes toward suicide. Suicide Life Threatening Behav. **21:** 374–384.
63. Doron, A., D. Stein, Y. Levine, *et al.* 1998. Physiological reactions to a suicide film: suicide attempters, suicide ideators, and nonsuicidal patients. Suicide Life Threatening Behav. **28:** 309–314.
64. Gibson, J.A.P. & L.M. Range. 1991. Are written reports of suicide and seeking help contagious? High schoolers' perceptions. J. Appl. Soc. Psychol. **21:** 1517–1523.
65. Higgins, L. & L.M. Range. 1996. Does information that a suicide victim was psychiatrically disturbed reduce the likelihood of contagion? J. Appl. Soc. Psychol. **26:** 781–785.
66. McDonald, D.H. & L.M. Range. 1990. Do written reports of suicide induce high-school students to believe that suicidal contagion will occur? J. Appl. Soc. Psychol. **20:** 1093–1102.

67. RANGE, L.M., W.C. GOGGIN & K.K. STEEDE. 1988. Perception of behavioral contagion of adolescent suicide. Suicide Life Threatening Behav. **18:** 334–341.
68. STEEDE, K.K. & L.M. RANGE. 1989. Does television induce suicidal contagion with adolescents? J. Community Psychol. **17:** 166–172.
69. MARTIN, G. 1996. The influence of television in a normal adolescent population. Arch. Suicide Res. **2:** 103–117.
70. GANZEBOOM, H.B.G. & D. DE HAAN. 1982. Gepubliceerde zelfmoorden en verhoging van sterfte door zelfmoord en ongelukken in Nederland 1972–1980. Mens en Maatschappij **57:** 55–69.
71. PHILLIPS, D. 1980. Airplane accidents, murder, and the mass media: towards a theory of imitation and suggestion. Soc. Forces **58:** 1001–1004.
72. PHILLIPS, D.P., K. LESYNA & D.J. PAIGHT. 1992. Suicide and the media. In Assessment and Prediction of Suicide. R.W. Maris, A.L. Berman, J.T. Maltsberger, et al., eds. :499–519. The Guilford Press. New York.
73. WASSERMAN, I.M. 1984. Imitation and suicide: a re-examination of the Werther effect. Am. Sociol. Rev. **49:** 427–436.
74. STACK, S. 1987. Celebrities and suicide: a taxonomy and analysis, 1948–1983. Am. Sociol. Rev. **52:** 401–412.
75. GUNDLACH, J. & S. STACK. 1990. The impact of hyper media coverage on suicide: New York City, 1910–1920. Soc. Sci. Q. **71:** 619–627.
76. STACK, S. 1990. Audience receptiveness, the media, and aged suicide. J. Aging Stud. **4:** 195–209.
77. JOBES, D.A., A.L. BERMAN, P.W. O'CARROLL, et al. 1996. The Kurt Cobain suicide crisis: perspectives from research, public health, and the news media. Suicide Life Threatening Behav. **26:** 260–271.
78. MARTIN, G. & L. KOO. 1997. Celebrity suicide: did the death of Kurt Cobain influence young suicides in Australia. Arch. Suicide Res. **3:** 187–198.
79. STACK, S. 1983. The effect of the Jonestown suicides on American suicide rates. J. Soc. Psychol. **119:** 145–146.
80. SCHMIDTKE, A. & S. SCHALLER. 2000. The role of mass media in suicide prevention. In The International Handbook of Suicide and Attempted Suicide. K. Hawton & K. van Heeringen, Eds. John Wiley & Sons. New York.
81. FEKETE, S. & A. SCHMIDTKE. 1995. The impact of mass media reports on suicide and attitudes toward self-destruction: previous studies and some new data from Hungary and Germany. In The Impact of Suicide. B. L. Mishara, ed. :142–155. Springer. New York.
82. FEKETE, S., A. SCHMIDTKE, E. ETZERSDORFER, et al. 1998. Media reports on suicide in Hungary, Austria, Germany and Lithuania in 1981 and 1991. In Suicide Prevention. D. DeLeo, A. Schmidtke & R.F.W. Diekstra, Eds. Kluwer Academic Publishers. Leiden.
83. CASTELLANOS, D., M.S. GOULD, A. MORISHIMA, et al. 1990. Television movies and suicide: a content analysis of suicide dramatization. Paper presented at the meeting of the American Academy of Child and Adolescent Psychiatry, Chicago, IL.
84. WEIMANN, G. & G. FISHMAN. 1995. Reconstructing suicide: reporting suicide in the Israeli press. Journalism Mass Commun. Q. **72:** 551–558.
85. FREY, C., K. MICHEL & L. VALACH. 1997. Suicide reporting in the Swiss print media: responsible or irresponsible? Eur. J. Public Health **7:** 15–19.

86. MICHEL, K., C. FREY, T.E. SCHLAEPFER, *et al.* 1995. Suicide reporting in the Swiss print media: frequency, form and content of articles. Eur. J. Public Health **5:** 199–203.
87. MICHEL, K., C. FREY, K. WYSS, *et al.* 2000. An exercise in improving suicide reporting in print media. Crisis **21:** 1–10.
88. GOULD, M.S., S. WALLENSTEIN, M.H. KLEINMAN, *et al.* 1990. Suicide clusters: an examination of age-specific effects. Am. J. Public Health **80:** 211–212.
89. GOULD, M.S., K. PETRIE, M. KLEINMAN, *et al.* 1994. Clustering of attempted suicide: New Zealand national data. Int. J. Epidemiol. **23:** 1185–1189.
90. BARRACLOUGH, B.M., D. SHEPHERD & C. JENNINGS. 1977. Do newspaper reports of coroners' inquests incite people to commit suicide? Br. J. Psychiatry **131:** 528–532.
91. FEKETE, S. & A. SCHMIDTKE. 1996. Suicidal models—their frequency and role in suicide attempters, non-suicidal psychiatric patients and normal control cases: a comparative German-Hungarian study. Omega **33:** 233–241.
92. STACK, S. 1988. Suicide: media impacts in war and peace, 1910–1920. Suicide Life Threatening Behav. **18:** 342–357.
93. 1995. CDC Media Guidelines Adopted by Board. News Link Am. Assoc. Suicidol. **21:** 5–6.
94. AMERICAN FOUNDATION FOR SUICIDE PREVENTION. ANNENBERG SCHOOL OF PUBLIC POLICY. 2001. Consensus Workshop on Media Guidelines for Coverage of Stories about Suicide. Jan. 16, 2001, New York, NY.
95. MARTIN, G. 1998. Media influence to suicide. Arch. Suicide Res. **4:** 51–66.
96. LITTMAN, S.K. 1985. Suicide epidemics and newspaper reporting. Suicide Life Threatening Behav. **15:** 43–50.
97. MOTTO, J.A. 1967. Suicide and suggestibility—the role of the press. Am. J. Psychiatry **124:** 156–160.
98. CANTOR, C.H., P.J. TUCKER & P. BURNETT. 1991. The media and suicide [letter to the editor]. Med. J. Aust. **155:** 130–131.
99. KOEPPING, A.P., H.B.G. GANZEBOOM & P.G. SWANBORN. 1989. Suicide increase after newspaper reports. Ned. Tijdschr. Psychol. Haar Grensgeb. **44:** 62–72.
100. JACKSON, E.D. & C.R. POTKAY. 1974. Audience reactions to the suicide play *Quiet Cries.* J. Community Psychol. **2:** 16–17.
101. PLATT, S. 1989. The consequences of a televised soap opera overdose: is there a mass media imitation effect? *In* Suicide and its Prevention: The Role of Attitude and Imitation. R. F. Diekstra, R. Maris *et al.*, eds. :341–359. E.J. Brill. Leiden, the Netherlands.

DISCUSSION

D. SHAFFER: Behavioral contagion is frequently observed on college campuses. As a psychiatrist on a college campus, what advice would you give about whether a suicide or a suicide attempt should be communicated to the rest of the student body?

M. S. GOULD: I think one should first consider the newsworthiness of the suicide attempt or completed suicide. I expect that some will disagree with what I am about to say: the suicide or suicide attempt need not be shared with the community, the campus as a whole. It depends on the circumstances. If it was a very public suicide, then clearly it does have to be shared because a number of other students would have witnessed the death. If it occurred while the student was home on spring break, then perhaps it doesn't have to be shared. If a student killed himself (the epidemiology of suicide suggests that it would be a male) in his dorm room, it doesn't necessarily have to be made public, but if he was found by a roommate, rumors will fly if you don't do something. I don't think presenting it in the school newspaper is necessarily the way to inform the other students. If it took place in a dorm, you may want to have grief counselors come in and have discussions with people living in the dorm. You could have drop-in centers. You don't have to say there's been a suicide, but can invite anyone who is feeling distressed to go to the college health service.

What we're doing as a project in high schools, although not directly comparable to colleges because the students do not live on the campus, might be useful: we are conducting ongoing screenings of the total student population in schools that have had a suicide, because there are a lot of kids at risk for suicide beyond the social network of a suicide victim. The youngsters who seem to be most vulnerable to the impact of a suicide are not necessarily the victim's best friends. We're finding from our research on suicide clusters that it's people far more distant in the social network or even people who know of the death through indirect means who may be most at risk. So the best way to prevent suicides or to have a program that deals with the impact of a suicide may be general screenings, rather than a newspaper article in the school newspaper that says so-and-so killed himself or to just limit follow-up counseling with the victim's best friends.

SHAFFER: I agree with Madelyn. I think you are faced with a fairly general dilemma with respect to suicide if you are the psychiatrist or psychologist at a school or college. On the one hand, there is the remote possibility that what you do may induce some form of copycat behavior or imitation, and, on the other hand, there is the much higher likelihood that two phenomena will occur. There will be friends or acquaintances who are be directly affected by the death and who will, according to David Brent's study on the consequences for friends of a suicide, experience quite significant impairment during the period following the death. It's probably worthwhile to follow some strategy to identify those people and try to use some preemptive intervention because we know that that morbidity is going to occur.

The other phenomenon that very frequently occurs in a closed community and can have quite serious consequences is scapegoating. It's common both within a family and within a small community after a suicide occurs that people are blamed. In a family it will often be the parents, or maybe an older sibling, for treating the child unfairly or bullying the child. In a college or school community it will often be another peer, or perhaps a teacher or professor, who is blamed for allegedly unfair behavior. We know it's very rare that that's the whole story. By simply closing the whole thing off by not exploring the prevailing rumors and beliefs, you deny yourself the opportunity to correct the scapegoating myths that go around, and this may actually have a role in allowing imitative suicide to occur. I think you are caught in a dilemma. The truth is we don't yet know how best to handle these psychological events, but I suspect that Madelyn's suggestion of screening that doesn't involve saying too much that might be misunderstood to too many people, coupled with discreet inquiries about the nature of the prevailing myths and trying to correct them, are a fairly safe compromise.

Another question: what are the high-status elements you said were sometimes associated with suicide?

GOULD: We know from a number of studies that the celebrity status of a suicide victim increases the impact of the suicide. A movie star or "all-American" athlete who commits suicide is usually not presented as a person with psychiatric problems, so the suicide can appear to be acceptable.

SHAFFER: While suicide contagion may be real, what about the idea of developed immunity? Perhaps there is a suicide contagion pattern because suicide has been so suppressed, stigmatized, and judged, particularly by faith communities. When suicide is heard about in the media, people who have been struggling experience relief and become free to act accordingly. On the other hand, if suicide prevention were to becme a common concern and seeking mental health services were destigmatized, we might not see suicide contagion. Do we deliberately repress ideas about suicide, and does seeing it in somebody else allow it to be unrepressed?

GOULD: We're not saying to not report about suicide. What we're hoping is that if you report about suicide in a realistic fashion without misinformation, if you provide resource lists and so on, people who are vulnerable may then seek help. That's why we would like to develop a collaboration with media representatives and journalists to find that balance where you avoid negative influence but present just enough information so that those who don't know what to do with their inner turmoil and perhaps aren't in treatment will know where to go. We want responsible reporting. Reporting about suicide in itself is not the problem, but how suicide is reported is a critical concern. It can be done in such a way that people who are vulnerable may learn how to get help or, unfortunately, it may contribute to the problem.

SHAFFER; This is a fantasy question: what do you recommend we as a professional group do to control or reduce the strong hold of the media on the public mind?

GOULD: That's what we're trying to do now with the American Foundation for Suicide Prevention. It's such a tough nut but it cheers me to think about 20 years ago: I don't think we public health professionals would ever have dreamt that we could have had the impact on cigarette smoking that has occurred in this country. I see our attempt to have some impact on the media as a similar process that will go on for the next couple of decades. I think we must start with nonfictional media stories. We have evidence that the artistic media can have a negative impact, but I don't think it would be realistic to attempt to curb it at this point. I don't think media professionals are going to be willing to be talked at. Rather, we need to build collaborations with journalists and other media representatives and get them involved so that this may become their issue rather than our issue—a fantasy, perhaps, but I hope not too much of a fantasy.

Firearms and Suicide

DAVID A. BRENT

Division of Child and Adolescent Psychiatry, Western Psychiatric Institute and Clinic, Pittsburgh, Pennsylvania, USA

ABSTRACT: The evidence linking firearms in the home to risk for suicide is reviewed. These data come from epidemiological, case-control, quasiexperimental, and prospective studies. The convergent finding from this wide range of studies is that there is a strong relationship between firearms in the home and risk for suicide, most firmly established in the United States.

KEYWORDS: Firearms; Risk of suicide; Adolescent suicide; Gun control legislation

EPIDEMIOLOGICAL STUDIES

Epidemiological studies have consistently shown that firearms are the most common method of suicide for all demographic groups in the United States.[1] The dramatic increase in the American youth suicide rate since 1960 is attributable primarily to an increase in suicide by firearms[2,3] (see FIGS. 1 and 2). In one study of youth suicide in Allegheny County from 1960 to 1983, the rate of suicide by firearms increased 330%, but the rate of suicide by other means only increased 150%.[4] The more recent increase in the suicide rate by African-American males is also attributable primarily to an increase in suicide by firearms.

There is evidence of a relationship between the increasing prevalence of alcohol abuse in adolescents over this period of time and the increase in suicide by firearms. First, the proportion of youthful suicide victims who were drinking at the time of the suicide has increased dramatically over the two decades beginning in 1960.[4,5] In turn, those youths who were drinking at the time of their suicide were much more likely to use a gun than were youths who were not drinking.[4,6,7] This finding is consistent with the observation that alcohol and illicit drug abuse in the home greatly increases the risk of violent death, including suicide.[8] Furthermore, these findings suggest that the increase in

Address for correspondence: David A. Brent, M.D., Division of Child and Adolescent Psychiatry, Western Psychiatric Institute and Clinic, 3811 O'Hara Street, Suite 112, Pittsburgh, PA 15213. Voice: 412-624-5172; fax: 412-624-7997.

brentda@msx.upmc.edu

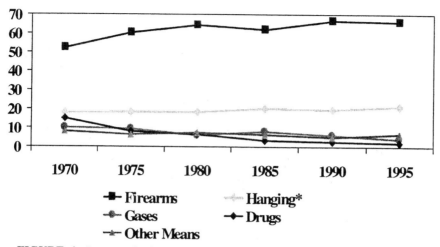

FIGURE 1. Percent of suicides for males 15–24 years of age by method of suicide; United States, 1970–1995. *Also includes strangulation and suffocation.

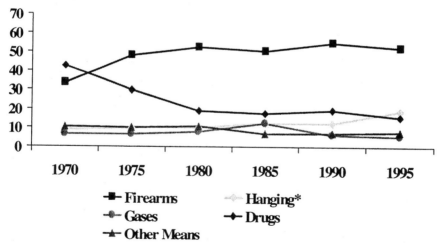

FIGURE 2. Percent of suicides for females 15–24 years of age by method of suicide; United States, 1970–1995. *Also includes strangulation and suffocation.

youth alcohol abuse and in firearms availability over the past three decades may be related to the increase in youth suicide in general, and in youth fire-arms suicide in particular. However, it is important to note that youth suicide has also dramatically increased in geographical regions where firearm own-ership and firearm suicides are relatively rare (e.g., New Zealand).[9] Therefore, it would be an oversimplification to say that the increase in youth suicide in the United States or anywhere else in the world is *solely* a function of increased firearms availability.

CASE-CONTROL STUDIES

Case-control studies performed in the United States have consistently shown a relationship between the presence of guns in the home and completed suicide. It is important to note that in a case-control study one can establish only the relative prevalence of guns in the homes of suicides vs. controls and assume that, if the sampling is performed without bias, this odds ratio is an estimate of the relative risk that having a gun in the home conveys for suicide.

Several case-control studies have been conducted comparing the prevalence of firearms in the homes of suicide victims and matched living controls.[6,9–12] These studies have focused on youth suicide primarily, although one, the largest by far, encompassed the entire life span.[12] In the Kellermann *et al.* study,[12] in contradistinction to the others, *only* suicides that occurred in the home were studied. All were conducted in he United States, with the exception of the study by Beautrais *et al.*,[9] which was conducted in New Zealand. Issues that were addressed (to a variable degree) in these studies were: (1) the likelihood that, if a gun was in the home, it was used for the suicide; (2) whether the gun was purchased recently for the express purpose of committing suicide; (3) the relative prevalence of guns in the homes of suicides and controls; (4) the impact of gun-related variables on suicidal risk (e.g., type of gun, number of guns, method of storage); and (5) the influence of demographic and psychiatric variables on the relationship between guns and risk for suicide.

With respect to these case-control studies, all the above-noted studies show that the presence of a gun in the home is highly predictive of its use for completed suicide (see TABLE 1). If a gun was already in the home, the odds of its being used for the suicide were markedly increased (31.1–107.9-fold). This was true even in New Zealand, where use of firearms is a much less common method for suicide than it is in the United States (14% vs. 55–60%).[9] Conversely, if a gun was not in the home, it was used as a method of suicide quite infrequently. Furthermore, in the one study that examined this issue, only 3% of the suicide sample of Kellermann *et al.*[12] had bought a gun within 2 weeks of the suicide. These data strongly suggest that it is the immediate gun availability that conveys the risk for firearms suicide and support method restriction as one means to prevent firearms suicide.

With regard to the odds of association between guns in the home and suicide, all the American studies have found a significant association between

TABLE 1. Case-control studies: guns in the home and method of suicide

	Brent et al.[6]	Kellermann et al.[12]	Beautrais et al.[9]
Use of gun if kept in home	87.8%	88%	33%
Use of gun if not kept in home	18.8%	6%	0.5%
Guns in home and firearms and method (odds ratio)	31.1	69.5	107.9
Firearms and alcohol use (odds ratio [95% confidence interval])	7.3	—	—
Bought gun within 2 weeks of suicide	—	3%	—

guns in the home and suicide. Two American studies of adolescent suicides, with referred suicide attempters and nonattempter psychiatric patients as controls, found an odds ratio in the range of 2–3.[10,11] In studies comparing suicides to a community sample of controls and adjusting for potentially confounding variables such as psychopathology, guns were four to five times more likely to be found in the home of suicide victims than in the homes of community controls.[6,12] It is of interest that firearms variables were unrelated to parental or adolescent psychopathology and therefore appear to convey risk relatively independently of these other important risk factors.[6,11] In the New Zealand study, the odds of association were in the predicted direction but escaped statistical significance (odds ratio [OR] = 1.4). Beautrais et al.[9] speculated that the paucity of firearms in the homes in New Zealand, along with the relative rarity of firearms use as a method of suicide, mitigated against finding an association. These results, at variance with American studies, indicate that cultural factors can clearly moderate the relationship between gun availability and risk for suicide.

While there is a relationship between guns in the home and suicide regardless of method of storage, type, or number of guns, these firearms-related variables do appear to modify risk substantially. There is a gradient of risk, with higher odds of association for handguns vs. long guns, loaded vs. unloaded guns, and unlocked vs. locked guns[6,12] (see TABLE 2). There appears to be some interaction with demographic factors, at least in adolescents, insofar as long guns convey an increased risk to males but not to females and handguns convey a particularly increased risk to females.[6] Furthermore, in adolescents long guns but not handguns convey an increased risk in rural areas (ORs 4.5 vs. 1.0), whereas in urban areas this situation is reversed, with handguns conveying a much higher risk than long guns (ORs 5.6 vs. 1.3).[6]

In the American studies, guns in the home are associated with suicide in both males and females (TABLE 3). In fact, firearms are the first choice as a method of suicide for both males and females, notwithstanding females' lower absolute rates. As noted above, handguns are particularly closely associat-

TABLE 2. Risk of suicide in the home in relation to various patterns of gun ownership[a]

Variable	Adjusted odds ratio	95% Confidence interval
Type of guns in the home		
One or more handguns	5.8	3.1–4.7
Long guns only	3.0	1.4–6.5
No guns in the home	1.0	—
Loaded guns		
Any gun kept loaded	9.2	4.1–20.1
All guns kept unloaded	3.3	1.7–6.1
No guns in the home	1.0	—
Locked guns		
Any guns kept unlocked	5.6	3.1–10.4
All guns kept locked up	2.4	1.0–5.7
No guns in the home	1.0	—

[a]Abstracted from Kellermann et al.[12]

TABLE 3. Guns in the home and suicide (odds ratio): gender

	Any	Long gun	Handgun	Loaded
Brent et al.[6]				
Male	4.0[a]	2.3	4.0[a]	4.0
Female	1.5	0.8	9.0[a]	1.0
Kellerman et al.[12]				
Male	6.4[a]	—	—	—
Female	3.3[a]	—	—	—

[a]95% confidence interval excludes 1.0.

ed with suicide in females, whereas long guns are more often used by males.[6,13] Beautrais et al.[9] found absolutely no relationship between firearms in the home and suicide in males, with the modest association that was noted coming from the relatively small female subsample.

In the one study that focused on the entire life span, it appears that the association between suicide and firearms in the home is strong across all age groups but was particularly high in the 24 and younger group (ORs 10.4 vs. 4.0–7.2 for those 25 and older).[12] In a comparison of risk factors for older (≥ 16 years) and younger adolescent suicide victims, it was found that young-

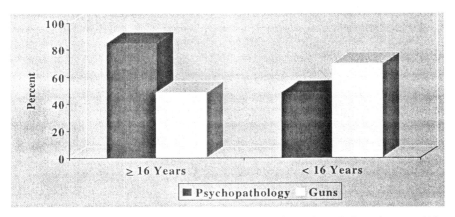

FIGURE 3. Population-attributable risk: guns and psychopathology by age. (Abstracted from Brent et al.[13])

er suicide victims have lower suicidal intent, lower rates of psychopathology in general, and lower rates of substance abuse in particular. The population-attributable risk for suicide due to the availability of firearms was actually more substantial than that due to psychopathology in the younger group, whereas this relationship was reversed in the older adolescent group[13] (see FIG. 3). This suggests that firearms availability may play a particularly important role in suicide risk in the young and that method restriction may therefore be relatively more important in the prevention of younger suicides.

The samples reported have been almost entirely Caucasian; the relationship between firearms availability and suicide has not been carefully studied in other ethnic groups. However, the increase in the suicide rate among young African-American males is accounted for mostly by an increase in suicide by firearms.[1]

In the above-noted community studies, guns in the home convey a four- to fivefold increased risk for suicide, after adjusting for the impact of psychiatric disorder.[6,12,13] However, guns in the home appear to convey a particularly increased risk for suicide in those with no apparent psychopathology (see TABLE 4). Kellermann et al.[12] reported that guns in the home conveyed a threefold elevated risk for suicide in those with psychiatric disorder, but a nearly 33-fold increased risk for completed suicide in those without apparent psychopathology. Similarly, Brent et al.[6,14] found that a loaded gun in the home conveyed a 32-fold increased risk for suicide in those without apparent psychopathology. These results, which may initially appear counterintuitive, are a consequence of the dramatic increase in risk for impulsive suicide that having a loaded gun in the home conveys even to persons without psychopathology.

TABLE 4. Guns in the home and suicide (odds ratio): psychiatric disorder

	Any	Long gun	Handgun	Loaded
Brent et al.[6]				
Psychiatric disorder				
Yes	3.4[a]	2.0	6.2[a]	0.6
No	11.5	5.6	12.9[a]	32.3[a]
Kellerman et al.[12]				
Psychiatric disorder				
Yes	3.0[a]	—	—	—
No	32.8[a]	—	—	—

[a]95% confidence interval excludes 1.0.

One study specifically addressed the ratio of the benefit of having a gun in the home for protection to the risk of suicide and other untoward outcomes. The frequency of firearms homicides in the home that occurred due to self-protection were compared to the frequency of other types of homicides, accidental deaths, and suicides in metropolitan Seattle.[15] For every homicide that occurred out of self-protection, there were 37 suicides, strongly suggesting that there is a high cost of maintaining a gun in the home for the purpose of self-protection.

GUN CONTROL LEGISLATION, FIREARMS AVAILABILITY, AND SUICIDE

Several approaches have been taken to link differences in gun control legislation and firearms availability to suicide rates. First, there have been cross-sectional comparisons between countries on gun availability and on suicide.[16,17] Second, there have been cross-sectional correlational examinations of the relationship between the restrictiveness of gun control laws and suicide rates in the United States. Third, there have been a number of quasiexperimental studies that have examined the impact of gun control legislation on suicide rates. In general, these three types of studies support an inverse relationship between restrictiveness in firearms legislation and the firearms suicide rate. However, there is also some evidence in some of these studies for method substitution. Also, some of the findings may be attributable to an overall secular trend rather than simply to the legislation.

In a particularly elegant cross-country comparison, the suicide rates in two quite similar cities, Seattle and Vancouver, were compared, with the assumption that there would be lower suicide rates in Vancouver due to the much more restrictive gun control laws in Canada.[17] In fact, the overall suicide rates were quite similar in the two cities, albeit with a higher proportion of firearms suicides in Seattle. However, the suicide rate among 15–24-year olds was 40% higher in Seattle, attributable almost entirely to a 10-fold higher rate of suicide by firearms in that city. Therefore, these results suggest that the greater availability of firearms is particularly deleterious for younger people, consistent with the above-noted case-control studies that have found a higher odds ratio and greater population-attributable risk for suicide due to firearms for younger populations.[12,13]

One study examined the relationship between the overall rate of suicide and the percentage of households with a gun in the home in 14 Western countries and found a strikingly strong correlation ($\rho = 0.52$).[16] While international comparisons are always fraught with difficulties due to variabilities in methods for certification of suicide, these findings do support a relationship between method availability and suicide and suggest that method substitution does not override the overall impact on suicide rate.

Several studies have examined correlations between different aspects of firearms control legislation—such as the requirement for a waiting period, requirement for licensing, and restricted availability based on psychiatric and/or criminal records—and the suicide rate.[18–20] All of these studies have shown an inverse relationship between the restrictiveness of firearms legislation and the overall suicide rates, using American states as the unit of analysis. Although there was some evidence of method substitution, the overall impact on the suicide rate was still favorable. Lester also noted in one study[19] that the prevalence of gun ownership, rather than the strictness of gun control laws per se, was the best predictor of overall suicide rates. Boor and Bair took these statistical analyses further[18] by adjusting for other sociodemographic factors that may differ between states and at the same time may be related to the suicide rate and still found a significant inverse correlation between the restrictiveness of gun control laws and the overall suicide rate (correlation coefficents $-.25$ to $-.48$). Therefore, within the limitations of correlational analyses of ecological data, these results are consistent with the view that greater restrictiveness of firearms legislation is associated with a lower overall suicide rate.

Four studies have examined the impact of changes in firearms legislation upon the suicide rates. Two examined the impact of the same law, but over shorter[21] and longer[22] periods of time, respectively. The results of neither study show an impact of legislation upon the suicide rate. A third study examined the impact of legislation on the suicide rate in Washington, D.C., documented significant change, and compared these trends to those in adjoining areas where no such legislative initiatives had taken place.[23] Finally, another study, conducted in Australia, found a positive impact of restrictive gun legislation on the suicide rate, albeit with some evidence of method restriction.[24] While these studies, taken collectively, are modestly supportive of a role for greater restrictiveness of gun legislation in the reduction of the suicide rate, they cannot control for other temporal trends and often do not survey a long enough period of time to document whether these positive trends are maintained. Another limitation is that it is impossible to document the extent to which these laws have been successfully enforced.

Rich *et al.* examined the impact of a 1978 law enacted in Canada that made ownership of handguns forbidden, required guns to be either registered or surrendered, and restricted from gun ownership those with either a conviction or psychiatric history related to violence.[21] In examining trends in the province of Ontario, a significant decrease in male firearms suicides was documented, but this decrement was offset by an increase in suicide by jumping.

Carrington and Moyer revisited the impact of this law by extending the period of observation and excluding the year 1978 from data analyses; they observed a significant reduction in firearm, nonfirearm, and total suicides.[22] Clearly, the decrease in nonfirearm suicides could not be attributable to a change in firearms legislation and suggests that some other social factors were operating over this period of time that might account for this decrease. This type of result illustrates the ambiguities of ecological studies.

In the best designed of these quasiexperimental studies, Loftin *et al.* examined the relationship between legislation enacted in 1976 in the District of Columbia and subsequent time trends in suicide and homicide.[23] This legislation mandated that all firearms be registered, that new purchasers meet "fitness" and knowledge of safety standards, and that owners store guns unloaded and disassembled, with certain occupational exceptions, such as law enforcement. The relatively unique aspect of this study was that changes in the rates of suicide and homicide in the District of Columbia were compared to changes in the rates of suicide and homicide in neighboring Maryland and Virginia counties, where no such change in firearms legislation had taken place. In the District of Columbia subsequent to the enactment of this legislation a 23% decline in firearm suicide and a 9% decline in nonfirearm suicide was noted. Over the same period of time in the adjoining Maryland and Virginia counties a 12% increase in firearm suicide and a 2% decline in nonfirearm suicide were observed. One weakness of all ecological studies is that it is impossible to monitor the extent to which these regulations were enforced or circumvented. However, one might have expected diffusion of unlawful firearms from neighboring counties into the District of Columbia, which would have diluted the potentially salutary impact of the legislation. The inference of a causal relationship between the change in legislation and the decline in suicide is bolstered by the greater effect on firearm vs. nonfirearm suicide and the geographic specificity of this effect. Method substitution did not occur to any substantial degree, and an overall decline in the suicide rate prevailed.

The impact of firearms legislation on suicide was examined in Queensland, Australia.[24] In this legislation, both current and prospective owners of long guns were required to obtain a license. In addition, new applicants were required to wait 28 days prior to obtaining their gun (a "cooling off period") and were required to pass a safety test. The suicide rate by firearms declined among men in metropolitan areas and in provincial cities, but not in rural areas. This effect was most notable among individuals under the age of 30. However, method substitution occurred in all regions but the provincial cities, where overall suicide rates did decline. Two limitations of the study are the absence of a control community, where no change in legislation had occurred, and the brevity of the observation (only 1 year pre- and postlegislation).

PROSPECTIVE STUDIES

Wintemute et al.[25] examined the standardized mortality rates (SMRs) of purchasers of handguns in California, who are registered by state law. In 1991, 238,292 purchasers of handguns were registered, and the standardized mortality ratios for suicide were examined for the 6 years after the initial purchase. The SMRs due to suicide were increased for the entire 6-year period of observation, although the risk for suicide declined exponentially with the

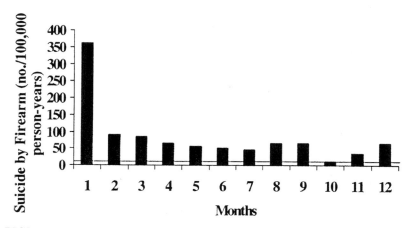

FIGURE 4. Rates of suicide by firearm within the first year after purchase among persons who purchased handguns in California in 1991. *Horizontal line* indicates age- and sex-adjusted average annual rate of suicide by firearm in California in 1991 and 1992 (11.3 per 100,000 persons per year). (Abstracted from Wintermute et al.[25])

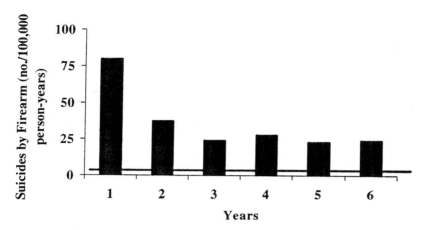

FIGURE 5. Rates of suicide by firearm during the 6 years after purchase among persons who purchased handguns in California in 1991. *Horizontal line* indicates age- and sex-adjusted average annual rate of suicide by firearm in California from 1991 through 1996 (10.7 per 100,000 persons per year). (Abstracted from Wintermute *et al.*[25])

time after the purchase. For example, in the first week, month, and year after the purchase of a handgun, the suicide rates by firearms were elevated 57-, 30-, and 7-fold over the expected rate, respectively, although even at 6 years after the purchase, the rates were still about double the expected rate (see FIGS. 4 and 5). This effect was observed both across the life span and in both sexes, although it was more pronounced in the young and among women. The latter finding is consistent with women's more specific use of handguns for suicide.[6,13] The extremely high rate of suicide right after purchase is consistent with the purchase of firearms for the purpose of committing suicide. This appears to be contradictory to Kellermann *et al.*'s observation[12] that only around 3% of all suicides are committed with guns purchased within the past 2 weeks. The findings in this study indicate only that *if a gun is purchased, it is often purchased for the purpose of committing suicide.* Most of the suicides that occurred among these purchasers occurred more than 2 weeks after the purchase, with the risk for suicide remaining elevated for the entire 6-year period of observation.

CONCLUSIONS AND RECOMMENDATIONS

The convergent evidence from epidemiological, case-control, quasiexperimental, and prospective studies is that there is a relationship between gun availability in the home and completed suicide by firearms. In the United

States, firearms are by far the most common method of completed suicide, and the prevalence of firearm suicide is closely correlated with firearm ownership rates in international comparisons.[1,16] Case-control studies indicate that firearms are much more likely to be in the homes of suicide completers than the homes of controls and that if a gun is in the home, it is highly likely to be used as the method of suicide.[6,9–12] Handguns, compared to long guns; loaded guns, compared to unloaded guns; and unlocked guns, compared to locked guns are all more closely associated with suicide.[6,12] The risk conveyed by the availability of guns may be particularly high among adolescents and young adults.[12,13,17] The firearm suicide rate and in general the overall suicide rate are related to the strictness of gun control laws and the prevalence of gun ownership.[16,18–20] Quasiexperimental studies suggest that greater restrictiveness in gun control laws is associated with declines in firearm suicide, sometimes without compensatory method substitution (e.g., Ref. 23). Finally, one prospective study indicates that the risk of suicide among handgun purchasers is markedly elevated, especially in the first year after purchase.[25] Therefore, method restriction, either on a case-by-case basis or via population methods, may substantially reduce the rate of suicide, particularly in the United States, where suicide by firearms is the most common method for both males and females. A "cooling-off" period may avert suicide by those who purchase handguns for the purpose of committing suicide.

With regard to case-based approaches to method restriction, remarkably little is known about the efficacy of standard approaches. For example, only two studies have examined the impact of firearms counseling on the parents of youth at risk for suicide. In one study, the parents of suicide attempters were counseled about the danger of having firearms in the home; 5/8 of the parents either removed the guns or stored them in a more secure manner.[26] In a study of depressed adolescents who entered a randomized psychotherapy clinical trial, only 27% of the parents who reported having guns in the home at intake removed the guns on follow-up.[27] Therefore, it is unwise to assume that providing recommendations on removal of firearms from the home will automatically result in compliance. One factor that may have led to noncompliance with recommendations in the above-cited study was the insistence that the gun, which may have been kept for protection, be removed. A compromise recommendation to improve the security of gun storage might have been more favorably received.[28] In addition, it is important that the clinician be aware of who owns the gun, since it is often the non–gun-owning parent who brings the child to the clinic. This being the case, the non–gun-owning parent may underestimate the number, type, and method of storage of firearms in the home and may not be able to persuade the spouse of the need to take action. Furthermore, in the above-noted study 18% of households that initially had no guns in the home eventually acquired them.[27] Therefore, it is vital that all parents of at-risk youth be counseled about firearms, not just those who happen to have firearms in the home at intake.

A population-based approach in which the primary care physician ascertains the presence and method of storage of all firearms and counsels the family accordingly may be helpful. While firearms counseling has gained acceptance as an important component of health supervision, in reality it often fails to occur.[29] Moreover, similarly to the above-noted experience with depressed adolescents and their parents, patients surveyed indicate that they are often noncompliant with physician recommendations to secure or remove firearms.[30] Nevertheless, because of the findings relating increased risk for suicide to having a loaded gun in the home even in the absence of psychopathology, it is incumbent upon the primary care physician to emphasize the risk of having a gun in the home to all children, not just to those who have serious psychiatric illnesses.

Finally, there are population approaches, through legislative initiatives, that alter procedures for firearms acquisition and ownership. Cross-sectional and quasiexperimental studies provide modest support for the utility of such approaches for the reduction of firearm suicide and of the overall suicide rate as well.

ACKNOWLEDGMENTS

This work was supported by William T. Grant Foundation Grant 1063-85; NIMH Grants MH44711, MH46500, and MH5512; and Services for Teens at Risk (STAR), an appropriation from the Commonwealth of Pennsylvania. The expert assistance of Beverly Sughrue in preparation of this manuscript is gratefully acknowledged.

REFERENCES

1. CENTERS FOR DISEASE CONTROL. 1994. Deaths resulting from firearm and motor vehicle related injuries. United States, 1968–1991. JAMA **27:** 495–496.
2. BOYD, J.H. 1983. The increasing rate of suicide by firearms. N. Engl. J. Med. **308:** 872–874.
3. BOYD, J.H. & E.K. MOSCICKI. 1986. Firearms and youth suicide. Am. J. Public Health **76**(10): 1240–1242.
4. BRENT, D.A., J.A. PERPER & C.J. ALLMAN. 1987. Alcohol, firearms, and suicide among youth: temporal trends in Allegheny County, Pennsylvania, 1960 to 1983. JAMA **257:** 3369–3372.

5. FORD, A.B., N.B. RUSHFORTH, N.M. RUSHFORTH, *et al.* 1979. Violent death in a metropolitan county: II. Changing patterns in suicides (1959–1974). Am. J. Public Health **69**(5): 459–464.

6. BRENT, D.A., J.A. PERPER, G. MORITZ, *et al.* 1993. Firearms and adolescent suicide: a community case-control study. Am. J. Dis. Child. **147**: 1066–1071.

7. HLADY, W.G. & J.P. MIDDAUGH. 1988. Suicides in Alaska: firearms and alcohol. Am. J. Public Health **78**: 179–180.

8. RIVARA, F.P., B.A. MUELLER, G. SOMES, *et al.* 1997. Alcohol and illicit drug abuse and the risk of violent death in the home. JAMA **278**(7): 569–575.

9. BEAUTRAIS, A.L., P.R. JOYCE & R.T. MULDER. 1996. Access to firearms and the risk of suicide: a case control study. Aust. N.Z. J. Psychiatry **30**: 741–748.

10. BRENT, D.A., J.A. PERPER, C.E. GOLDSTEIN, *et al.* 1988. Risk factors for adolescent suicide: a comparison of adolescent suicide victims with suicidal inpatients. Arch. Gen. Psychiatry **45**: 581–588.

11. BRENT, D.A., J.A. PERPER, C.J. ALLMAN, *et al.* 1991. The presence and accessibility of firearms in the homes of adolescent suicides: a case-control study. JAMA **266**: 2989–2995.

12. KELLERMANN, A.L., F.P. RIVARA, N.B. RUSHFORTH, *et al.* 1992. Suicide in the home in relationship to gun ownership. N. Engl. J. Med. **327**: 467–472.

13. BRENT, D.A., M. BAUGHER, J. BRIDGE, *et al.* 1999. Age and sex-related risk factors for adolescent suicide. J. Am. Acad. Child Adolesc. Psychiatry **38**(12): 1497–1505.

14. BRENT, D.A., J. PERPER, G. MORITZ, *et al.* 1993. Suicide in adolescents with no apparent psychopathology. J. Am. Acad. Child Adolesc. Psychiatry **32**: 494–500.

15. KELLERMANN, A.L. & D.T. REAY. 1986. Protection or peril? An analysis of firearm-related deaths in the home. N. Engl. J. Med. **314**: 1557–1560.

16. KILLIAS, M. 1993. International correlations between gun ownership and rates of homicide and suicide. Can. Med. Assoc. J. **148**(10): 1721–1725.

17. SLOAN, J.H., F.P. RIVARA, D.T. REAY, *et al.* 1990. Firearm regulations and rates of suicide—a comparison of two metropolitan areas. N. Engl. J. Med. **322**: 369–373.

18. BOOR, M. & J.H. BAIR. 1990. Suicide rates, handgun control laws, and sociodemographic variables. Psychol. Rep. **66**: 923–930.

19. LESTER, D. 1988. Gun control, gun ownership, and suicide prevention. Suicide Life Threatening Behav. **18**(2): 176–180.

20. LESTER, D. & M.E. MURRELL. 1986. The influence of gun control laws on personal violence. J. Community Psychol. **14**: 315–318.

21. RICH, C., J. YOUNG, R.C. FOWLER, *et al.* 1990. Guns and suicide: possible effects of some specific legislation. Am. J. Psychiatry **147**: 342–346.

22. CARRINGTON, P.J. & S. MOYER. 1994. Gun control and suicide in Ontario. Am. J. Psychiatry **151**: 606–608.

23. LOFTIN, C., C. MCDOWALL, B. WIERSEMA & T.J. COTTEY. 1991. Effects of restrictive licensing of handguns on homicide and suicide in the District of Columbia. N. Engl. J. Med. **325**: 1615–1620.

24. CANTOR, C.H. & P.J. SLATER. 1995. The impact of firearm control legislation on suicide in Queensland: preliminary findings. Med. J. Aust. **162**: 583–585.

25. WINTEMUTE, G.J. C.A. PARHAM, J.J. BEAUMONT, *et al.* 1999. Mortality among recent purchasers of handguns. N. Engl. J. Med. **341**(21): 1583–1589.

26. KRUESI, M.J.P., J. GROSSMAN, J.M. PENNINGTON, *et al.* 1999. Suicide and violence prevention: parent education in the emergency department. J. Am. Acad. Child Adolesc. Psychiatry **38**(3): 250–255.
27. BRENT, D.A., M. BAUGHER, B. BIRMAHER, *et al.* 2000. Compliance with recommendations to remove firearms by families participating in a clinical trial for adolescent depression. J. Am. Acad. Child. Adolesc. Psychiatry **39**: 1220–1226.
28. WEBSTER, D.W., M.E.H. WILSON, A.K. DUGGAN & L.C. PAKULA. 1992. Parent's beliefs about preventing gun injuries to children. Pediatrics **89**: 908–914.
29. GROSSMAN, D.C., K. MANG & F.P. RIVARA. 1995. Firearm injury prevention counseling by pediatricians and family physicians: practices and beliefs. Arch. Pediatr. Adolesc. Med. **149**: 973–977.
30. WEIL, D.S. & D. HEMENWAY. 1992. Loaded guns in the home: analysis of a national random survey of gun owners. JAMA **267**(22): 3033–3037.

DISCUSSION

DAVID SHAFFER (*Chairman*): David, how many of the 106 patients in the last study had firearms in the home? Of the 106 what is 26%? What is the denominator?

DAVID A. BRENT: I think it was about half.

SHAFFER: About half? Is it an increase in suicide by firearms or a general increase in attempts that are lethal when guns are chosen? That goes back to your earlier observation that most of the increase was attributable to firearm deaths. Could you clarify this?

BRENT: What I was trying to say is that if you look at the time trends of suicide and you look at, for example, the period of time say from the mid-'60s to the early '80s in Allegheny County, the suicide rate went up about 2.5-fold. The suicide rate by firearms went up 3.5-fold. The suicide rate by other methods went up about 1.4-fold; the 1.4 was not statistically significant, so the increase in the suicide rate seemed to be mostly suicide by firearms.

SHAFFER: There is an interesting comment here to the effect that the importance of the Carrington and [Moyer] study is that there was no displacement to suicide by other methods.

BRENT: Right, that's true.

SHAFFER: But the follow-up was how long?

BRENT: I think the law was enacted in the mid-'80s. I think they had about 10 years of follow-up.

SHAFFER: Finally, is there any correlation between the kinds of fathers who own guns and their relationship to sons who kill themselves? What are the selection factors for the purchase of firearms by men who have sons?

BRENT: I don't know. That's a great question that would come up from that California study.

SHAFFER: Yes. Are there any data relative to the experience in using firearms? Do we know whether people who commit suicide with a firearm in the home have actually been using a firearm for sporting, hunting, or target practice, as opposed to just having them there?

BRENT: I don't think I can answer that directly. I would just say, based on the interviews I did, that many of the kids who killed themselves either used their own gun or were quite familiar with the use of guns. But I don't think I can answer that in a quantitative way; I'm just not sure.

Index of Contributors